HD
1379
.P378

Petersen, Kristelle
L.

The single person's
home-buying
handbook

THE SINGLE PERSON'S
HOME-BUYING
HANDBOOK

THE SINGLE PERSON'S HOME-BUYING HANDBOOK

Kristelle L. Petersen

HAWTHORN | DUTTON | New York

For my readers, in the hope that this book will make home buying a secure and satisfactory experience.

For information contact:
Elsevier-Dutton Publishing Co., Inc., 2 Park Avenue,
New York, N.Y. 10016

Library of Congress Cataloging in Publication Data
[Library of Congress Catalog Card Number]

ISBN:0–8015–6840–4 (cloth)
0–8015–6842–0 (paper)

Published simultaneously in Canada by Clarke, Irwin & Company
Limited, Toronto and Vancouver

Designed by Nicola Mazzella

10 9 8 7 6 5 4 3 2 1

First Edition

Contents

ACKNOWLEDGMENTS

I would like to thank the following professionals for lending their expertise in the creation of this book: Donald E. Brotherson, A.I.A.; Jackie Blank, Blank and McCune, The Real Estate Company; Dorothy Johnson, Banco Mortgage Co.; James N. Kendall, U.S. League of Savings Associations; Stanley D. Kolb, ASA, SRA, RM; Lyle Kreps, Unique Real Estate Corp.; Anita A. Mandelbaum, C.P.A., Coopers & Lybrand; Ronald J. Passaro, American Society of Home Inspectors, Inc.; and Tom Stanton, Federal Trade Commission.

Special thanks for their encouragement and inspiration are also due to Wendy Lipkind, Robert G. Owens, and Robert W. Seery.

Last and perhaps most significantly, I wish to express my appreciation to the many home buyers who so candidly shared their experiences with me. Their stories and confidences nurtured my original hunch that a special home-buying book was needed for single persons and provided the material that enabled me to develop this manuscript fully.

PREFACE

This book could most aptly be subtitled: Caveat Emptor or Let the Buyer Beware. Although thousands of books have been written on housing and how to procure shelter, the majority take an industry perspective which I believe does an immeasurable disservice to the consumer.

The result is that the buyer, who is not expected to be privy to the intricacies of this powerful and multi-faceted industry, becomes embroiled in a dissatisfactory and harrowing transaction which frequently leads to victimization. Indeed, the single buyer is all too often the pawn in a complex game whose rules are never disclosed by the major players—seller, broker, builder, lender, and providers of settlement services. And there are so many competing forces, contradictions, and vested interests within the real estate industry that it is extremely difficult, if not impossible, for the consumer to ferret out the truth vital to a satisfactory purchase. Recently, it has become expedient to blame inflation and high costs as the culprits and most books address themselves to overcoming those obstacles. But that is a simplistic approach to a much more complicated problem.

As the Federal Trade Commission, which has undertaken an unprecedented nationwide investigation into the industry, notes, "Housing is of enormous importance to consumers and appears to be a sector of the economy rife with problems of consumer and competitive injury."

The single buyer in particular needs guidance and insight into the type of situations to anticipate. This book, based on several years of research and numerous interviews with single home buyers across the country, is an effort to lay bare the facts. It specifically tackles the problems that the single person encounters and the pitfalls for which the buyer must beware. And it provides a spectrum of economical alternatives that the person with a limited budget should explore.

The horror stories of persons I interviewed are included with the hope that you will benefit from their bad experiences and avoid similar misfortunes. I do believe there are many reputable professionals working to improve the real estate and housing industry. By uncovering some of the abuses and bad actors, this book can save you from paying the price of illegal and unethical practices.

I think government has a role to play in helping consumers to obtain affordable shelter fairly, but I do not advocate government regulation and enforcement as the answer. I believe that informed, aware consumers must play the major role in any reform of home-buying practices.

   This book is designed so that you can easily refer to any home-buying facet of special interest to you, although I believe you will derive the greatest benefit from a thorough reading of the entire text.

   While some persons might take offense at my reliance on the male reference pronoun, this stylistic choice was made to facilitate presentation of the vast amount of material to be covered.

                                                                Kristelle L. Petersen

THE SINGLE PERSON'S HOME-BUYING HANDBOOK

1

The Advantages of
Ownership for You

"April 15 was my reason for buying a home," reports Sally, a young attorney whose purchase of a $70,000 bungalow saved her more than $2,000 in federal income taxes.

While she was renting, Sally realized that Uncle Sam was getting the lion's share of her $22,500 income because she had no sizable tax deductions to claim—the kind that only home ownership could give her. As a renter, Sally could only claim the standard deduction and personal exemption on her federal income taxes, which left her with a $4,289 tax bill. However, as a home owner, she is eligible to file an itemized tax return, claiming her mortgage interest payments and property taxes as deductions. In Sally's case, that reduced her federal tax bill to $2,268.

In addition to giving the well-salaried single person immediate tax benefits, home ownership also provides you the best and most secure investment of your money. On the average, homes have been appreciating at an annual rate of 12 to 15 percent, and many home buyers have seen their homes' value increase 20 percent in just one year.

Pete, a college professor, bought a huge Victorian house in town for $33,500 a few years ago. The elderly owners had let the house deteriorate, and so Pete, who enjoys working with his hands, fixed up the place in his spare time. He then rented out three rooms and now has a house valued at $95,000, as well as an income property that pays for itself.

Home ownership is the best hedge against inflation, which is now running at an annual rate of about 18 percent. Since most salaries can't keep pace with inflation, the trick is to put your money in an investment that will. And house prices are virtually recession resistant. So even when there is a downturn in the economy and house prices drop a bit, they will escalate even more when the economy picks up. Of course, the best time to buy is when prices dip.

Timothy, a minister whose salary was lagging way behind inflation, capitalized beautifully on a recent economic slump. While most investors were hestitating, Tim charged ahead and offered $20,000 for a Civil War-vintage house on four acres of land. He managed to befriend the elderly woman who had spent her life in the house, which needed complete overhauling. He was so enchanted by the possibilities of the house and the prospect of owning land, that he returned several times to visit with the owner, who was forced to sell because of ill health.

Convinced that Tim would continue the tradition of her family home in a manner that suited her wishes, the woman turned down several higher bids and sold it to him for $20,000. Tim has spent the past year improving his property, which is now appraised at $75,000. However, because of special tax breaks for owners who improve their property, Tim doesn't pay taxes on that amount.

Tim, whose $18,000 salary barely supported him and his two young sons in town, says "I'm a very urban person, and I had never owned property, so it's very strange that I started looking toward the country. But economic factors forced that. I think there are worse times ahead with prices of everything continuing to rise drastically and my salary growing smaller proportionately.

"Now I grow most of my own food, live more and more simply, and don't have any major monthly bills. Ownership has given me a great sense of security. And I know my savings are better invested than they would be in stocks or bonds."

Although you probably aren't planning to make such a radical change in your life-style, you should realize, as Tim did, the urgency of investing now. Home prices will continue to rise at unprecedented rates, in part because of the intense demand. Between now and 1985, as the post–World War II baby-boom generation comes of age and 30 million more adults enter the housing market, the demand for houses will be the greatest of any time in American history.

At the same time, no-growth moratoriums and government regulations are limiting land development and, hence, the supply of houses. Meanwhile, rising labor and materials costs are driving up home prices even further.

Moreover, the Census Bureau reports that renters spend about 24 percent of their incomes on housing, while home owners with mortgages spend only 18 percent, and rents are expected to increase at a rate of between 7 and 10 percent per year. In many areas rents will rise drastically over the next few years as housing demand increases and apartment availability decreases. Because of rent controls, government regulations, and high construction costs, very few apartment complexes are being built, and existing apartments are being converted into condominiums and cooperatives to get away from controls.

If you delay purchasing, you will face substantially higher monthly mortgage payments. And although today's interest rates seem steep, remember that as you build equity in your home, you pay off your mortgage debt with money of declining value. With inflation at 18 percent, a mortgage loan at 13 percent actually costs you less than 15 percent in terms of real dollars.

As an enforced savings plan and hedge against inflation, home ownership is your best bet. Plus, once you build up some equity in your home, you've got something to borrow against if you should need a large sum of cash for any purpose.

True, buying a house today requires a lot of up-front money. But there are resources you can tap to get that money for your down payment and other costs. Those alternatives will be explained in subsequent chapters. You'll also learn about tax incentives and financing plans designed to help first-time buyers, as well as special tax breaks for persons who buy homes following job transfers and relocations.

2

What's Your Life-Style and Where Do You Want to Live?

Before you actually start looking at houses, you first should take time to consider your life-style, your values, and your needs. These factors should determine the location and type of dwelling you choose. Since buying a home is apt to be the single largest investment of your life, you want to assure a compatible match between you and your house. Therefore, you want to charter a rational course in your house hunt.

The worst mistake you can make is buying on impulse or emotion. Don't base your decision on sentimental appeal or a real-estate broker's pitch. Plotting a home-buying approach will help you avoid the plight of Susan, a young professional woman in Chicago.

Susan decided she simply had to have a place of her own, and on her first day of looking put in a bid, at the broker's urging, on a one-and-a-half story suburban house, framed in lilac bushes. To all her friends, Susan bragged about her super find with lilacs, rose bushes, and all the homey features with which she had grown up. However, her tune changed rapidly after she'd settled in and found herself isolated from her friends in town and saddled with unending maintenance and fix-up chores. She soon discovered that the one hour commute to her job was a real hassle—especially when she had to take off work during the day to come home and let the plumber in.

Think first about location. Do you want to be close to work? If you're career-building and that's the most consuming focus of your life now, you may opt for the convenience of a condominium or cooperative apartment near your place of employment. Ask yourself if you want the stimulation of city life, with entertainment, shopping, and business resources readily available. Or is your job such a pressure cooker that at the end of the day and on weekends what you really need is the slowed-down pace of suburban life? The suburbs offer a quieter atmosphere, more personal space, and privacy. You'll have your own yard and can garden or get up a volleyball or badminton game if that's your way of relaxing. Or maybe you just want to have a few friends in for a backyard barbecue.

Dan, a thirty-year-old executive who spends his work week flying to other cities calling on clients, found the perfect haven in a San Diego suburb. His two-bedroom ranch home is close to the ocean and provides the one feature upon which he insisted—a window in the bathroom.

"I like to look out the window while I'm showering, and I never could find an apartment with a bathroom window," he said.

Moreover, the location met Dan's other requirements. He hates driving and sought a place where he could walk to the grocery store, commute to work in thirty minutes, and find some peace, quiet, and sanity in the evening. However, the real luxury, he admits, is finally being able to play his music as loud as he wants without worrying about other tenants complaining.

If you have children, you may need a suburban home that offers sufficient play space and is close to schools and day-care centers. In fact, you may want to look into some planned unit developments (PUDs), which provide such amenities as shared open spaces, nearby shopping, schools, community services, and often recreational facilities. In an effort to combat escalating housing costs and provide maximum convenience for working persons, more developers are putting up PUDs on the edges of the suburbs.

PUDs usually offer a variety of dwellings at various price ranges to accommodate all ages, family sizes, life-styles, and budgets. In a typical PUD, you're likely find single-family detached units, town houses, and condominium apartments.

Also, in the exurbs, those outermost fringes of the metropolitan area where most new construction occurs, you'll find a variety of town-house developments. Many of them are geared specifically to single persons and offer such recreational facilities as tennis courts, swimming pools, party rooms, and nearby golf courses. If your main interest is meeting other single persons, particularly if you're new to an area, you'd do best to check out town-house complexes geared to this crowd.

If you have a pioneering spirit, you may desire a house in the country. But remember, then you're buying a good commute and quite a drive to the grocery store or other shopping facility. Also, if you're in a northern climate, you'll have to contend with snow in the winter and grass to mow in the summer. If a country home is what you think you want, contemplate carefully all the aspects of rural living.

Reared on a farm, Jill, returning from California to the Midwest for a high-paying job, decided she wanted a two-story frame house on some acreage. However, after two weeks of house-sitting for vacationing friends who lived twenty miles outside of the city on twelve acres, Jill settled on a two-story house in town.

"I realized what I could afford required more fixing up than I had time or money for, and I also realized how isolated it could be out in the country. If I got snowed in or anything happened to me, I would be stuck out there alone," Jill explained.

Phillip, on the other hand, started out looking for a duplex in town and ended up with an old farmhouse in the country. A psychologist, Phillip had always lived in the city and decided he needed the challenge of country living to find out whether he could be self-sufficient.

"I felt very badly about myself as a carpenter because I didn't know the skills of hammer, nails, and saw. So I decided the best way to learn how to build was to work on a place, and this house I found was one of the worst looking houses and in great need of repair. I have completely gutted and rebuilt it, and I now feel really good about knowing that I can work with my hands."

Phillip said he realized what he really wanted was "almost sort of a lodge—a retreat house" that would enable him to escape from the cerebral concentration his counseling required. As it turned out, the physical labor of the remodeling became the therapist's therapy, and in the process, Phillip built a gigantic fireplace out of hand-picked rocks. As one project followed another on the house, a whole new life-style evolved for Phillip.

"My life kind of slowed down, and I found I didn't go to as many events in town. You see, it's the kind of house that when you get here you just like to stay here.

"The pattern of my day in the winter is to get up at six-thirty, come downstairs, and immediately build a fire. Many times, the temperature is about fifty-five degrees when I get up. And it's such a good feeling to stand in front of that big fireplace with the fire crackling."

Of course, in addition to considering location, you must also decide what type of home you want. If you're seeking convenience and security, then you should look into a high-rise condominium, a modern cooperative apartment, or a town house. With a condo or co-op, the maintenance is taken care of for you, although you pay a fee for that service. If you want more space and privacy, but all modern appliances, then direct your attention to new detached homes. Patio homes, so-called because they're built on a minimal amount of land, require relatively little maintenance, but still give you your own space.

However, if you really want to get involved in a house, committing a lot of time and effort to remodeling, then you should look at older homes. They offer big rooms and unique characteristics that you can't find in most new houses, but they require much more maintenance.

You honestly need to ask yourself how much of a time and money investment you want to make in your home. If it's to be primarily an investment that will build equity for you, then by all means purchase a new house that will demand little upkeep. On the other hand, if you're willing to sacrifice entertainment, travel, and other things to get the house you want and make it a reflection of you, analyze closely the older homes on the market.

Warren, a forty-five-year-old professional, suddenly found himself in the housing market after a divorce and two unhappy years of apartment living and said he didn't know what kind of house he wanted. He just knew what he didn't want.

"I really hate most new houses. In fact, during that two-year period in which I was looking around, I would go to the outskirts of town, where those masses of new houses are located. I swear to God I'd go into those places and I'd come out and want to know where the gas chambers were afterward. I mean it was just the most antiseptic, sterile, concentration-camp kind of environment. I couldn't stand it."

Warren, who had built a new house with his former spouse, but really loved old houses because of their "fantastic potential for being fixed up," finally bought a three-story, 1906 house in town. He then proceeded to paint the entire house, inside and out, insulate and finish off the attic, and tear up all the carpet and finish off the wood floors. And he says the place now is "much more of an expression of me than anyplace I have ever lived."

His large, high-ceilinged living room with the home's original brick fireplace draws together the important elements of Warren's life. His extensive collection of books line one wall, and his grand piano takes up the front quarter of the room. A sunny plant room with ceiling-high windows leads into a spacious kitchen.

Before launching your house hunt, there are some other questions you should ask yourself. How much entertaining do you do—will you need a guest bedroom or a large kitchen to accommodate your culinary inclinations? How well prepared are you for home ownership—do you have minor carpentry, plumbing, and wiring skills? If not, avoid older dwellings unless they've already been remodeled. How much time do you have to spend cleaning and maintaining your home?

What amenities do you require? Must you have a dishwasher, washer, dryer, garbage disposal, self-cleaning oven, microwave oven, and trash compactor? How important is a fireplace? Do you need a basement, attic, or garage for storage or setting up an extra workroom? Do you want a place that you could expand at some future point? Will you live alone, purchase it with someone else, or have a roommate? If you plan to share your home, you perhaps should consider a floor plan that provides separate spaces for you and your housemate. Are you an avid indoor gardener, needing a plant room and lots of southern and eastern exposures?

After thoroughly contemplating your needs and desires in a home, sit down and make a list of the absolute essential requirements. Note also the additional features you want and the points on which you can compromise. Now you've established a standard by which you can judge each house at which you look. Be sure to take that list with you when you go house hunting, and stick to your priorities. Don't make any snap decisions, allow yourself to be hyped by any brokers' or sellers' pitches, or be overwhelmed by any particular feature of a home.

One final word. The location you choose will, to a certain extent, determine the type of house in which you'll end up. For example, you'll find older homes and row houses in town or in the suburbs near town, and you'll find new homes and town-house developments in the outlying areas. To assist you in your shopping, Chapter 4 provides detailed information on each type of dwelling.

3

How Much Home Can You Afford?

Since your monthly housing costs will probably double when you buy your home, it's important to calculate now exactly how much of your income you can afford to allocate for housing. On the average, single buyers who paid rents between $260 and $390, make monthly house payments ranging between $500 and $640.

The best approach is to visit with a mortgage loan officer, who can advise you how much he will lend you based on your monthly cash flow. An experienced real-estate broker will also be able to tell you the price and type of home for which your income qualifies and will know lending practices in your locale. The whole objective is to get a ball-park figure now of how much home you can afford based on your income and assets. This will prevent you from wasting time looking at $90,000 dwellings when you need to be looking in the $60,000 price range.

Lenders used to say that no more than 25 percent of your monthly income should go for housing, but economic conditions have caused some lenders to modify that guideline. Lenders today may allow you to spend up to 35 percent on your gross monthly income on housing and may even give you credit for income potential. At this point, the key is to remain flexible and explore all the financing options, especially if you're working with a limited budget and limited cash reserves.

You also need to exercise some caution. As with any profession, in the banking and real-estate business there are some unethical and incompetent lenders and brokers, who see the single person as an easy mark. Knowing a bit about mortgage lending procedures will help you avoid those individuals and put you on the track to a sound business transaction.

First, you need to familiarize yourself with the factors the lender and broker will consider when qualifying you for a loan. They will want to know your gross monthly income from salary and other sources. By law, the lender must consider income from part-time employment, alimony, child support, public assistance programs, disability insurance, Social Security, and unemployment payments, if these are steady items.

Lenders also will evaluate your job stability—the type of job you have and the time you have held your current position. If you've just moved into a city to take a new position, which is a career advancement, the lender will give you credit for that. However, if you've recently changed types of employment, the lender may consider you a loan risk. For example, if you leave a secure job in hotel management to go into sales, the lender may not write you a mortgage loan until you have a proven track record in your new field. Likewise, the self-employed person may be considered a bad risk, unless that individual has a proven, steady income over several years.

The main thing to understand about mortgage lending is that the loan officer's ultimate consideration is whether you offer a secure investment of his institution's money. To determine that, he will check out all aspects about you and your business that he feels he needs.

The lender will consider whether you are at the low end of your income potential. If you're just starting out in your career, the lender may give you credit for future income and allow you to commit a larger percentage of your cash flow to housing. However, if you choose to invest a major chunk of your income in housing, be prepared to make sacrifices in some other areas.

Next, the lender will look at your outstanding debt obligations. Any installment debts, such as car payments or revolving charge accounts that extend beyond six months, will be subtracted from your income to determine your funds available for housing.

The lender also will review your financial history and credit record. He will want to verify that you have enough money set aside for the down payment, closing costs (all charges due at the time you sign your mortgage note), and ongoing house expenses.

In qualifying buyers for loans, lenders now take into account the cost of monthly utility and maintenance bills, as well as the cost of property taxes and home insurance. Lenders are increasingly concerned about utility bills, which in some places are now as high as monthly mortgage payments. Because the average income can't keep pace with escalating energy costs, some lending institutions even require homes to meet minimum energy requirements in order to qualify for loans. To estimate maintenance costs, the lender looks at the age and condition of the home.

From all these factors, the lender calculates what percent of your income he will allow you as a monthly housing allowance. He then consults a mortgage schedule, which shows monthly principal and interest payments for various loan amounts, to determine how much loan you qualify for based on your monthly housing allowance.

To illustrate how this whole process works, consider how Connie, a young professional, was qualified for the home and loan she could afford (see Chart A, page 12). Twenty-nine-year-old Connie had saved $5,000, owed about $2,900 on her car, earned about $1,900 per month, and had a raise upcoming. Her broker gathered these figures in the initial interview. He then deducted her monthly car payments of $120 from her monthly income, leaving $1,780. Then he estimated her monthly payments for utilities, maintenance, taxes, and insurance for the type of house and location she wanted. After plugging in those figures, he consulted a mortgage schedule to determine the size loan for which Connie qualified based on the $487 she had available for monthly mortgage payments.

Allowing Connie to allocate 40 percent of her monthly income for housing, the broker qualified her for a $56,000 loan at 10 percent interest over thirty-five years. Her monthly payments for principal and interest would be $481.42. If she made a 5 percent down payment ($3,050), she could afford a $61,000 home and would have $1,950 left in savings to pay her closing costs.

Before visiting a lender, you can get a clear idea of how much of your monthly income you can spend for housing by filling out Chart B (page 12). Breaking down your monthly expenses this way will help you decide where you can make some sacrifices to increase your housing allocation, if necessary. Most single buyers forgo discretionary expenditures such as travel, entertainment, or a new car for a few years in order to purchase their first homes.

Says Paul, who bought a $40,000 house when he entered law practice, "Fifty percent of my net income goes into the house, so I know I can't make the payments and drive a new car. But I learned a lot about finances and the money market early in my career by purchasing this home.

"I was willing to make the sacrifice and now realize that owning my own home has made me a better person, because I am responsible for this property and its upkeep. I don't always rely on someone else to do things for me as I did when renting. In my opinion, anyone who owns a house learns a lot more about life."

As you're working out your housing budget, you also need to figure how much money you have on hand for the down payment and closing costs. Keep in mind that the higher your down payment, the lower your monthly payments will be. The mortgage schedule in Chart C (page 13) shows how much your monthly payments will be for several different-priced homes, based on the size of the down payment. Payments are shown for loans of 11 through 17 percent interest, since these rates are apt to vary, depending on market conditions and where you live.

From this chart, you can see that if you have $5,000 to put down and $500 per month for house payments, you can afford a $50,000 home with a thirty-year mortgage loan at 13 percent.

You will need to find out what size down payments lenders in your area are requiring. Recently, lenders have made loans with only 5 percent down for new homes, but in times of tight money they may require 20 or 25 percent or more. If the latter is the case and you don't have enough cash for the down payment requirement, there are other avenues for you to explore. You may be able to get a FHA-backed loan, which has low down payment requirement; or you may have to take out a second mortgage. Then, too, you might get a loan from parents or other relatives or you may borrow against the cash value of certificates of deposit, your whole life insurance policy, or an interest-paying savings account.

At the same time you're thinking about the down payment, you should figure how much you will need for other expenses involved with the purchase. Ask your broker or lender how much you'll need to set aside for the closing costs. Then think about moving expenses, appliances you'll have to buy (refrigerator, stove, air conditioner, etc.), new furniture, and condominium association fees, if applicable. There will also be a host of miscellaneous items for which you should plan—lawn mower, hoses, snow shovel, garbage cans, tools, and minor remodeling (such as painting or carpeting a room) if you're buying an older home. If you'll have a costly commute when you move, include transportation expenses into your calculations.

Don't underrate any of these expenses. And be sure to get accurate quotes on taxes and insurance. That will enable you to avoid the plight of Karen, a journalist in Washington, D.C. Karen stretched her budget to the limit to buy her home—a $61,500 two-story town house near Capitol Hill. Her $490 monthly payments left her just enough for food and transportation. However, after moving in, she received notice that her property value had been reassessed when she purchased, which boosted her taxes and resulted in monthly payments of $560. She was forced to rent out a room to meet the higher payments.

When you're given an estimate of the yearly taxes on a particular piece of property, it's a good idea to call the county tax assessor's office to find out when the most recent rate and assessment increase occurred. The tax assessor's office can also tell you when the next assessment will be made, but not how much it will increase or decrease, since this depends on the house's market value on the day it is appraised.

If you think you're going to have trouble coming up with the money for the down payment and other expenses, don't panic. There are a variety of financial plans geared for single persons with limited cash reserves and incomes. These programs and methods for getting funds for the down payment will be fully explained in Chapters 8 and 9, which deal with financing. In addition, each chapter will suggest options you can investigate to help you get the most home for the least money, and techniques employed by other single buyers will be described.

CHART A

GROSS MONTHLY INCOME	SAVINGS		INSTALLMENT DEBT	
			PER MONTH	BALANCE
$1,900	$5,000	Car loan	$120	$2,900
−120				
$1,780				

ESTIMATED EXPENSES*

Utilities	$ 80
Maintenance	25
Taxes	100
Home insurance	20
	$225

HOUSING ALLOWANCE

40% of $1,780 = $712

$712 − $225 = $487 (Amount available for monthly principal and interest)

Your real-estate broker should be able to quote you estimated costs for utilities, maintenance, taxes, and home insurance based on his knowledge of the housing market in your area.

CHART B

AVERAGE MONTHLY INCOME

Total take-home pay (gross pay less taxes) $_____

Other regular income   _____

Total monthly income $_____(A)

AVERAGE MONTHLY NON-HOUSING EXPENSES

Food and household supplies $_____

Clothing   _____

Medical costs and insurance   _____

Life and casualty insurance   _____

Automobile insurance   _____

Education   _____

Commuting (fares, gas, parking)   _____

Automobile payments   _____

Other installment loan payments   _____

Recreation   _____

Entertainment   _____

Telephone   _____

Contributions, dues, fees, etc.   _____

Personal expenses   _____

Regular savings or investments   _____

Miscellaneous expenses (newspaper, etc.)   _____

Total monthly non-housing expenses $_____(B)

MONTHLY INCOME AVAILABLE FOR HOUSING

(Subtract B from A) $_____(C)

CHART C
MORTGAGE SCHEDULE

MONTHLY PAYMENT* (PRINCIPAL PLUS INTEREST)

COST OF HOUSE	LOAN DURATION	DOWN PAYMENT %	$	11%	12%	13%	14%	15%	16%	17%
		10	5,000	$441	474	508	542	576	612	647
	25	20	10,000	392	421	451	482	512	544	575
		30	15,000	343	369	395	421	448	476	503
		10	5,000	429	463	498	533	569	605	642
$50,000	30	20	10,000	381	411	442	474	506	538	570
		30	15,000	333	360	387	415	443	471	499
		10	5,000	422	457	493	529	566	602	639
	35	20	10,000	375	406	438	470	503	535	568
		30	15,000	328	355	383	411	440	468	497
		10	6,000	529	569	609	650	692	734	776
	25	20	12,000	470	505	541	578	615	652	690
		30	18,000	412	442	474	506	538	571	604
		10	6,000	514	555	597	640	683	726	770
$60,000	30	20	12,000	457	494	531	569	607	645	684
		30	18,000	400	432	465	498	531	565	599
		10	6,000	506	548	591	635	679	723	767
	35	20	12,000	450	487	526	564	603	642	682
		30	18,000	394	427	460	494	528	562	597
		10	8,000	706	758	812	867	922	978	1,035
	25	20	16,000	627	674	722	770	820	870	920
		30	24,000	549	590	632	674	717	761	805
		10	8,000	686	741	796	853	910	968	1,026
$80,000	30	20	16,000	609	658	708	758	809	861	912
		30	24,000	533	576	619	663	708	753	798
		10	8,000	675	734	789	846	905	964	1,023
	35	20	16,000	600	650	701	752	804	857	909
		30	24,000	525	569	613	658	704	750	795
		10	10,000	882	948	1,015	1,083	1,153	1,223	1,294
	25	20	20,000	784	843	902	963	1,025	1,087	1,150
		30	30,000	686	737	789	843	897	951	1,006
		10	10,000	857	926	996	1,066	1,138	1,210	1,283
$100,000	30	20	20,000	762	823	885	948	1,012	1,076	1,141
		30	30,000	664	720	774	829	885	941	998
		10	10,000	843	914	986	1,058	1,131	1,205	1,278
	35	20	20,000	750	812	876	941	1,005	1,071	1,136
		30	30,000	656	711	767	823	880	937	994

Figures rounded to nearest dollar.

NOTE: *For about $3, you can buy a monthly amortization booklet at your bookstore. This booklet will give you monthly payments required to amortize a loan at a given percent over a given number of years.*

4

The Single Buyer's Guide to Housing Alternatives

This chapter will advise you how to conduct an efficient, successful house hunt. It will describe different types of housing suitable for your single life-style and tell you how to find the affordable options in your area. You'll learn how to judge and compare various prospects.

There are a few things you should keep in mind as you're looking. Since your utility bills and property taxes will be determined by the size and cost of the home you buy, shop for only as much house as you realistically need. The smaller and more energy efficient the home, the less you'll have to heat and cool, as well as to maintain.

If you're planning to relocate, it's advisable to check into home prices and the cost of living in your new locale before moving. Home prices vary drastically from region to region. For example, buyers in southern California and Washington, D.C. often pay twice as much as buyers in other parts of the country. House costs in the north-central United States and in *some* southern states are considerably lower than in other regions.

Home costs are also much higher in major metropolitan areas than in medium-sized cities. Home buyers in cities exceeding 1.5 million population pay roughly 16 percent more for their homes than buyers in cities with populations of 250,000 to 1.5 million. Homes and real-estate taxes are usually less expensive in the suburbs than in the inner city.

First-time home buyers in large cities have the hardest time getting into the market. Young urban buyers, therefore, need to shop for lower priced, high-density dwellings, such as condominium and cooperative apartments or town houses. It's also a good idea for first-time buyers to scout around the suburbs for older, less expensive detached houses. In any event, with a thorough, organized search you can find quality for your limited housing dollar.

Your location will determine the type of house you'll eventually buy. In New York City, cooperative apartments and lofts are abundant, but in California, the main forms of attached housing are condominiums and town houses. There are no condos or co-ops in some midwestern communities, where those forms of housing simply haven't yet gained popularity. Single-family detached houses still predominate.

So to launch your search, the first thing you need to do is familiarize yourself with the housing market in your area. You want to find out the types and locations of homes available in your price range. You can start by reading the real-estate sections of your newspapers, as well as any local publications on housing. Also, tell friends, relatives, and work associates about the type and price of home in which you think you're interested.

You might also go into a real-estate broker's office and ask to see the multiple-listings book, which pictures all the for-sale houses, their prices, square footage, number of rooms, and other pertinent data. However, it's best to hold off enlisting the aid of a broker, as you want to do your initial research unpressured. Or like David, who spent several months doing his homework, you might visit open houses, where you can inspect different styles of homes.

"I wanted to develop a sense of prices relative to locations and square footage in the absence of any buying pressure. Plus I wanted to educate myself about the market without taking up a broker's time, because at the outset I really didn't know what I could afford or exactly what I wanted," said David, who is now snugly settled into a beach home.

By thoroughly familiarizing yourself with the market, you'll be in a strong position to negotiate the best sales price when you do make an offer on a home. As you're looking, take along a tablet to jot down your likes and dislikes about particular homes and any questions you may want to ask later. Also, carry a camera so you can get a few interior and exterior snapshots and a tape measure to check window and door dimensions. Once you get serious about a prospect, try to visit the home several times, preferably once during the day and once at night to get a more total feeling for the place. This can save you a terrible case of buyer's remorse later.

If possible, avoid buying in the spring and fall, when prices are usually highest, and understand that you're better off buying the least expensive home in any given neighborhood as you will realize a greater appreciation because of the more expensive surrounding properties. Above all, remain flexible, and be ready to settle for something less than what you wanted in order to break into the market. Once you've built up some equity in your home, you can sell it for a higher price and move up to exactly what you want.

In the following sections, you'll learn the basic advantages and disadvantages of the various types of dwellings. But as you're shopping, talk with sellers, brokers, builders, and other buyers to find out what the common housing problems are in your area. Houses wear differently in different climates. In southern California, for example, houses often experience roofing problems; in the Midwest, it's frequently wet basements. In any case, you want to know what you're buying into.

Existing Single-Family Houses

An existing, or resale, single-family house is any home from one to 150 years old. The distinguishing characteristic is that it has been lived in. Older homes, particularly those built twenty or more years ago, usually can be purchased for considerably less than a comparably sized new house. Whereas the national median price for a new house was about $63,000 in 1979, the national median price of an existing house was approximately $56,000.

Because older homes cost less, monthly payments and property taxes are less. Plus you can be assured of a stable tax base in an established neighborhood, where you won't be footing the bill for new schools, roads, parks, and the other expenses of a new development. You'll probably get a yard already landscaped, which will save you the considerable cost of buying new shrubs, trees, and grass.

Now is an excellent time to buy an older home, because during high inflation, lenders are eager to take back outstanding lower rate mortgages and exchange them for mortgage loans at the going rates. Also, the federal emphasis on recycling of existing dwellings requires lenders to loan money in inner-city and older low-income neighborhoods, where you can find some truly gracious, large, old homes at bargain prices.*

You're apt to find these big, older houses in the city or in the inner-ring suburbs. Check with your municipal housing department to find out where programs are underway to restore older houses. In many cities, neighborhood groups form to rebuild older sections of the community. Often, a number of young single persons with a pioneering spirit join forces to revitalize an area and create their own neighborhood. Where this happens, there's usually a constant trade-off of information and labor. You should also ask your city housing department and the local Federal Housing Administration (FHA) office whether you qualify for any of the government programs funding the refurbishing of older homes. (For further information on these programs, see "Rehabilitation Housing," page 57.)

With a large, older home, you can get substantially more space for your housing dollar. You also can get distinct architectural features not available in new houses. And these older homes are usually extremely well built, with substantial materials that have withstood the test of time.

One young architect involved in rehabilitation and remodeling maintains that pre-World War II houses were better built and are more energy efficient than houses built after the war, when poorer thermal insulating materials were used and glass facades were fashionable. He says that prior to 1940, families built their homes to last for a hundred years—a claim that can't be made for many newer homes.

You'll find a much greater variety of styles and sizes in older homes. However, it's important to consider from the outset how much time and money you want to invest in revamping the house. If you're an enthusiastic

---

*Escalating costs, coupled with increased consumer demand for housing, has prompted passage of state and federal legislation prohibiting the practice of red-lining. Many lenders traditionally drew red lines around ethnic and racially mixed low income and inner-city neighborhoods where they refused to make loans in order to channel their money into more alluent neighborhoods.

do-it-yourselfer, then you would do well to buy a much older house and remodel it to suit your tastes. That can be a creative and deeply fulfilling project. You may want to duplex the house for additional income or simply fix it up and rent out several rooms.

If your main objective is to get into a minimally priced, sound home that won't need lots of work, check out the post–World War II housing stock in your area. In the fifties and sixties, scores of tract houses were built in large subdivisions around major cities. These homes, which sold then for about $10,000, now go for $50,000 and more, depending on how much they've been remodeled or expanded. Today these tracts can provide reasonably priced homes in pleasant suburban neighborhoods. As you're shopping, analyze each house for the amount of maintenance and yard work it will require.

Sarah, who recently moved to Los Angeles from Washington, D.C. to take a new job, articulates the kind of concerns the shopper for an older home should keep in mind.

"My top priority was getting into a safe neighborhood that would also be reasonably close to work so I wouldn't have a long commute," Sarah said. "With each house I looked at, I had to ask myself whether I would feel comfortable coming home there after a dinner party or whether my friends would feel safe leaving late at night.

"I wanted a house that was structurally sound and would not require remodeling, because working full-time I can't be at home to let in subcontractors or oversee their work. Nor could I tackle stripping wallpaper or redoing a fireplace. I needed a house that would only require some cosmetic repairs, such as painting a room. Therefore, I did have to pay a little more. On the other hand, some of my friends have bought houses requiring a lot of work, because that's the only way they could afford to get into the market."

After several months of looking, Sarah bought an older, two-bedroom home in Santa Monica for $127,000, which she claims was "a heck of a deal at the time." (New house prices in the Los Angeles area averaged about $200,000 then.) She lives in a nice, quiet neighborhood where she feels secure and has a small, private backyard. She's close to the bus line and can commute to her downtown office in eighteen minutes.

Two things you need to evaluate carefully when buying an older home are the status of the neighborhood and the condition of the house. You need to find out whether the neighborhood is stable, is declining, has deteriorated seriously, or is just making a comeback. If it's declining or really deteriorated, you might have trouble getting a loan in that area. However, you can get some terrific bargains in areas that are just starting to be revitalized. The trick is to know your market well enough to invest at the right time.

Usually, once the recycling process starts in a neighborhood, prices skyrocket, so you want to get in one step ahead of that happening. Good sources for that kind of information are real-estate agents, lenders, and officials of local housing agencies involved in rehabilitating older homes. Also ask those sources about purchasing a house on which the mortgage has been foreclosed. Lenders don't like to leave those houses sitting empty, so often you can get an excellent home at a rock-bottom price this way. Check also with your local FHA office about reclaimed houses.

The next step is to thoroughly check out the condition of any house you consider. The nice thing about older houses is that they've shifted every way they're going to and so they usually don't hide their flaws. Defects such as cracked plaster, low water pressure, and inadequate electrical service are apparent. If you doubt your ability to conduct an adequate inspection, it's well worth your money to hire a home inspector or other professional (engineer, independent general contractor, or architect) to get an informed opinion on the structural condition.

Don't rely on the real-estate broker for a final opinion on the condition of the house. Many brokers know very little about the structural components of houses. And bear in mind, the broker is interested in his commission, which he receives from the seller. The U. S. Department of Housing and Urban Development (HUD) estimates that in one year buyers of existing houses paid more than $750 million to repair undisclosed defects.

If serious structural defects are discovered at this point, you can use them to negotiate a lower price for the house or ask the owner to repair them. However, if you decide to assume responsibility for the repairs, you should get bids on them before closing your transaction. You want to make sure the repair costs don't exceed the amount you save by buying an older home. Usually, when you sign the sales contract, or the offer to buy, it stipulates that the house will be conveyed to you in good working order. So make certain that clause is included; if you find something to the contrary in your inspections, you can void the purchase agreement.

If you're moving from a modern apartment into an older home, realize that you will probably be sacrificing such conveniences as a garbage disposal, dishwasher, central air conditioning, as well as other updated facilities. Decide ahead of time how much inconvenience you can tolerate. And if you elect to buy a house requiring substantial remodeling, figure cost and inconvenience in advance. That means getting time frames and bids for the work before you buy.

If your remodeling budget is very limited, you may have to space out improvements over several years. Can you bear to sweat out that first summer without air conditioning? It's also a good idea to visit with some other persons who have been through the process and to browse through some books dealing specifically with older house renovations.

When you're inquiring about financing, ask about purchase programs incorporating property improvement loans. Many lenders offer improvement loans with the mortgage. Some lenders even give loans at preferred rates for energy upgrades on existing homes. A number of progressive lenders insist that older homes meet minimum energy requirements in order to qualify for loans.

If you do buy an older home and make energy-conserving improvements, you'll qualify for a tax credit of up to $300, depending on how much you do. The current Energy Act allows you to deduct from your income taxes any money spent for insulation, storm windows, weather stripping, thermal windows, and the like. Check with the local FHA office or your tax accountant for more details. If you install solar, wind, or geothermal equipment, you'll qualify for an even larger tax break.

Of course, there are some drawbacks to buying an older home. Usually lenders require larger down payments (ranging from 20 to 40 percent) for older homes. Also, utility bills are apt to be higher because older homes often lack insulation. You should ask to see the past year's utility bills for any home you consider and then figure whether you can afford the heating and cooling expenses and what energy improvements are needed. Also, older homes require more maintenance, and you will eventually face such major expenses as reroofing, exterior painting, and replacing furnaces and water heaters. So include these items in your figures, as well as yard maintenance.

If you decide to have a local contractor or builder do some remodeling on the house, check out that individual's credentials thoroughly before signing any contracts. As the remodeling business has picked up, many incompetent characters have gotten into the act. To make sure you're working with a reliable professional, ask for the names of some of his previous customers and contact them for information. You can also check his credentials at the Better Business Bureau and with the local association of home builders.

If your house is fifty years old or older, make sure the contractor or remodeler you select is familiar with the construction of older houses, which were built much differently than houses are today. Ask to see some of his previous work on older homes, and visit with the owners to see if they are satisfied with his work.

Row Houses

In most older cities, particularly those in the East, you'll find blocks of row houses on a sweat-equity basis. In Atlanta, for example, a group of reddish-brown sandstone). Built in the 1800s or at the turn of the century, many of these row houses have gone through several phases. Starting out as residential town houses, they were converted to light industrial use as the neighborhood changed and later divided into apartments. Now they're being restored as individual dwellings, often offering up to 3,500 square feet of living space.

In many cases, neighborhood associations are formed to restore these row houses on a sweat-equity basis. In Atlanta, for example, a group of singles who decided to build their own community pooled funds to buy up a section of old row houses. They then set to work to rehabilitate their homes, doing what labor they could themselves and contracting for the rest. They got the dwellings for substantially less money than they could a new house and scheduled remodeling as they could afford it.

Other cities, recognizing the strengthened tax base they gain by bringing people back in town, offer financial programs for urban homesteaders. Baltimore auctioned off individual row houses for $1 each, with the requirement that the purchaser rehabilitate and live in the unit. (See "Rehabilitation Housing," page 57.)

Of course, speculators and developers are also getting into the act. They buy out inner-city blocks of row houses, rehab them, and resell them at rates of $50 per square foot or more. Some units go for as much as $120,000. If you can afford these prices, you can get a modern home with traditional charm. Often the developer will arrange mortgage loans for his buyers. In any event, you pay top dollar when you buy an already refurbished row house.

To get a row house at a modest price almost anywhere today, you have to buy before the renovation boom hits a particular neighborhood. And that entails some speculation on your part. You have to take the chance that if you buy while the area is still in the deteriorated stage that other like-minded people will later invest. Of course, the way to assure that is to organize a group to buy out a block or organize a homesteading cooperative (see "Cooperatives," page 45.)

Check with your city housing department about the possibility of purchasing repossessed row houses. Many cities offer financial assistance and construction counseling for homesteaders. Watch the newspapers for reports of upcoming auctions of row houses and rehabilitation programs, and get in touch with other neighborhood associations involved in restorations.

If you go the row house rehab route, you'll need to be exceedingly resourceful. But it can be a true entrepreneurial experience—you'll encounter lots of unanticipated snags, learn more than you ever imagined, and in the end, reap the rich rewards of your efforts.

One final note: If you decide to buy a row house, make sure you find out in advance who owns the common wall. If your neighbor holds title to the wall, he may elect to remodel and tear it down, and you'll have no say in the matter.

New Houses

Despite all the talk of escalating costs, many new houses are still within the economic reach of the single person. In fact, to meet the growing demand of the single market, many builders finally are developing some scaled-down, less expensive dwellings. Recognizing that a growing segment of the population has been denied access to the housing market, smart builders are turning away from the costly two-thousand-square-foot house designed for the three-child family. Instead they're constructing a variety of smaller affordable homes that cater to the single life-style and budget.

If what you're seeking is maximum convenience, you should explore these compact new options. You can get all the modern amenities—central air conditioning and appliances such as self-defrosting refrigerators, self-cleaning ovens, trash compactors, dishwashers, and microwave ovens. When you move in, the house is clean and you can decorate it as you wish—choosing your own carpeting, drapes, and appliances, which the builder will install. (Depending on your budget, you can custom order such luxury items as fireplaces, greenhouse windows, a hot tub, or sunken bathtub.) There will be less maintenance with a new home, and you should get a warranty against defects for the first year you occupy the home.

One of the big advantages of buying a new house is easier financing terms. Most lenders will finance a new home with only 5 to 10 percent down. Frequently, builders have prearranged financial packages with local lenders to assure that their buyers get loans, which is especially helpful in times of tight money. You may be able to get a substantial discount on a new home from a builder who has overbuilt and needs to sell his houses immediately. In such cases, you're in a good bargaining position to get the house at a reduced price. This, again, is where doing your homework can pay big dividends. Study your local real-estate market and read the real-estate section of the newspaper.

Sometimes, builders will advertise discounts. If you follow the ads closely, you'll know who has overbuilt. Then you can make a bid on the house that is considerably lower than the asking price and possibly save several thousand dollars. Always ask the builder how long the house has been on the market, but don't expect to get an honest answer every time. You may have to check with neighbors to get the real story.

Another warning: Big write-ups in the newspaper or a housing magazine about developers, builders, or subdivisions are *not* endorsements of quality. These stories often fail to point out the pitfalls of a project because the builder or development company is a large advertiser with the publication or has other connections. Furthermore, a lender's willingness to write you a loan for a new house is not indicative of structural quality. Often major builders and developers keep large cash reserves in local lending institutions to assure that their buyers will be serviced. In these instances, the lender will be the last one to warn you about the builder's less-than-impeccable reputation.

Town Houses

The first thing to find out about a town-house development is how the units are sold. Many town homes are sold in the form of condominiums, meaning that you own only the interior space, plus the patio if you have one, while the grounds in the project are jointly owned by you and your neighbors and managed and maintained through a home-owners' association. (See "Condominiums," page 37). Other town homes are sold like conventional houses: You buy your unit and the land upon which it stands, usually a small yard in front and back with a patio. This is called ownership in fee simple.

Fee simple town-house developments may also have home-owners' associations to look after various community interests, especially if recreational facilities are offered with the development. Membership is usually mandatory, and you pay a monthly association fee for such services as grass mowing, snow removal, and maintenance of recreational facilities.

Town houses are available in a variety of price ranges, designs, and configurations. While many units (often the least expensive ones) are constructed in the traditional row pattern, builders also cluster some models into duplexes, fourplexes, and sixplexes. One builder, for example, features fourplexes deftly disguised as mansionlike single units. On sloping sites, pairs of two-story town houses are piggybacked over one-floor units. In the higher quality developments, rows of units are short and arranged along curving streets or around cul-de-sacs, with landscaped spaces between buildings. To provide maximum privacy, individual units often have staggered setbacks and rooflines and differing exteriors.

The economy of a town-house development derives from the higher density of dwellings and shared common walls, which add up to energy savings for you. Understand, however, that there are high-end town-house developments, as well as the economy packages. Some developers market to the older, single person whose family has left the nest and who is now seeking to get rid of a large, high-maintenance, single-family home. These town houses usually offer all-custom luxuries, and prices may exceed $100,000.

On the other hand, for the economy-minded, first-time buyer, there are town houses that offer just the basics: a modern two-bedroom unit with no recreational facilities. Of course, you usually can opt to have a fireplace and microwave oven installed, but everything else is standard to all the units, which is how the builder keeps his costs low. Therefore, you can't custom-order appliances or other amenities.

Many developers offer town houses with age and no-children-allowed restrictions, geared specifically to the single buyer. These developments generally have commonly owned recreational facilities, such as swimming pools, clubhouses, and tennis courts. To find out what's available in your area, read real-estate ads and check with a knowledgeable broker or mortgage lender. Be advised, though, that brokers interested in large commissions may not want your business and may know little about town-house complexes. Then, your best source of information may be other single persons like yourself, and you'll deal directly with the developer or his agent.

Before you buy, there are several things you should look into. Above all, check for quality construction. Ask some owners who have been in the development for a while if they're satisfied or if they've had any particular problems. Unfortunately, paying a premium price doesn't assure premium quality, as Marilyn can attest.

Marilyn, ironically a public relations representative for home builders, bought a $67,000 town house from a builder she knew in Fairfax County, Virginia, a suburb of Washington, D. C. After signing the final papers and moving in, she noticed that the walls were curving in several rooms, the finishing job was very poor, and the grading around her unit was so inadequate that she had a swamp in her backyard.

"There were just a lot of problems," said Marilyn, who commutes one hour to work each day. "And it's a real hassle when you continually have to be arranging for someone to be home to let workmen into your *new house* to make repairs." (See "Defective Housing," page 35, for tips on how to avoid Marilyn's plight.)

You should find out how well the walls are soundproofed and if the builder offers double-walled construction. You don't want to be the constant captive audience of your neighbor's stereo or television. Avoid floor plans that place your bedroom next to your neighbor's recreation room.

Analyze the setup of any home-owners' association. The monthly assessment fee can—and will—go up with inflation. Many times, dues are pegged abnormally low to begin with as a sales strategy. If there are shared recreational facilities, find out how much you'll pay for them, and be sure that what is provided is adequate for the community. Also, make certain there are adequate parking facilities in the development, for you as well as visitors. There should be at least three parking spaces per unit.

It's advisable to review, with your attorney, covenants and documents you'll have to sign relating to the association. They may bind you to restrictions you'll find intolerable—such as no parking of recreational vehicles and boats on the premises or landscaping and uniformity restrictions prohibiting you from adding a fence or changing the exterior color of your house.

New House Locations

Before continuing the discussion on new house options, a word is in order regarding their location. Generally, you'll find new homes in the outlying suburbs, where raw land is available. In some cases, where urban renewal has occurred and older structures have been razed, you'll find new homes in the city. Because of the recent migration back to the city, you're apt to pay top dollar for these in-town homes, unless your city has developed some special programs for moderate income buyers. Check with the municipal housing department.

In the suburbs, you'll find new homes in the standard builder subdivisions and in the new planned unit developments (PUDs). In the standard subdivision, tract houses by the hundreds are laid out in rows throughout the community. Usually, a single builder puts up these tract houses, so called because they are all variations of a few standard floor plans. Production crews familiar with the stock plans put these homes up at a rapid pace. Uniformity is the key feature of these subdivisions: a grid arrangement of houses, with the same lot sizes and smiliar exteriors.

PUDs, on the other hand, offer a variety of housing arranged in clusters and around cul-de-sacs to make maximum use of the land and provide open spaces for the entire community. Because of astronomical land prices (more than $100,000 per acre in many areas), more developers and builders are working together to create PUDs. These developments provide housing to accommodate all ages, life-styles, and budgets.

Basic community facilities, such as shopping, schools, churches, fire and police protection, and other services, are integrated into the planning of the PUD. Builders arrange houses in clusters and around cul-de-sacs to reduce costs for streets, sidewalks, utility connections, sewer systems, and construction time. These savings help to keep house prices low. However, home-owner privacy is assured in the PUD through careful design and siting of each dwelling.

Houses are built on smaller, less expensive lots to conserve land, so there are large open spaces, where trees and streams are preserved. In many standard subdivisions, natural land features are plowed under when the developer razes the ground before platting it.

Many PUDs offer recreational facilities—swimming pools, tennis courts, playgrounds, clubhouses, picnic areas, and bike paths. You may be required to pay for these amenities, as well as maintenance of open spaces and residential streets through membership in a home-owners' association. (Some super-exclusive PUDs favor special interests. For example, they may offer man-made lakes for sailors or equestrian trails for horse owners. In these instances, the usual economics of the PUD don't apply.) If you buy into a PUD with a home-owners' association, you'll be required by a covenant to pay your pro rata share of the community's costs, for which you'll have one vote in determining operation changes and capital improvements. Before buying into a PUD, make sure the association is strong and solvent and review the covenants carefully.

PUDs are a viable alternative to existing housing patterns, particularly for first-time buyers priced out of other markets. In addition to condo apartments and town houses, you'll find some other very affordable detached dwellings in PUDs. However, study your entire market for these new home concepts.

Affordable New Home Concepts

These compact, new concept homes resulted from the demand by young singles and older empty nesters on fixed incomes for affordable, detached homes. These houses save money because they can be built on smaller, less expensive lots; they require fewer materials (wood has become extremely costly); and they use less energy. Maintenance is low as are real-estate taxes.

Zero-Lot-Line Houses

First started in southern California, these well-planned little homes are built on the minimum amount of land. Often, lots are only 34 feet wide, providing enough space for a patio and small yard, yet not so much that it requires lots of maintenance and interferes with busy life-styles. The house is placed on or near one of the side boundary lines. Thus, the name zero-lot-line homes (ZLL).

Builders across the country report that ZLLs are selling faster than any other type of house, primarily because they can be bought so inexpensively in a time of escalating land prices. Reports one Texas builder: "Lot costs amount to around 32 percent of the sales price of a house. When we can get ten homes rather than four or five on an acre of land, we can sell them for two-thirds the normal price. We trade side yard space for higher densities. Our buyers like them."

Most noteworthy is the fact that mortgage lenders also like them. Builders in many areas report that it's easier for buyers to get financing for single-family houses than for town houses or condominiums (although this is not universally true).

Zero-lot-line houses have come on strong in many cities since municipal zoning officials gave them the stamp of approval. Zoning officials, who tend to be adamant about the type and size of homes they'll approve for a community, traditionally have insisted that detached houses be built a certain minimum distance from the boundary lines of their lots. Fortunately, many of these officials now realize zero-lot-line houses reduce urban sprawl and enable persons to buy homes who would otherwise be priced out of the market.

To assure your privacy, the wall of the house abutting the boundary sidelines contains no windows or only windows placed higher than usual. The rest of the house is specially designed, often with skylights and arches, to bring in sunlight. The single side yard is large enough for a garden, barbecue, or patio area. In the drought-prone West, the smaller yards prove particularly economical. As the cost of public water goes up, buyers want less lawn to water.

Many zero-lot-line houses sell in the $45,000 to $75,000 range, though prices where you live will be determined by your local market. You may also find some zero-lot-line houses sold as condominiums.

Patio Houses

Basically the same as zero-lot-line houses, these detached dwellings are marketed in some areas as "patio homes." They may have slightly more yard space than a ZLL house, depending on the specifications of the development. However, the concept is the same: reduced cost achieved through putting a smaller home on a smaller lot.

No-Frills Houses

During the fifties and sixties, first-time buyers bought the majority of new homes. Because of rising costs, currently only one out of four new home customers is a first-time buyer. To battle this problem, some builders are introducing "no-frills homes," which lack many of the extras that contribute to higher prices.

One California builder (as you'll notice, many of these new concepts originated in California where land prices and real-estate inflation are highest) who previously offered high-end custom homes has turned to constructing single-family, no-frills homes. He said he found a crying need for housing among persons earning less than $20,000 per year. The builder offers three models, including a 1,000-square-foot two-bedroom and a

1,200-square-foot three-bedroom. When the houses came on the market, they ranged in price from $28,500 to $37,100, on a lot about 60 by 120 feet.

The houses include insulation, tile flooring throughout, sliding patio doors, two-car garages with storage, air conditioning, fiberglass tubs and shower enclosures, kitchen cabinets with hardware, light fixtures, and small patios. They exclude such "extras" as kitchen appliances, washer and dryers, carpeting, drapes, and landscaping.

By prearrangement of the builder, many of these homes are financed through government-insured mortgages, which require small down payments and low monthly payments from the buyer. Ask a mortgage lender, broker, or FHA official about similar homes in your area.

Expandable Core Houses

Also geared for the under $20,000-per-year income crowd, these compact starter homes are designed to be expanded as the buyer's income increases. One Sacramento builder reports he developed four core models ranging in price from about $30,000 to $35,000 for young working persons who had been priced out of the conventional market.

His smallest house, an 816-square-foot, two-bedroom model, no bigger than an apartment, can grow into a four-bedroom, two-bath unit with a large den or game room. This home is ideal for the single person who would later decide to take a roommate or marry, or for the single parent who later wishes to add more space for growing children. You should realize that adding onto or remodeling the typical house is at best an expensive proposition, and often it's impossible to get what you want. However, these homes are especially designed to be expanded at minimal cost and inconvenience to you.

To keep costs low, these homes are sold with only the basics—gas ranges, garbage disposals, hookups for washers and dryers, and ceiling and exterior insulation. Options the builder will include, as your budget allows, are carpeting, dishwasher, fireplace, and butcher-block cabinetry.

All of these models qualify for FHA, minimum down payment mortgages. That means first-time buyers can get often into these homes for about $2,000 to $2,500 cash up-front.

Unfinished Houses

Many builders offer houses with unfinished upper levels for about $2,000 less than if the builder finished the house. Usually one floor is ample for the live-alone single person, and you can finish the upstairs later as time and money allow. Plus you have the flexibility to create a music room, study, library, or whatever suits your needs and tastes.

Some builders will also give you a discount on a house if you agree to do some of the finishing work yourself, such as interior painting. Before jumping into one of these arrangements, make sure you have a written agreement in advance as to who will do what and what the savings passed on to you will be.

Duplex Units

One of the latest affordable concepts builders have developed is the purchase of one-half of a duplex. Most builders and developers are putting a number of these units into their projects. They claim that these units provide the square footage and amenities of the single-family detached house for about $10,000 to $15,000 less. These duplexes come in all forms and styles—split-levels, two-stories, and back-to-front units.

You own your half of the duplex and the land it sits on (fee simple ownership) and you're responsible for upkeep of the exterior and the yard. Warranties are usually provided on these units. To accommodate first-time buyers, many builders arrange for graduated-payment mortgages with low down payments and government-backed financing. Builders in some areas even pay part of the closing costs to help market these units. You should also know that federal savings-and-loan associations can write conventional loans on half a duplex with only 10 percent down.

These units appreciate at the same rate as detached houses and are used by many first-time buyers as a stepping stone to a more expensive home. As this concept gains popularity, builders are also providing luxury units, with up to two thousand square feet of space. These units, however, are not designed for economy and sell for about the same as a median-priced, single-family house.

Where this marketing concept is not available, many single persons pool their funds to buy duplexes together, and one person lives on each side. (See Chapter 11, "Special Tips for Single Persons Buying Together.") Other single persons with the available capital buy duplexes as investments, living in one half and renting out the other half. (See Chapter 14, "Investment Opportunities for the Single Person.")

Buying on the Basis of a Model

If you decide to have your home built on the basis of a builder's model that you visit, you should have several things in writing before putting any money down. Get the floor plans and specifications on everything, including interior decorating and landscaping. Don't assume that the model you visit is exactly what you'll get. Higher quality appurtenances, such as light fixtures, appliances, carpeting, and drapes are often used in the sales models.

Moreover, interior designers hired by the builder sometimes furnish the rooms with scaled-down furniture or extensive wall mirrors to make the rooms appear larger. Get the builder or his sales representative to explain clearly the different options, extras, and decorator items shown in the model and those available for your home. And get precise prices for each item. Many volume builders have detailed brochures showing floor plans and outlining options.

Evaluate the character of the builder or salesperson. How responsive is he or she? Does he quote exact prices and know his product well? Or is there a lot of hesitation before your questions are answered? These initial reactions probably will indicate the type of relationship you can expect with the builder or sales rep while the house is under construction. Ideally, you want to work with a person who will answer your questions at each stage of construction and who knows the process thoroughly. If you encounter a less-than-seasoned professional, keep on shopping.

Make sure you get a minimum one-year written warranty from the builder, and don't put down any money or sign a contract until your lawyer goes over all the details. You also should check in advance to see what regulations there are, if any, governing the development in which your home is to be built.

The advantage of buying on the basis of a model as opposed to an existing new house is that you can choose your own wall paint, floor coverings, and appliances. You can choose top-of-the-line items all the way or hold down your costs with some items and splurge with others. You can have a fireplace, the color and type of bathtub you want, wallpaper and other built-ins that you wouldn't get with a new home already built—the so-called speculative-built home.

Manufactured Housing

Manufactured housing is another option you should consider if you're trying to break into the market with a moderately priced new home. These homes, often geared to first-time buyers with limited budgets, are produced in factories and shipped to the site for erection. (Conventional "site-built" houses are completely assembled on your lot by carpenters and other tradesmen.) Savings result from the production-line manufacturing process, which also reduces the time it takes to put up the house. Often, a manufactured house can be assembled on your lot within three weeks.

As the prices for land, materials, and on-site labor escalate, manufactured housing can provide affordable shelter for many single persons. It is now possible to get a manufactured house as durable and energy efficient as a site-built structure. Manufacturers have refined their technology to the point where they can turn out dwellings with precise fits and closer tolerances that reduce air infiltration. Some manufacturers offer such special energy-efficient options as added roof and ceiling insulation, six-inch exterior wall insulation, triple-glazed windows, and a heat-pump heating/cooling system. Beware though of manufacturers who make claims of energy efficiency to which they don't live up.

You will probably choose your house from several standard models offered by the manufacturer, who like the tract-home builder keeps his costs low by offering a limited number of floor plans that can be rapidly reproduced. However, nationwide there are more than five hundred manufacturers in operation, offering a variety of floor plans, exteriors, and design alternatives. They produce ranch homes, split-foyers, bi-levels, two-stories—the gamut of styles. Some manufacturers specialize in small—850-square-foot, two-bedroom—starter homes. Others include interior design packages providing drapes, furnishings for six rooms, and wallpaper for bedrooms, kitchen, and bath. You'll also find manufacturers who will alter floor plans and add certain custom features for you.

Most manufactured houses are marketed through local builder/dealers. The manufacturer, in essence, franchises the product to local builders, who deal directly with customers in their areas. These dealers often have display models which you can visit. Often, these dealers are also real-estate brokers or affiliated with real-estate firms. It is essential that you choose an established and reputable builder/dealer who understands the building process and knows how to schedule subcontractors. Step one, however, is to familiarize yourself with the basic types of manufactured homes— components, panelized packages, and modular, or sectional, homes.

Components

The basic structural components of the home—roof and floor trusses and interior and exterior wall panels—are built at a manufacturer's plant and sold as a package to the builder. This production technique eliminates the costly and time-consuming step of measuring and cutting lumber at the site. It also means the house can be started away from bad weather, which is why many progressive builders go this route. This is the main manufactured housing process in the country.

Panelized Packages

One step up the manufacturing ladder from the component house, these packages come to the site in ready-to-assemble sections—floors, walls, and ceilings. The wall panels usually include sheathing, siding, windows and doors, and often factory-applied insulation. Panelized packages come as either open-wall or closed-wall systems. In the open-wall system, one side of the wall is left open so the builder can install electrical wiring, heating, and plumbing on the job site. With the closed-wall product, the manufacturer installs the electrical wiring, heat ducts, and plumbing on the panels. Then after an in-plant inspection by a state-approved building inspector, the walls are closed with an interior dry-wall finish.

Producers of panelized housing fall into two categories—custom and catalog manufacturers. Custom manufacturers will fabricate a home to your specifications. Catalog manufacturers produce only those houses which are included in their catalogs, usually architect-designed homes. Catalog homes generally offer a number of floor plans with a variety of exterior sidings.

Modular or Sectional Homes

The most complete form of the manufactured packages, these homes are shipped from the factory to the site in several sections or modules. When the modular/sectional home leaves the factory, it is complete in nearly every detail. All exterior siding, windows, and doors are installed, and the roof is installed and shingled. Interiors are complete with carpeted and tiled floors, walls papered or painted, interior doors hung, and all kitchen and bathroom cabinets, fixtures, and appliances installed. A modular/sectional home can be moved onto its permanent foundation within a few hours and ready to occupy in less than one week.

Non-Traditional Homes Utilizing the Manufactured Process

Dome homes, log homes, and A-frames may also have components manufactured in plants with parts shipped to the site for erection. All of these structures offer a certain unique ambiance. However, manufacturers of these products often make claims of energy efficiency and low cost to which the homes don't live up. A couple of A-frame occupants who bought their house situated on a wooded and secluded lot for its "openness and captivating possibilities" chronically complain that their paychecks go increasingly for heating, cooling, and termite treatments.

New to the marketplace is the "modified A-frame," which has a flat section on the top of the roof, unlike the traditional A-frame, which comes to a point. The reason for this modification is to increase the amount of insulation in the roof and to decrease heat loss. However, a number of modified A-frames have collapsed under snow loads. Therefore, if you are going to buy one of these structures, make sure it has an engineering certification geared to the snow loads of your area.

Dome homes, on the other hand, have been known to withstand loads of snow, heavy winds, and earthquakes when other houses have crumbled. Moreover, dome dwellers brag about the energy efficiency of their homes. Domes have less exterior surface exposed to the outside environment in proportion to the number of square feet of interior floor space than any other structures. Domes are fine alternatives to traditional rectilinear houses, provided the components are ordered from an established and reputable manufacturer and properly constructed. For more information and a list of manufacturers, write: American Dome Co., 1026 Sunset Trail, Webster, New York 14580.

Log home manufacturers sell everything from a one-room cabin to a large two-story or split-level, contemporary-style dwelling. With the increasing popularity of these structures, the Log Homes Council of the National Association of Home Manufacturers warns that there are many firms "selling little more than green logs and pretty pictures to unwary buyers." In addition, many log home manufacturers make blatantly false claims of high-insulating properties of their logs. A log home requires an engineering analysis to ensure structural integrity and livability. The council requires all of its members to have their home plans approved by one of the state or nationally recognized building-code-writing bodies. For more information, write the Log Homes Council, care of the National Association of Home Manufacturers, 6521 Arlington Boulevard, Falls Church, Virginia 22042.

If you're interested in any of these alternatives, you should investigate the market thoroughly before buying and read the available literature—that distributed by the manufacturer as well as some general guides on the subject. And by all means, talk with some persons residing in those kinds of structures to learn their satisfactions and problems.

The Sweat-Equity Concept

Some manufacturers sell building kits, including all the materials for a home and an instruction manual, to the home buyer, who then puts the components together himself. This procedure, known as sweat equity, enables the buyer to get his home at a rock-bottom price and to build up equity through the sweat of his own brow. These owner-built homes can be bought in almost any stage of construction. Some manufacturers will erect the shell and then leave the finishing work for the buyer.

To illustrate, consider Hal, an outdoors-minded young executive, who bought four acres of land outside the small community where he worked and ordered a sweat-equity house package for $20,000. He paid the manufacturer about $3,500 to erect the foundation on his woodsy lot. He paid another $3,000 for the plumbing, heating, and air conditioning, bringing the total cost of his 1,300-square-foot ranch house to about $26,500. Hal then put on the roof shingles, installed the insulation and electrical wiring, laid the floors, painted the house, and landscaped the property himself.

One shell-kit company even provides financing with a three-year construction loan. However, the buyer usually has to agree to give the company a note and first mortgage lien on his land. Or the buyer must furnish the manufacturer a recordable land contract or deed showing he is purchasing or has purchased the land. The buyer is then expected to complete his home within three years and arrange with a local lender for a long-term loan.

If you decide to go the sweat-equity route, a couple of warnings are in order. First, make sure you know exactly what you're getting into. The Federal Trade Commission (FTC) has already intervened to prevent one manufacturer from misrepresenting the ease with which its pre-cut, build-it-yourself houses can be constructed. The FTC complaint against Insilco Corporation and its subsidiary Miles Homes, Inc. alleged that the companies falsely advertised that their houses could be easily and completely assembled by anyone, without the help of skilled building tradesmen, and that the instructions for each house were simple enough for anyone to follow.

The consent agreement that Insilco and Miles reached with the FTC requires the companies to disclose certain essential facts to consumers. For example, the firms must inform buyers, in writing, prior to sales, that they may need the help of experienced tradesmen, that some localities *require* that licensed tradesmen perform certain home-building work, and that the house will be subject to a mortgage lien as security. The firms are further required to provide each buyer a three-day period in which to cancel the transaction and to establish a fast system for handling consumer complaints. The FTC investigation also uncovered allegations that buyers often paid undisclosed delivery charges and were not told everything about their financial obligations and the housing.

Second, realize that you may have difficulty getting financing for a sweat-equity home. Lenders often hesitate when asked to invest mortgage money in an unfinished house. (If for some reason you can't get a local lender to go along with you, you may have to work through a manufacturer who offers financing.)

Third, you need to analyze carefully the extent of the project and your building ability and aptitude. Building your own home is apt to demand all of your spare time for a year or more. In addition, you may need expert help, which can be expensive if you have to call in a plumber or electrician. If you get in over your head, your dream home can become a disaster. Says one experienced builder, who has frequently been called in to help shell-kit buyers salvage their homes: "Selling owner/builder kits is like selling the crate parts for a 747 with an instruction manual on how to put it together. A house is a complex environment in terms of assembly, and you have to know how the components are put together. For a company to give 20 to 25 percent of the parts to owners and then let them fend for themselves is less than ethical, and the results are often tragic."

Some manufacturers protect themselves by interviewing prospective buyers to see if they have the necessary building experience. If you doubt your abilities, you would do well to go with such a firm. Discuss with the manufacturer what he will do, as well as writing some contingencies into your agreement. Then if you can't complete the home, the manufacturer will step back in and help.

Also, consider buying a package where all you finish is the interior. But before entering into any agreements, shop carefully for a reputable shell-kit dealer. Usually, you'll find advertisements for sweat-equity homes in newspapers and shelter magazines. Check your library, too, for shelter books listing shell-kit manufacturers.

Prices of Manufactured Houses

Some manufacturers claim their units sell for $2 to $4 less per square foot than site-built houses, while others claim savings of up to $11 per square foot. Check your local market. You may find the larger manufacturers offer more lower priced models, but it's a fair bet that you can find a house in the $30,000 range. Of course, you can get a much more expensive package, too, depending on the size and number of options you choose and how far the house has to be shipped. In any case, ask the builder/dealer for a firm price quotation, which he should be able to give you weeks in advance.

Your price will be pegged to how far the house has to be transported. To cut costs, deal with a local manufacturer. Ask each builder/dealer you visit the location of the manufacturer, since some plants ship houses as far as three hundred miles. Others limit distribution to a relatively small area. Manufactured housing, primarily a regional industry, is much stronger in the northeastern, north central and midwestern states, where harsh winters cut down on-site building time. If you live in one of these states, you'll have a number of manufacturers from which to choose, and you may even be able to arrange a visit to the plant. Most fabricated houses are erected in rural areas and in the suburbs, where you may find whole developments of manufactured housing, as well as manufactured town-house and condominium units.

All manufactured housing must comply with local building codes. In some areas, building code restrictions prohibit manufactured houses, so check with your local housing department about this possibility. Sometimes, local builders opposed to manufactured housing lobby municipal officials to maintain codes that preclude manufactured structures.

Financing for Manufactured Houses

Manufactured homes appreciate at the same rate as conventional homes do and can be conventionally financed. In addition, most manufactured homes qualify for government-backed financing. The builder/dealer may offer a financing package for the house, but you should check the overall costs of his financial package against the cost of financing through a local lending institution. Check what it will cost you over the life of the loan.

Further Information on Manufactured Housing

The National Association of Home Manufacturers publishes an annual *Guide to Manufactured Homes*, which describes in detail the various manufacturing processes and their advantages. The book also lists more than a hundred home manufacturers, the types of houses they produce, and the person to contact for further information. You can order a copy for $3 from the National Association of Home Manufacturers, 6521 Arlington Boulevard, Falls Church, Virginia 22042.

When you order a manufactured house, have the local builder/dealer put in writing the day your new home will arrive at the lot and the occupancy date. A reputable, established dealer should be able to give you firm time frames and should offer a minimum one-year, *written* warranty on structural components of the house. Ask the dealer for energy-efficiency specifications on the house. Then get the names of a few other customers and visit with them about their experiences with the dealer and the quality of their homes. This preliminary research will help you avoid the predicament of Elaine, whose inept builder/dealer landed her in court and left her with an improperly constructed and unfinished home.

Elaine, a teacher living in the heart of the midwestern manufactured-housing belt, decided that she wanted a new house as an investment and a place of her own to decorate. Her annual salary of $15,000 dictated that she shop for the most affordable options, and after visiting several builder/dealers, she settled on a modular home, which she felt she could get with the minimum of hassles. Unfortunately, the established dealer she selected got very busy with a bunch of orders and refused to make earlier agreed-upon alterations on the model she chose. However, that dealer referred her to another manufacturer, represented by a young man, Tim, who had just become a full-fledged dealer.

Accepting the referral on good faith, Elaine placed her order with Tim in mid-July and plunked down $2,000, with the promise that she would be in the house by mid-August. Since she was moving from one town to another to take a new teaching position, she wanted a couple of weeks to get settled in her new home before school started.

On her slated occupancy date of August 15, ground had not even been broken for the basement. It took ten weeks to complete the house Tim said would be finished in three weeks. In the meantime Elaine had no place to live nor money to pay rent!

She had paid Tim an additional $21,000 when the house arrived and then was forced to set up temporary quarters in a "drafty, old barnlike place with no appliances" that an acquaintance found for her. Since she had nowhere to store her furniture, Tim offered to move it into the basement for her. On the appointed day, he failed to show up with his truck. Elaine discovered that not only were there no windows installed in the basement, but the neighborhood kids were using it as their gathering place. A call to Tim's home revealed that he was out of town for a golf tournament.

"That was when I decided I'd just as soon see him drawn and quartered," Elaine said. "I finally exploded and moved into a motel and billed Tim."

However, that was just the beginning. This was Tim's first house, and it turned out that he knew nothing about general contracting and how to manage subcontractors. The carpenters he hired didn't know how to hang doors or windows. The electricians he hired had to rewire the house three times before the city inspector would give the approval to turn on the electricity. Only after complaining to the mayor's office and staging a confrontation with Tim and the electricians in the code inspector's office did Elaine get an approval of her wiring.

Elaine did not advise her lender of the hassles she was having and, unbelievably, the savings-and-loan officer issued Tim's final payment without requiring lien waivers from the subcontractors. Elaine got no receipts from Tim for her payments, which she had relied on the lender to record as he issued money to Tim.

When Elaine moved in, Tim abruptly left town. Then the subcontractors started hammering on her door demanding their payments. Tim had either not paid them or written them bad checks. As the subs conferred and came to the brink of issuing a judgment on Elaine's house, she frantically consulted the district attorney. He was appalled that she had not sought legal counsel earlier. As a result, she lost her first battle in court and was ordered to pay the plumber for services Tim had requested him to provide.

Fortunately, the DA managed to locate Tim and negotiated a deal with the subs whereby Tim would pay them off in installments. Elaine has her house with a one-year warranty from the manufacturer, who refuses to repair warped windows, defective storm doors, improperly hung interior doors, cracks in the cupboards, and unpainted spots of dry wall. The manufacturer contends those are the dealer's responsibility. Tim obviously will be doing no more dealing. So Elaine is stuck footing the bill to bring her new house up to code standards.

"The whole thing was really discouraging, disgusting, and very depressing," Elaine laments. "Anybody who builds a house is totally at the mercy of those bastards who won't tell you a damn thing about what's going on."

She admits, though, that her initial mistake was not getting some references on Tim and then sticking with an established dealer.

"I was just green enough—having never bought or built a home before—that he got by with everything. Later when I talked with the DA, he said I should have had a lawyer who could have checked out Tim's procedures. My own feeling is if I had had a lawyer sitting at my elbow maybe Tim would have taken me a little more seriously. He was a totally brazen shyster."

Defective Housing

New home defects now rank among the top consumer problems in the country, report Federal Trade Commission (FTC) officials. Complaints pouring into the FTC cite such defects as exposed wiring, cracking and buckling walls, improperly installed plumbing, and poorly constructed foundations, roofs, and floors. Ten percent of the new homes built may have major defects, according to a preliminary FTC estimate.

One resident of a new town-house complex relates that carpeting worth $2,000 was ruined when her toilets backed up for the third time. To stop drafts, another resident had to stuff putty into electrical outlets. One young executive was forced to turn down a transfer and job promotion because he couldn't sell for $29,000 the condo unit that he had paid $24,900 for a few years before. Other owners complained of cracked foundations, faulty drainage, leaky roofs, inadequate insulation, and poor heating.

Kaufman & Broad, Inc., one of the nation's largest home builders, constructed that town-house complex. It took the intervention of the state attorney general to get the company to agree to a settlement with the aggrieved residents. Kaufman & Broad ultimately accepted a proposal requiring the company to buy back defective homes or pay the owners the amount by which any uncorrected defects lowered the value of their homes.

In a separate action, Kaufman & Broad also has agreed to a FTC consent order requiring the company to provide a warranty with each new home it sells across the country and to repair major construction defects in homes bought from it. In addition, the order prohibits Kaufman & Broad from selling or delivering housing that is not built in accordance with adequate standards of workmanship. The FTC is now investigating other major builders and has undertaken a nationwide survey of new home defects.

Federal investigators also have uncovered major defects in homes underwritten by Farmers Home Administration (FmHA) loans. FmHA finances homes for persons such as Elaine, who live in rural communities or small towns where it's difficult to obtain financing. Inspectors found backed-up sewers, leaky walls and floors, holes around ceiling lights, and new homes with no floor insulation or vents for clothes dryers. Builders sometimes completely ignored plans. In one case, the living room of a new home was walled off from the front entryway. In these incidences, the home owners ended up footing bills for thousands of dollars in repairs or simply defaulted on the loans when defects were too expensive for them to repair.

As a result of these investigations, FmHA has ordered its offices across the country to protect borrowers from shoddy workmanship. Under new rules, borrowers can report defects to local FmHA offices, which can then require the builder to make repairs. If he doesn't make the repairs within a reasonable time, the builder can be debarred from participation in the Farmers Home loan program.

In most states, the only protection new home buyers have is in the form of implied warranty laws that make builders liable for defects in material and workmanship. However, these laws are ineffective in dealing with builders who go broke or who refuse to make good on claims without a legal battle.

Thus, the FTC has warned the home-building industry either to clean up its act or face government regulation. Noting that less than 25 percent of the nation's builders offer warranties on their homes, the FTC says it will institute federal protection for buyers unless more builders provide warranties. As a model warranty, FTC officials point to the HOW program, a ten-year insured warranty against defects paid for by the builder. The Home Owner's Warranty Corp. (HOW) was formed in 1974 by the National Association of Home Builders (NAHB) as a step to avoid federal regulation. (For more about warranties, see "The Home Warranty," page 124.) Unfortunately, the HOW program is voluntary and those builders trying to cut costs and finish off houses rapidly are the ones most apt to experience problems.

Therefore, it is your responsibility as a buyer to inquire carefully about the workmanship and the type of warranty offered on each new home you consider—be it condominium, town house, or detached new house in a high-end development. Cost does not guarantee quality. Try to visit with some of the builder's other customers before putting down any money. Ask them what problems, if any, they've had and how well the builder followed up on repairs.

It's rare to find a new home owner who can say all work was finished when he occupied his house. Builders reply that where demand is high for new homes, labor and material shortages make it difficult to finish them properly by the time buyers want to move in. Some builders have warned consumers to expect a lot more houses with things missing from them.

The builders' response is valid in some cases. Builders, indeed, are hampered by shortages and high costs, and responsible members of the industry are attempting to work out these problems. NAHB, which has about 117,000 members nationwide, has urged all affiliated local home-builders' associations to establish systems for handling the complaints of new home buyers. If you're in the market for a new home, call your local builders' association, ask about the complaint system, and get the names of builders who offer the HOW program. Also, inquire about consumer protection legislation in your state for new home buyers. If you don't get the answers there, consult the consumer protection division of your state attorney general's office. Ultimately, of course, the quality of the home you get depends on the integrity of the builder with whom you deal.

If you encounter serious defects in a new home and can't resolve the problem locally, you can write the FTC's Division of Marketing Abuses, Room 272, Federal Trade Commission, Washington, D.C. 20580.

Buyers of existing homes also need to be wary of defects. The FTC estimates that undisclosed defects cost buyers of existing homes more than $750 million in one year. A survey revealed that 55 percent of the problems arose within the first six months of occupancy and 80 percent within the first year. About 45 percent of the home buyers surveyed had unexpected repairs costing an average of $500 in the first two years of ownership. Generally, these defects are discovered just after the buyer gives up all available cash in order to make the purchase. You can avoid these problems by having a thorough structural inspection prior to signing the final purchase papers.

Another difficulty that single buyers (especially single first-time buyers) may encounter is the developer who can't follow through with the roads or amenities he promised to provide. This is a common problem in areas where there is a high demand for housing. The developer runs into either financial or regulatory obstacles. Before accepting any developer's promise about a project in which you plan to buy, check out his reputation carefully. Ask what other developments he has done in the area, and then visit those developments to see if they are finished off and meet the quality which you expect. Try also to visit with some residents and see if all promises were met.

Throughout the eighties and into the twenty-first century, the trend will be increasingly toward high-density and association housing, where owners control shared amenities. Two of the most popular forms of association housing will be condonimiums and cooperatives, wherein residents work together to create and maintain their community. Buying a condo or co-op unit is a complicated business, distinctively different from buying a standard detached house. Therefore, you first must understand the concept of the organization and then be prepared to analyze its stability and acceptability for you, as well as all of the governing documents and rules.

Condominiums

A condominium is a form of ownership whereby you own your living quarters—the deed is made out to you—and you also own an undivided share in the common property. In other words, this common property— hallways, grounds, sidewalks, and laundry and recreational facilities—is owned jointly by you and your neighbors. More than half of all Americans will live in some form of condominiums within the next twenty years, according to the U.S. Department of Housing and Urban Development.

With a condo, you get all the advantages of ownership—equity buildup, appreciation, tax breaks—without the responsibilities of maintenance and yard work. You are responsible for your own living quarters and participation in the condominium association, which usually hires a property management firm to handle maintenance and other details. As an owner, you have one vote in determining everything the association does, and you'll probably be asked to participate in some association committees. You elect a board of directors, which oversees the affairs of the complex and deals directly with the management firm, and you pay a monthly fee to support the association's activities and to maintain the common grounds.

Varieties of Condos

When you buy a condo, you're buying a certain life-style as well. Indeed, the upsurge in condominiums results from builders' and developers' recognition of changing life-styles and demographics in America. They realize that the growing number of single buyers welcome this form of maintenance-free housing. And condo developers tend to cater to three distinct groups of singles: the young, first-time buyer; the single-again individual who often has children; and the older, retired single.

You will find condos in a range of prices—from the super-luxurious, with all the amenities, to the just-basics, economical, starter home—in a variety of styles and locations. Generally, there are more condominiums in and around major cities, where a scarcity of available land, limited resources, and high house prices have made them a necessary alternative. In the city, you can find self-contained condo villages offering everything from one-bedroom apartments to two-story town houses topping out at $200,000. These high-end projects usually offer units with varying floor plans and such amenities as garages, gyms, outdoor jogging tracks, saunas, swimming pools, and clubhouses with nearby shopping facilities.

In most cities, you'll also find old apartment buildings being converted into condominiums. Those conversions, done with quality and taste, offer suitable in-town housing, albeit usually at a premium price. On the other hand, some converters just stick in a few modern amenities, slap on an exorbitant price, and don't tell you about the failing roof and furnace. So proceed with caution if you're shopping the conversion market.

You'll probably find the greatest variety of condos in the suburbs. There you'll see attached town houses with a gamut of recreational facilities. And you'll also find no-frills condo projects with minimally priced units designed for the first-time buyer.

Condos are a logical starting point for the first-time buyer. If the high priced, in-town condos scare you, head for the suburbs, and consider enlisting the aid of a real-estate broker knowledgeable in the condo market.

Above all, as you look at various condos, try to find out about the other residents, who will be your co-owners and with whom you will have to work. Try to find a complex that will suit your life-style and where your co-owners will be both socially compatible and financially dependable. If you have a high-tension job and seek peace and solitude at home, you may want to buy into an adults-only complex. Avoid complexes where most of the residents seem to be straining financially. When maintenance costs go up, such marginal owners may default on their mortgages. You and the other remaining owners will pay the accumulated maintenance charges on those foreclosed units. That could result in a chain of defaults that jeopardizes the whole project.

Using a Condo Broker

If you're in an area where there are lots of condos and you have some specific requirements, you might do well to consult a broker *specializing* in condominium sales. For example, if you want a complex that will allow you to keep a dog, a condo broker can help you find such a place. Also, the broker should be able to match your requirements in price, location, and amenities with an appropriate condo.

One brokerage firm that exclusively handles the sale and resale of condos keeps a file of every condo association in the area and provides explanations of the history of the association and how well it works. Some speciality brokers keep detailed records of the ownership history of individual condo units—who the various owners were, how many times the unit has been sold, and what the sales price was each time. Such a broker can advise you about the rules and regulations of each condo complex, as well as tell you about any impending policy changes or special assessments. Since special legislation governs the sale and resale of condos in each state, you should consult a broker well versed in these laws and the documents involved in the condo transaction. That way, if you run into serious problems, you'll have recourse—you can come back to the broker if he or she misled you in any way.

Selecting a knowledgeable broker can spare you the grief Ken experienced. A bachelor who prides himself on being a gourmet cook, Ken decided to buy a condo—his first home—as an investment.

"I know precious little about finance and investments," said Ken, who has a hefty $60,000 annual salary as an academic and professional consultant. "I wanted an investment, but I didn't have the time to go down and find out everything about buying a condo—that would be a hassle and my schedule is too demanding for that. So I dealt with someone I thought I could trust to take care of me."

Unfortunately, that someone was a broker who knew precious little about condominiums. Ken's chief requirement was a gas stove, which the broker promised he could get. As it turned out, not only did he not get his gas stove, but he didn't occupy his condo until three months after his scheduled move-in date because of construction delays.

A seasoned condo broker would have known that the developer had a track record of delays. Moreover, the broker should have known in advance about the appliance package and allowable alterations and should not have made unfounded promises to Ken. Call your local Board of Realtors for the names of brokerage firms specializing in condo sales.

If you're in a community where there are only a few condo developments, it's probably wise to school yourself on the particulars of condos and handle the purchase yourself. If you do your homework, you're apt to know more than any brokers you might consult. And if you're buying a resale condo, you should be able to negotiate a lower price if the seller doesn't pay a broker's fee. One developer/architect in a medium-sized community reports that brokers won't show prospective buyers condos that aren't listed with their firms. If you run into this situation, watch the newspaper real-estate sections for condo ads.

Financial Aspects

Condos can be financed in most communities exactly like any other home—with a conventional or government-backed loan. However, in communities where condos have not gained wide acceptance or where there have been serious problems with condo developments, financing may be a problem. For example, in some areas lenders don't like to get involved with the legal documents entailed in a condo purchase, and they'll write mortgages only for condo units where they have handled the developer's financing. Unless a lender has money already invested in the project, he may refuse to write you a mortgage for a new or used condo apartment. Check with local lenders before you sign anything.

In most places, condos appreciate as rapidly as detached houses. Where condos are in hot demand, notably the Sunbelt states, they may appreciate at a higher rate. In any event, when you buy, consider the resale value of your unit. The best assurance of good resale value is a good location, and the best location is in a stable neighborhood where property values are rising.

Regulations and Abuses

There is no uniform law governing condominiums—operation, management, construction standards, or conversions. Each state has enacted its own laws regulating condos, which were first introduced in the United States in the early sixties. Naturally, with a new industry there were bound to be abuses. Initially, numerous instances surfaced of low-balled monthly dues, sweetheart contracts between developers and management firms, and recreational leases, which benefited the builder/developer. For example, the developer would retain title to the swimming pool and lease it back to the owners at a higher rate each year. Enactment of the state laws and pressure from lenders has cleaned up most of these abuses.

However, as a buyer, you still have to be on your toes. First, you need to check out the reputation of the builder or developer and don't take anything on face value. One well-known developer of a nationally recognized, award-winning adult community is on the verge of being sued by disgruntled residents. They cite such defects as decaying wood, leaking roofs, faulty sewer pipes, interior dampness, sinking carport floors, flammable Sheetrock, rotting decks, broken water pipes, and cracked steps and walks.

As you're shopping, find out what other projects the developer has built or converted and visit one. Ask the residents their opinions of the builder. If they complain of constant problems and the building appears run down, look for another developer. Also, keep in mind that good developers usually offer structural warranties on each condo unit.

Buying into an Incomplete Complex or on the Basis of a Model

Often, the builder will sell condos on the basis of a few already constructed models with the promise that when completed the complex will contain a certain number of units. With rising construction and interest rates, this can be a hazardous undertaking.

Ken learned this lesson the hard way. In March, he put down $1,000 in earnest money on a $40,000 condo that was to be completed May 15. He didn't occupy until July 17, by which time the interest rate for his mortgage loan had gone up, as had the closing costs. Moreover, when he did move in, there was no hot water, and he inherited "a swimming pool of rainwater" in his backyard, which had not been properly graded.

"I was ready to move in the spring and ended up losing money because I had to forfeit my rental deposit. I refused to move in until the unit was finished, and because the builder didn't plan very well, he had a hell of a time getting the place finished," Ken said.

Bob bought a town house in one of the first condo complexes constructed in his community. The developer promised that eventually there would be a street in front of Bob's unit. He's lived there two years, and there's still no street.

Bob, an attorney specializing in real-estate and tax law, warns: "If you're buying an unbuilt unit, be sure to examine the abstract before you sign anything to make sure what the developer promises will actually be provided."

Also protect yourself regarding promised recreational facilities. Have it written into your sales contract that any money you put down for unbuilt recreational facilities will be placed in an escrow account and refunded if the facilities aren't up within a certain time period. Likewise, if the developer wants a sizable deposit on your unit, make sure the money goes into an escrow account rather than into construction costs—otherwise you won't get your deposit back if the developer goes bankrupt. Avoid developers who want an advance payment for the maintenance fund while the project is still under construction—there's no maintenance on an unfinished building.

If the project is being built in stages, that can affect the amount of your monthly assessments and your ownership share. If the developer constructs fewer units than originally planned, you wind up paying more in maintenance fees, especially if there are recreational facilities. Again, this is where checking the developer's track record is the best recourse. Also, as new units are added, your share may diminish, so you need to find out in advance what your minimum interest in the common property will be when all phases are finished.

A final word of advice: You'll encounter fewer problems and surprises if the buildings and facilities are up when you buy.

Condominium Conversions

The back-to-the-city movement has spurred the conversion of many apartment buildings into condominiums. When landlords realize renting is no longer profitable, many sell out to the developer/converters who make some cosmetic repairs to the building and then slap $50,000 price tags on apartments valued at $17,000.

Because of widespread misrepresentation—developers passing off defective structures on unwilling tenants and unsuspecting buyers—many cities have enacted ordinances governing conversions. Some municipalities have even enforced moratoriums on conversions in cases where the rental stock was being depleted, older citizens were being forced out of their apartments, and flagrant abuses surfaced. The owner may only have to give a ninety- or one hundred twenty-day notice on a conversion, which can force out tenants who have lived in the building for years.

Says Margaret, a thirty-two-year-old professional, who had recently been transferred to Chicago by her company, "I was shocked when I heard about the conversion. I just assumed if you were a good tenant you could stay indefinitely. The rental agent said there was no conversion in sight, and I really resent this. I'm just not prepared to buy here, and I'm certainly not prepared to move—I just did that. Now I'm forced to move again, and I really don't know where to go."

If your building is about to be converted, check your state laws and local ordinances for your rights as a tenant.

Of course, there's a bright side to the conversion market. Some outstanding condos are being created from turn-of-the-century apartment buildings. When executed with quality and taste, these renovated units offer distinctive, in-city living. Architectural features often include bay and leaded glass windows, skylights, large, high-ceilinged rooms, and beautiful wood trim. Plus you get all the modern amenities of a brand-new home, including an intercom security system.

These units can be excellent investments if they are reasonably priced. Unfortunately, demand has driven up the per-unit prices to unaffordable levels in many areas. In one city, renovated condos are going for $140 per square foot.

If you're looking at a converted condo, check first for structural integrity. Old buildings, unless they have been remodeled from the basement up, have old furnaces, roofs, plumbing, and wiring. If you buy in and then find these systems have to be replaced, you pay for them. Ask to see an engineer's report on the condition of the building before you buy. The report should state the condition of various systems and their remaining useful life. Be wary of cosmetic changes, such as new paint and a redecorated lobby; often that's just camouflage. Keep in mind that the number-one problem with conversions is inadequate rehabilitation prior to sale.

Finally, before signing anything, make sure you can get a loan for a converted unit or one under conversion.

Resale Condos

If you're looking at a resale condo, check with the association to see if there are any problems with the unit. It's a good idea to make your own structural inspection to assure there is no damage within the unit. Also, make sure that all assessments have been paid and that no unapproved changes have been made to the property.

Documents and Procedures

Prior to purchasing any condo, there are certain documents you must examine and procedures you must check out. Condos can be fraught with hidden costs, and if you don't analyze the details carefully, you may find yourself locked into a contract that costs you more every year. Before signing a sales contract or any binding agreement, read all the legal documents for the development and make sure you understand them. Have your attorney go over them and clarify anything you don't understand.

Specifically, you need to review:

- The declaration, or master deed, which details each owner's property rights and the conditions on the use of his property, as well as his rights and obligations in the community association.
- The bylaws, which establish rules for the operation of the association through officers, a board of directors, committees, and membership meetings.
- The operating budget, which sets the monthly assessment each owner pays and the services he receives.
- The management agreement, which spells out who will manage the complex and maintain the property.

Other points you should consider:

- How energy efficient is the building? Is it adequately insulated and sited on the land for maximum energy efficiency? What kind of heating and cooling system is provided? What will your average monthly fuel bill be?
- How much will your taxes be?
- Is the monthly assessment rate unreasonably low? Condo salespersons often quote unrealistically low maintenance fees, and once the developer moves out and the tenants take over, the assessment doubles. Ask to see a full breakdown of the maintenance budget, and ask a real-estate pro (attorney or accountant) if it's reasonable.
- Does the budget provide reserve funds for major maintenance, replacements, and emergencies? If not, you'll dig into your pocket for extra snow removal or removal of a diseased tree.

- Is the management adequate? Other residents should be able to answer that. Avoid condos with long-term maintenance contracts made by the developer. The association should be able to cancel any contracts the developer made with outside firms.
- What amenities are provided? If there are recreational facilities, will you use them and are they worth the added expense?
- Who owns the recreational facilities? Be leery if the developer holds title to the swimming pool and tennis courts and leases them to the association. After a few years, rental costs can be enormous.
- Who owns the land on which your condo unit sits? Some developers, particularly in Florida, retain ownership of the land and lease it to the condo owner for ninety-nine years, often with a cost-of-living escalator clause. Don't buy if there's a rent escalator and no option to buy after ten years or less. If your deal includes a lease and you don't pay the rent, you can lose your unit. Also, when the developer owns the land, you shouldn't pay as much for the condo as you would for a unit that includes the land on which it was built.
- What is the time frame for transition of the operation and management from the developer to the owners' association? Under most legal documents, the developer has a majority of the association votes until 75 percent of the units are sold. If the developer is honest and experienced, he can help the new owners get off to a good start. But the developer's control should end within a reasonable time, usually one year. Beware if the transfer of control is contingent upon the sale of all units. By withholding just one unit, the developer can retain control indefinitely and hike your assessments each year.
- Does the master insurance policy covering the common elements protect co-owners from loss or damage by fire and other hazards? This policy should include coverage for liability.
- Do you have a structural engineer's or home inspector's report on the condominium? That report can save you from buying into a shoddily built development or dilapidated conversion.
- In the case of a converted condo, ask to see proof that the building meets all local building and construction codes. If it doesn't, make sure that you won't have to share the costs involved in updating the building's systems.
- What kind of warranty does the builder or developer provide? Make sure you understand what it covers. If none is offered, see what protections you have under state laws.
- Are there provisions in the association rules that you will find intolerable? You may be prohibited from having a business office in your home, painting your front door, owning a pet, or putting up a fence. Read the bylaws throughout before buying.
- Does the association have the first right of refusal if you decide to sell your unit? That means you must offer it to the association first. Determine how much say the association has regarding sales.
- Is the association run in a compatible and amicable manner? Visiting with a few residents and reading the minutes of a few association meetings can prevent you from buying into a place where there's constant bickering.
- Are most of the units owned by their residents? If you buy into a complex where a large number of units are rented out by owner/speculators, you'll have less say in how the association is run and price increases. In many areas, it's common for speculators to buy large chunks of converted condos, thus driving up prices to all other purchasers.

These are some of the major issues to consider in buying a condo. For further information, there is an excellent, forty-eight-page, free booklet published by HUD that you can send for: "Questions About Condominiums." Direct requests to the Consumer Information Center, Dept. 586E, Pueblo, Colorado 81009.

The Community Associations Institute, a non-profit organization created to provide membership services and assistance to all parties involved in community associations, also has some good literature on condos. Request information from CAI, 1832 M Street, N.W., Washington, D. C. 20036. Also inquire whether there is a local CAI chapter in your area.

Cooperatives

Cooperatives, which have been around much longer than condos, are non-profit corporations with shareholders, and elected directors and officers. Credit unions are probably the most well known form of co-ops in America. The earliest U.S. housing cooperatives were formed in New York City during the 1880s. Immigrant industrial workers needing affordable housing joined forces to buy their apartment buildings. The concept, then, is essentially one of self-help enterprise—people pooling their resources to satisfy mutual needs.

If you live in a cooperative, you are simultaneously a resident, member, and shareholder. You buy a share of stock in the non-profit cooperative corporation, and this gives you occupancy rights to a housing unit, as well as the tax advantages of ownership. You can deduct from your federal income taxes your part of the mortgage interest and real-estate taxes, as well as interest on money you borrow to finance your share.

Several features distinguish cooperatives from all other forms of housing. A cooperative is a representative democracy, where the members, and not an outside developer, call all the shots. Together, the co-op members own a whole community—not just their own homes—and they can protect the community against undesirable changes. Members cooperate to hold down costs and to maintain quality standards that protect the rights of all residents. Active involvement in the organization results in low turnover and a stable community, which reduces crime, vandalism, and urban alienation. Through the cooperative association, members, jointly, can exert influence on municipal officials to change tax and utility rates and to obtain improved services from local government.

Documents and Procedures

Before proceeding to a discussion of types of co-ops and financial aspects, it's necessary to have a firm understanding of the co-op structure. When you apply to move into a co-op, you will be asked to sign a subscription agreement (which is basically a sales contract), stating that if you are approved by the co-op board for membership, you will pay a certain amount and pledge to become a resident. You will be interviewed by a membership committee, and a credit check, for which you pay, will be run on you.

If accepted as a member, you will be required to sign an occupancy agreement. This document, also sometimes called a proprietary lease, states how much you will pay in monthly maintenance fees, your responsibilities as a resident, and the rules and regulations (bylaws) of the co-op. The occupancy agreement is similar to a lease in a rental unit, except that it is usually renewable over a long term and it protects you from eviction.

Next, you pay the agreed-upon amount of money to the corporation and receive your stock certificate, which is your proportion of ownership in the co-op. In some co-ops, the number of shares you receive depends on the size of the unit you occupy. Sometimes, it's figured on the basis of square feet of your unit, and you should inquire about this.

As a shareholder, you help determine the policies and bylaws of the co-op. You vote to elect the board members, who make the business decisions for the corporation. As a resident, you have the right to occupy your unit and to use all mutual facilities. Many co-ops hire management firms to handle the day-to-day details of the organization and the maintenance. You will pay a monthly carrying charge to cover such operating expenses as maintenance and management fees. This carrying charge, basically the equivalent of rent, also goes to pay the monthly mortgage payment on the co-op and property taxes. The monthly fee generally runs 10 to 20 percent below going rental rates.

Types of Cooperatives

Cooperatives exist in a variety of forms—town houses, garden apartments, mid- and high-rise apartments, lofts, duplexes, detached houses, and mobile homes. Area generally dictates form—in the city you're most apt to find co-op apartments, lofts, and row houses. In the suburbs, you'll find town-house complexes, duplexes, and detached houses.

However, what really distinguishes the *type* of cooperative is the method of financing, because that establishes the groundwork for how the organization must be run. Because it's often hard to get financing, most co-ops for middle-income persons involve some kind of government funding. The U. S. Department of Housing and Urban Development (HUD) has helped finance many co-ops, and nationwide there are now about 500 HUD-insured co-ops.

HUD also subsidizes many co-ops to provide housing for low-income persons. To qualify for occupancy in a subsidized co-op, one must fall into certain low-income brackets. This category of co-ops is mentioned only so you will be aware of them and not confuse them with HUD-insured co-ops in your shopping.

Numerous other cooperatives are established through a combination of local, state, and federal financing. Location is a big factor, because in some states, such as New York, where co-ops are very popular, citizen demand and lobbying efforts have led to government allocations for co-ops. Then citizen groups take over from that point to create the cooperative associations.

Because of the great demand for moderate-priced housing in the cities, many tenants organize themselves to convert their apartment buildings into cooperatives. In fact, the majority of new co-ops being formed are conversions of existing dwellings. Usually, the converters apply for government financing and/or grants to accomplish their project. There are also a number of completely privately financed co-ops. Often, these are in the luxury class, and the buy-in fee ranges anywhere from $50,000 up to $100,000 or more. Most likely, a private investor or developer has put together the co-op and sells units at going market rates. In New York City and Washington, D. C., the strongholds of the co-op movement, you can expect to pay a minimum of $50,000 buy-in fee for a privately developed, one-bedroom co-op apartment. And you'll pay anywhere from $250–$650 for the monthly carrying charge, in addition to money you borrow to buy your share. At the Watergate in Washington, one-bedroom units, which sold for $28,000 ten years ago, now sell for more than $100,000.

Many cooperators believe these privately financed co-ops that are resold at prevailing market rates betray the essence of the cooperative movement. Most moderate-income-level co-ops, and especially those with government funding, set a limit on the amount any member can make by selling his share. The idea is to hold costs down to provide affordable shelter for like-minded individuals.

Therefore, with a moderate-income-level cooperative, you don't realize the appreciation rewards that you do with conventional housing. In most co-ops, your stock value increases by the amount you pay on the principal each year and the improvements made in the community. In some cases, there's an escalation clause for inflation so you receive some return on the increased value of your stock if you sell. Before buying into any co-op, ask how the appreciation rate is set.

Prices and Availability

Nationwide, there are now about a half million co-op units, located primarily in a few major cities. However, the co-op movement is gaining impetus as people needing affordable shelter learn about the economies and advantages of cooperative living. Co-ops are not as well known as condominiums; and developers, lenders, and real-estate brokers haven't jumped on the bandwagon for them because they're not a for-profit proposition. Nevertheless, HUD officials predict that thousands of co-op associations will be created throughout the country within the next decade, spurred by recently enacted legislation.

In most cities, the waiting lists for co-ops are long. As in New York and Washington, there are a number of established middle-income co-ops in Los Angeles, San Francisco, Atlanta, Chicago, Detroit, and Minneapolis. To locate these cooperatives, check with a local housing referral service, your local HUD office, or the Yellow Pages. Brokers aren't apt to help you find housing where there's no guaranteed commission for them.

Most co-ops belong to regional associations, which could direct you to the managing agents of co-ops in your area. To obtain the names of those associations, contact the National Association of Housing Cooperatives (NAHC), Suite 805, 1012 Fourteenth Street, N.W., Washington, D.C. 20005 (telephone: 202–628–6242). NAHC will send you a National Directory of Housing Cooperatives for $5 and can supply you with detailed information on the formation and operation of cooperatives.

NAHC has a slide/tape presentation, "The Cooperative Way to Home Ownership," which you can rent. The association also conducts training seminars around the country for tenant groups interested in co-op conversions and for local advocacy groups wanting to form co-ops. NAHC has prepared a tenant handbook on co-op conversions and a booklet informing community groups how to apply for federal funds to form co-ops. In addition, NAHC has literature for local officials outlining how they can help citizen groups organize co-ops.

Financial Aspects

Cooperatives have been held out of many communities where lenders and builders blackballed them. Many lenders consider these non-profit enterprises uncredit-worthy and won't make a blanket mortgage for the corporation. It has also been very hard to get a loan for an individual cooperative unit. Lenders write mortgages with real property as collateral. But when you buy into a co-op, instead of receiving title to a specific piece of property, you get a stock certificate, which most lenders won't accept as security for a loan.

Hence, existing co-op units usually have been resold for cash, or by the seller taking back a loan from the buyer, or by the buyer tapping private resources for a loan. Only rarely would lending institutions grant a loan secured just by the buyer's stock. Such loans were generally for less than 50 percent of the buy-in fee.

Fortunately, the tide is changing. California has enacted legislation permitting banks and savings-and-loan associations to finance the purchase of individual leasehold interests in cooperatives. And HUD is launching a program to make available low-rate loans for persons wanting to buy into cooperatives. Inquire at your local HUD office about this program. Also visit with your local lender. Banking rules change frequently, and lending institutions are having to reassess their policies constantly in light of increased housing inflation.

The best news of all is implementation of the National Consumer Cooperative Bank, hailed as one of the major consumer political coups of the century. Created to provide loans and technical assistance to non-profit cooperatives, the bank began functioning in April 1980. Proponents claim it lays the groundwork for building a strong national cooperative movement.

The bank can make and service loans for cooperative enterprises and furnish financially related services, such as insurance. (Co-ops have often experienced difficulty obtaining insurance, as well as financing.) Loans from the bank can be combined with other funding sources to create total financial packages to start up new co-ops or convert existing dwellings. The bank is expected to play a prominent role in the redevelopment of inner-city neighborhoods.

It's anticipated that loans will be made to cooperators for the rehabilitation of abandoned and deteriorating buildings, which will then be co-oped. The bank is also empowered to provide money for energy-saving improvements, such as solar heating and insulation, as well as community facilities. However, the bank does not make loans to individuals to buy into co-op units. For further information, contact the National Consumer Cooperative Bank, 2001 S. Street, N.W., Washington, D.C. 20009. Information about loan applications can be obtained by calling the bank's toll-free number: 800–424–2481.

Co-op Conversions

Cooperators are already heavily involved in urban revitalization on a grass-roots level, from Sioux City, Iowa to New York City. In these so-called "sweat-equity" and "moderate rehab" co-ops, persons needing affordable shelter do much of the remodeling themselves to bring deteriorating buildings up to livable code standards. These conversions, often accomplished with city funding, have proven so successful that HUD has earmarked monies for low-interest loans to aid in the renovation of selected city-owned buildings by homesteaders as cooperatives.

Another major co-op movement is the conversion of old factories and warehouses into livable spaces. This movement originated in New York's SoHo section in the early sixties, when artists started converting the upper levels of old buildings in this industrial area into living/working quarters. These conversions were primarily sweat-equity projects. And, as they proved successful and the concept caught on, other like-minded people began forming corporations to buy and co-op their own buildings. Often, these conversions are welcomed by landlords who no longer make profits on their buildings and are unwilling to maintain them.

Andrea, a thirty-year-old professional woman, lives in just such a building north of Greenwich Village in Manhattan. Constructed in the 1890s as a rooming house, the building was later made into thirty-one apartments. Several years ago, the landlord stopped maintaining the building, and for fifty-two winter days there was no heat. At that point, the tenants organized an association and declared a rent strike. For three years, the tenants' association managed the building—collecting the rents, making the necessary repairs, and turning the balance over to the landlord.

Meanwhile, the landlord quit paying taxes on the building, and one of the three mortgages he held on the dwelling was foreclosed. The building was placed in receivership, and the court appointed a managing agent. Since the landlord had offered the building to several speculators, the tenants foresaw that the only way they could assure their continued residence at affordable rates was by co-oping.

Also about this time, the city put the building on the auction block, and at each auction the tenants turned out en masse to discourage any prospective buyers. Their delaying tactics worked, and they finally obtained a loan from the Consumer-Farmer Foundation to buy the building. In addition, they have applied for a loan from city-administered Community Development Block Grant funds to help pay for back taxes and rehabilitation of the building. They also have a construction loan with a commercial bank for major remodeling.

At the point that the building became an incorporated cooperative, each person had to pay $1,500 for his share, for which he received a proprietary lease entitling him to his apartment. The shareholder residents then elected a seven-member board of directors, which makes the policy decisions and conducts the business of the corporation. The corporation also hired a live-in managing agent, who handles daily maintenance and operation.

Andrea, who has a 583-square-foot unit, says that the whole process has been an arduous one, requiring much time and effort. She said there have been disagreements among residents on how the corporation should be structured and increasing maintenance costs with which to contend. She stresses that it takes a lot of legwork and perseverance to put together the necessary elements for a conversion.

The bylaws of Andrea's cooperative are designed to protect all tenants. They stipulate that if someone moves, the corporation has the first option to buy that individual's share. In this way, the corporation retains control of the co-op's makeup and can maintain quality and stability. A departing shareholder receives the amount of equity he put into the corporation, cash for capital improvements he made to his unit, plus a modest amount for increased value due to inflation.

Because of the large capital outlays required to rehabilitate the building, the buy-in fee is now $9,500. When an applicant is offered the subscription agreement, he is required to put down 10 percent of the buy-in fee. Then a careful character and credit check is made on the individual, who is asked for three references.

There's a long waiting list of applicants, and Andrea reports there is "a crying need for this type of moderate-priced housing that is not being met." She feels the answer is for more people to do conversions.

Fortunately, government is responding to this need by establishing new programs to assist co-op conversions. Now that you know about the tribulations that a conversion may entail, if you're willing to go this route, check with the Cooperative Bank, your local HUD office, city housing department, and state housing financing authority for assistance. Other sources of funding may be private or non-profit foundations sympathetic to the cooperative cause.

Additional Considerations

There are a few other points to keep in mind as you shop for a co-op or contemplate a co-op conversion.

Generally, the two- to three-hundred-unit co-ops are the best run and most successful. When co-ops get bigger, they often lose the community spirit. At the two- to three-hundred-unit size, they're small enough for people to know each other and yet survive financially.

Often, when you buy into a co-op, you gain the benefit of auxiliary services that spell big savings for you. Many co-op communities also organize buying clubs, day-care centers, insurance programs, health care and car repair services, food and clothing stores, and even cable-TV co-ops for their members. Ask about these extras as you're shopping.

Before you put down money for your share, check these things:

- Look at the newsletter, minutes of the board meetings, and membership turnover rate, and talk with members to get an idea of how well the co-op is run and how well members get along.
- The operating budget and most recent financial statement should show whether there are adequate reserves for replacement of major items, such as the heating or plumbing system. If not, you may get stuck paying a sizable emergency assessment.
- Ask other members whether they're satisfied with the management firm, and find out how often the firm has increased its charges.
- Read the bylaws, and make sure they're acceptable to you.
- Ask how often the carrying charges have been increased and if there's an upcoming increase. Also ask how the building is heated and cooled, how much the utility bills run, whether the major systems of the building have been updated, or what their existing life is.
- Find out how resales are handled. Is the equity of your unit frozen or can you make a profit if you sell?
- What are the provisions for subleasing? If there are no restrictions, you may wind up with an undesirable neighbor. Subleasing should be allowed only for short-term absences of members.
- Make certain the cooperative meets the building code standard.

Mobile Homes

Mobile homes can be an answer for single persons wanting homes of their own but who are priced out of other markets. Long considered the nadir of the housing industry, mobile homes are improving as manufacturers recognize the growing demand for sound, affordable shelter.

Costs And Trends

The *average* new singlewide home of 14 feet by 70 feet costs roughly between $16,000 and $20,000, depending on the manufacturer and the appurtenances. The average doublewide (also called multisection) of about

28 feet by 70 feet costs approximately $25,000 to $30,000. Some top-end mobile homes located in well-planned communities sell for as much as $50,000. These more expensive homes, available in a variety of floor plans offering up to 2,000 square feet, have such houselike features as wood siding, beamed cathedral ceilings, and tiled roofs. They also offer all the amenities of standard houses, including fireplaces and total appliance packages in the kitchens.

Most mobile homes today are mobile only to the extent that they are transported to a fixed site where they often are placed on a concrete foundation and landscaped as a permanent dwelling. The tin-can trailers of yesteryear, you'll remember, were propped up on concrete blocks and skirted—some of them still are. The trend, however, is away from that appearance and more toward landscaped mobile home communities.

One innovative manufacturer is developing mobile home subdivisions. The manufacturer, who does everything from acquire the land to arrange conventional long-term mortgage financing, claims the subdivisions will demonstrate that mobile homes can supply attractive housing for under $40,000. You'll find the majority of these modern communities in southern or western states, where land is plentiful and the population is increasing.

In other parts of the country, long-standing barriers to mobile homes are being broken down by state housing goals that require local communities to zone for a full price spectrum of housing. For instance, Oregon, a state known for its strict land-control policies, has approved mobile home subdivisions for several cities.

Typically, mobile home parks were located on the outskirts of town or in the so-called working-class sections of the city. Mobile homes, also called "mobes" within the industry, proliferated following World War II, when the demand for inexpensive housing burgeoned. That same intense demand exists today as the post-World War II babies come of age, and again, the industry is responding, albeit with a more sophisticated product. Mobile home manufacturers are attempting to shed their second-class image, and where they succeed, zoning officials are allowing mobile home communities into the nicer areas.

You will need to check with your city building department about the zoning regulations where you live. The placement of mobes on private land is severely restricted and even prohibited in some counties. Regulations requiring mobes to be placed on one acre or more of land often are intended to keep them out. It's imperative that you have a place to put a mobile home before buying one.

If you put your home on private property, you'll have to pay for site preparation—providing a foundation, hooking up utility lines, and possibly installing a septic system and well.

Appreciation or Depreciation?

Remember: Location determines value. So how much your home will appreciate or depreciate in value is based on where you put it. How lending institutions in your area handle financing of used mobile homes, as well as supply and demand and rate of inflation, also affect value. Many savings and loan associations, noting that mobile homes purchased with land do appreciate, are increasingly willing to write loans for them under liberalized banking rules.

Manufacturers claim that well-placed, permanent-sited mobes appreciate as much as site-built houses. And Foremost Corporation of America, the nation's largest insurer of mobile homes, contends that a mobile home bought in 1973 appreciates in value by 5 to 15 percent per year. However, the National Association of Realtors reports that over a recent five-year period the depreciation rate on mobes averaged from 12 to 50 percent of the original price.

Financing

The reason for the depreciation is that a mobile home is usually considered a piece of property or equipment rather than a piece of real estate and is financed accordingly. Many mobiles are financed like cars, with personal property loans. Interest rates are higher and payoff periods shorter, as a rule, than for mortgages. Down payment requirements sometimes are proportionally larger.

Most mobile home dealers will arrange the financing, including an insurance package. However, you usually pay a premium for the dealer's package, which may be financed through a mortgage company owned by the manufacturer; so before signing anything, you should check other sources. You may be able to get a government-backed loan, a credit union loan, or even a real-estate mortgage. Avoid finance companies where you'll pay top dollar.

Under liberalized lending regulations, federally chartered saving associations can now make twenty-year loans on new and existing mobile homes with only 10 percent down. Some lenders write twenty-five-year mortgages on mobile home/real-estate packages, where you own the land at a rate only slightly higher than that for site-built homes. It's estimated that within five years, 60 percent of all mobiles will be financed with real-estate mortgages. So ask several lenders about rates and terms they offer—these inquiries may save you a lot of money.

Presently, most mobile home loans are written for twelve to fifteen years, with down payments ranging from 10 percent to 25 percent. If you belong to a credit union, you may be able to get the best terms there. There are also three government-backed loan programs for mobile loans.

The Department of Housing and Urban Development's Federal Housing Administration (FHA) insures loans made by approved lenders to buyers with nominal down payments. The unit must be used as your residence, and you must have an acceptable site for it, either owned or rented. The FHA will insure up to $18,000 for fifteen years on a singlewide unit and up to $27,500 for twenty years on a singlewide and lot. It will insure up to $27,000 for twenty years on a doublewide and up to $36,500 for twenty-five years on a doublewide and developed lot. The maximum financing charge is subject to periodic review based on economic conditions. You can apply for FHA-insured loans at government-approved lenders, whose names you can get at your FHA area office.

For eligible veterans, the Veterans Administration will guarantee up to 50 percent of a loan to a maximum of $17,500 for fifteen years on a singlewide and for twenty years on a doublewide.

The Farmers Home Administration (FmHA) has also been authorized to include mobile homes in rural areas in its mortgage insurance and guaranty programs. If you're in a rural area, check with your local FmHA office for details on these programs.

Taxes and Deductions

Regardless of the type of loan you get, the interest is deductible from your federal income taxes. When you buy your mobile home, you will pay a sales tax, which is also deductible. Some states tax mobiles as personal property or real estate; others make special mobile home assessments; these charges are all deductible. In addition, some states charge license-plate fees, also deductible.

Insurance

You'll need fire, theft, and physical damage insurance on your home, as well as coverage of your personal effects inside your home. Many dealers will be eager to sign you up for home-owner's insurance and a credit life policy, which pays off the balance of the loan in the event of your death. Resist their offers until you do some independent shopping. You might find you can get cheaper rates and better coverage from an independent agent. Moreover, those credit life policies, often unnecessary, may entail kickbacks to the dealer from the underwriter.

Construction and Quality

Mobile home manufacturers proudly tout the fact that theirs is the only shelter industry regulated by the federal government, claiming this as proof of a superior product. Don't accept that claim on face value. Since June 15, 1976, all new mobile homes have been required to meet federal safety and construction standards issued by HUD. These standards were developed in response to a Congressional order to reduce the injuries, deaths, and property damage resulting from mobile home accidents.

Therefore, every mobile home you see should have a tag indicating it was inspected and complies with the HUD standards, which require more insulation among other things. Avoid any dealer who advertises his product as "HUD approved." Although HUD establishes the standards covering mobile home construction, the agency does not accept or approve any mobile homes. Dealers so advertising their products are subject to fines up to $1,000. Also, don't assume the HUD inspection tag is a guarantee of quality. Unfortunately, in some states, the inspection programs for mobile homes are very lax. Where this is the case, the HUD tag is meaningless. Your best assurance of quality is to order a proven model through a reliable local dealer.

You can check the construction caliber of any unit by examining the workmanship. Look closely at the molding around the doors, at the corner of the ceiling and sidewalls, and the shoe molds at the floor. Are they tightly attached, and do they fit together neatly at junctions? Also check for staples that aren't all the way into the wood.

You can buy or borrow publications from your library that will advise you on how to evaulate thoroughly the structural integrity and systems of a mobile home. Be sure you get one published after June 15, 1976, when the new regulations took effect. Check who the author and publisher are and avoid industry-oriented publications that merely endorse the product.

Warranties

HUD requires that all new mobile homes carry a minimum one-year warranty covering the home's structural soundness, energy efficiency, and workmanship. Be sure to get in writing the correct procedure for making a warranty claim if something goes wrong. Make certain you understand which claims will be honored by the dealer and which you'll have to resolve with the mobile home or appliance manufacturer. Most manufacturers warrant only the construction; the appliances and furniture are under their individual manufacturers' warranties.

Thus, the manufacturers that supply the stove, refrigerator, furnace, and the like should provide separate warranties. Study them thoroughly to determine whether they're as comprehensive as the warranties you would get from local retailers. Find out about service provisions for your appliances. Determine whether each warranty is "full" and covers both parts and labor throughout the entire coverage period or whether it's "limited" and covers parts fully, but covers labor for a lesser period of time.

Amenity Package

Most mobiles include a living room, fully equipped kitchen, dinette or dining room, one to three bedrooms, one or two baths, an automatic heating system, water heater, built-in and freestanding furniture, carpeting, and drapes. (Usually you can choose the color and style of your decor and furniture.) All of these items are generally included in the package price of the unit. A close look at the quality of these items can tell you a lot about the caliber of the manufacturer. If the furniture and drapes are cheap, chances are the construction of the unit is too.

If you don't like the furnishings or appliances, many dealers will sell the home unfurnished and allow you a *nominal* discount for excluding the package. Optional items—central air conditioning, washer and dryer, dishwasher, garbage disposal, and other amenities—can be purchased as part of the home. If you buy them from the manufacturer, you may pay top dollar, so you might check his prices against those of an independent retailer.

Choosing a Reputable Dealer

Your first step in shopping for a mobile home should be to find a reliable dealer. Ask any dealer you visit for references of former customers. Contact those customers, and inquire whether their homes are as good as they were represented to be and whether after-sale service, if required, was promptly provided.

Have a dealer itemize in writing all the costs. Avoid retailers who won't quote you the overall costs, but promise to put you in a home for so much per month. Ask each dealer what is included in the price. Does it include transportation to the site and setting up once there? Avoid dealers who try to pressure you into a purchase or signing any papers. Your local Better Business Bureau can advise you if there have been complaints lodged against a dealer.

Choosing a Mobile Home Park

It's essential that you have a place to put your home before buying. Many parks are owned by dealers who will only provide space for the units they sell. Get a written guarantee that your park space is reserved for you before you buy. Keep in mind that homes located in newer, planned development parks or subdivisions are most apt to appreciate. Also, you should select a park that's geared to your age and life-style. There are many adult-only communities for young singles and some age-restricted communities for older persons and retirees with the full range of recreational facilities.

Getting established in a mobile home park can add 15 percent or more to the base price of the home, so you should request in writing what services the dealer will provide and what costs you must assume. Although many states have banned them, sizable and non-refundable entrance and exit fees are still charged in some places. Monthly rental fees for sites depend on the park's age and facilities.

Your best protection is a written lease on the lot for at least one year. A good lease should protect you against arbitrary changes of rules without proper notice, arbitrary eviction and rent increases, or special assessments while the lease is in force. You should also find out what maintenance services the park provides and obtain a copy of the rules and regulations. Read them carefully for special restrictions that you would find unbearable.

Basically, the park will be only as good as its management. So visit with some residents to find out if they are pleased with the management and if the rules are enforced. Then find out whether your home can remain on its site if you sell and what the manager's right of review is regarding the sale. Usually, he can reject buyers he considers uncredit-worthy.

Some mobile home lots, particularly those in large parks located in the

Sunbelt states, are available on a condominium basis. That is, you buy the lot within the park and then have the right to put your mobile home there, subject to the home-owners' association's rules and guidelines.

Buying a Used Mobile Home

You may be able to get a better deal on a fairly new used home than on a brand new home because it will already have depreciated and you can buy it for "book" value. *The NADA Mobile Home Appraisal Guide*, published three times a year by the National Automobile Dealers Association, gives both the retail value and loan value on a used home based on its location, make, model, size, and age. Lenders will consult this book to determine how much they'll loan you on a used home. And this book price is the base you should work from to negotiate a sales price.

Also, find out what repairs have been made to the home, and ask to see utility and maintenance records. Do not buy a unit manufactured before June 15, 1976, which does not have the tag indicating that it was inspected and met the HUD construction standards.

Rehabilitation Housing

Urban revitalization is essential to meet the housing needs of the eighties—needs created by the increasing number of single households. For city-oriented single persons who want to avoid long commutes and driving expenses, a rehabilitated house in town is ideal. Realizing the importance of neighborhood and community support, many single persons are joining forces to renovate older, abandoned sections of cities all over the country. Once they get organized, they usually can win the support of a few local lenders and city officials sympathetic to their project.

Says one Atlanta mortgage banker who specializes in arranging the financing for mid-town rehab projects for single people, "Singles prefer the community kind of living that recycling older neighborhoods in town can offer them and where they can find great support from each other. They don't like the subdivisions out in the suburbs, because they find little social support in that kind of situation, where they're the odd person in the area."

Inner-city rehabilitation started as a grass-roots effort, where local citizens united to reconstruct neighborhoods. Initially, they had tremendous difficulty obtaining financing for their projects. Now, as the established housing industry—builders, lenders, brokers, developers—has recognized the lucrativeness of recycling, it has become big business. The result has been the "gentrification" of many inner-city areas. Gentrification refers to the displacement of lower- and moderate-income persons from their neighborhoods as developers acquire the properties, rehabilitate them, and sell them at market rates. You can, of course, buy a gentrified dwelling, but it will be expensive. In many cities, you'll find remodeled row houses or older, updated buildings converted into condos.

The other route you can go, and by far the more economical one, is to form a coalition with like-minded single persons and do your own rehabilitation project. It will be a pioneering effort, which will enable you to create your own living space—something that will be uniquely you and will reflect your own tastes and needs.

So how do you undertake such a project?

Step one is to find out what neighborhood rehabilitation programs are underway or available in your city. As federal government support for inner-city revitalization has expanded, the number of programs offering technical and financial assistance has ballooned. Contact your municipal department of community development or department of community affairs and inquire about urban homesteading programs and inner-city financial assistance projects.

Be forewarned that although many cities are getting millions of federal dollars for rehab projects, these funds are often diverted into civic and commercial projects. That's usually because the politically sensitive mayor's office wants to keep happy the influential building and business powers. So to achieve your goal, you may have to take the course of thousands of other grass-root rehabbers: Get organized and fight city hall. Many urban homesteaders have succeeded by forming neighborhood groups and becoming political activists.

In the process, they often exposed the misuse of federal money. For example, Citizens for Community Improvement in one city discovered that the mayor was diverting federal funds targeted for rehab programs into a street paving project for an exclusive new suburb. Neighborhood action groups in other cities revealed that housing rehab funds were being funneled into hotel and shopping-mall developments.

Unfortunately, just about anytime you deal with government, you run into red tape and some abuses. You can get valuable assistance in dealing with your local government from the Chicago-based National Training and Information Center (NTIC). NTIC, a non-profit educational institution, providing training and research for neighborhood groups, holds workshops across the country to teach people how to organize and get their rehab programs going. NTIC also has a number of books informing rehabbers what steps to take and how to overcome obstacles. The center publishes a newsletter, which reports on private, federal, and local programs on neighborhood revitalizations, as well as pertinent legislation. You can contact NTIC at 1123 W. Washington Boulevard, Chicago, Illinois 60607 (telephone: 312–243–3035).

In addition, NTIC can put you in touch with neighborhood organizations in other cities, which can provide helpful advice. Well-organized neighborhood groups have succeeded in getting better bus routes into their communities, and better street lights and parks. They have also solved zoning problems, reduced property taxes and crime, prevented cities from moving hospitals and schools, and established home repair programs. They have exposed illegal red-lining (lenders' practice of refusing to make loans in areas they consider high risk, usually inner-city neighborhoods) and insurance red-lining (insurance companies refusing to write policies for inner-city dwellings). Many states' insurance codes prohibit this practice.

As a rehabber, there are two key pieces of legislation you should learn about and put to work for you. The Community Reinvestment Act (CRA) of 1977 requires banks and savings-and-loan associations to demonstrate that they are meeting the credit needs of their communities. Specifically, CRA provides incentives for lenders to make loans in older, inner-city neighborhoods, which they have traditionally bypassed in order to invest their money in expensive new suburban housing. If lenders are found refusing loans to their local, inner-city constituencies, they can be prohibited from expanding their business by the federal regulatory agencies. However, it's up to the local neighborhood groups to monitor the lenders for compliance.

Other vital legislation, the Home Mortgage Disclosure Act, requires lenders to disclose where they make mortgage loans by zip codes so neighborhood groups can tell where red-lining may be occurring. For further information on how to make these laws work for you, contact the Center for Community Change (CCC), 1000 Wisconsin Avenue, N.W., Washington, D.C. 20007 (telephone: 202–338–8920). In addition to helping neighborhood groups force compliance with the federal laws, CCC provides technical assistance and help on how to put financial packages together for rehab projects.

Another tool available to you is *The Federal Domestic Assistance Catalog,* which informs neighborhood groups how to write grants seeking federal funds. The catalog, published by the Office of Management and Budget, lists more than a thousand government assistance programs, ranging from technical assistance and project grants to direct loans and insurance. You can find the catalog in the government documents section of most libraries, or you can order a copy for $20 from the Superintendent of Documents, U. S. Government Printing Office, Washington, D. C. 20420.

The Department of Housing and Urban Development (HUD) also issues a free booklet, "Programs of HUD," describing its urban rehab programs. Contact your local HUD office for a copy.

HUD has initiated a very successful urban homesteading program in about fifty cities and plans to expand the program. Under that program, HUD transfers one- to four-family homes that it has acquired to local governments to sell to selected homesteaders for as little as $1. The homesteader must agree to bring the property up to local code standards within eighteen months of occupancy and to live there for at least three years. Usually, city-assisted financing is available to the homesteaders for part or all of the rehabilitation costs. This program has proven successful for many singles.

Alice, a homesteader in Atlanta, Georgia, bought a one-and-a-half-story bungalow for $1 and enlisted the help of friends to restore her home.

"When I first saw my house-to-be, the windows were boarded up and weeds were knee-high in the yard," she said. "My friends thought I was crazy, but I knew it was a deal and I wanted a home of my own.

"Now I call on help easily. I'll call someone and say, 'Come over for dinner, I need some help on something.' A lot of times, friends have said they would really like to help with some specific project. So I can just call up and ask them if they'd like to help work on the house this weekend. In many ways, this has been almost a community project, and it's helped build friendships. When you work together on something this constructive, it really nurtures friendships."

Other cities have organized their own urban homesteading programs in which they award to a lottery winner, for $1, an abandoned house that the city has taken over for tax delinquency. It may cost $16,000 to $30,000 to rehab the house, but the initial cost couldn't be lower. So far, about 3,000 houses have been recycled this way in Baltimore, a city that has pioneered in urban rehabbing.

The Baltimore Housing and Community Development Department, which has made the successful $1 rehab project an ongoing program, requires the lottery winner to get his house ready to occupy within six months. (Often these homes—mostly row houses—are gutted structures with no plumbing, wiring, or heating and cooling.) The owner is required to live in the dwelling for eighteen months. During the initial period of occupancy and rehabbing, the owner lives in the dwelling tax-free. It is later assessed at market value, and then the city levies taxes.

Dick Davis, the information director for the Baltimore Housing Department, reports that the average income of rehabbers is $22,000. He notes that these projects appeal predominantly to the moderate-income, young professionals who enjoy the variety of an open and mixed ethnic community. Most of these inner-city Baltimore row houses, originally built in the 1840 to 1865 period, are three stories high, and each level is about fifteen feet wide and forty to fifty feet deep.

Baltimore also has a program to take over row houses, rehab them, and then either co-op them or provide low-interest loans for persons who can't afford the remodeling costs under the $1 homesteading program. The city has three cooperatives with about 250 row houses each. The buy-in fee is $500, in addition to a $35 application fee, and the resident pays $150 to $230 per month, depending on the size of his unit. These row house co-ops range from one- to four-bedroom units. The resident pays his own utilities in addition to the monthly co-op fee. Anyone is eligible to participate in this program—there is no income limit.

You should investigate if your city has programs or plans for programs comparable to these model efforts in Baltimore. If not, organize and get the city to establish such a program if it's not offering any means for single people to rehab inner-city dwellings.

HUD has recently launched a new neighborhood self-help program to offer technical assistance to inexperienced community groups. For further information on HUD programs, contact your local HUD office.

Keep in mind, the most important element in any rehab project is a strong, organized coalition as your base of support. Single persons involved in these efforts report that city administrations are notorious for foot-dragging when it comes to assisting self-help groups. Then it becomes necessary to mobilize and lobby elected officials.

One of the most successful recycling organizations across the nation has been the Neighborhood Housing Services (NHS). NHS, a coalition of private and public interests working together to stabilize and revitalize deteriorating neighborhoods through revolving loan funds, is now active in about a hundred cities. Basically, the way it functions is that a small staff of professionals, through NHS, brings together local citizen groups, government officials, and lenders to ensure community participation.

These coalitions then cooperate to overcome red-lining and other discriminatory practices. They make money available for urban homesteaders and help existing home owners renovate their houses. The NHS staff provides rehabilitation and financial counseling as well as construction assistance. To find out if this program is operating in your community, look for NHS in the phone book or contact your local community development office. If there's no NHS in your area, you can get further information from the Neighborhood Reinvestment Corporation, 1700 G Street, N.W., Washington, D. C. 20552. You will probably have to lobby elected officials to get the program established with local funds in your community.

Another urban rehabilitation initiative you should know about is that of the Federal National Mortgage Association (FNMA), a federally chartered corporation which makes mortgage funds available to local lending institutions through the secondary money market. FNMA has launched three new programs to pump almost $100 million into urban rehabilitations. You will have to check with local lenders to find out which ones are participating in the FNMA programs.

Here's how one FNMA program can work for you: You buy a deteriorated house for $20,000 that will have a completed value of $40,000. You can obtain a mortgage for up to $38,000—the after-rehab value, less a 5 percent down payment—from an FNMA-approved lender. After obtaining FNMA's commitment to buy the mortgage, the lender will close the loan, immediately selling it to FNMA. What this program essentially does is provide prefunding for your rehab project, reducing the risk to the local lender and thus making him willing to loan you the money.

Another avenue to explore is rehabbing and converting an existing building of four or more units into a cooperative. (See "Cooperatives," page 45.)

Be advised that you should exercise extreme caution in contracting for any work in a rehab project. First, there are many fly-by-night operators eager to make a fast buck off well-intended homesteaders who don't know a lot about construction. For example, Joe bought a beautiful old house in the Capital Hill district of Washington, D. C. and hired a heating and cooling man to do some duct work. After that was done, Joe wound up paying a carpenter $1,500 to repair the walls that were ripped up by the man doing the duct work.

Second, many builders are not familiar with the way older homes were built and don't know how to work on them. Houses are not built the same today as they were fifty years or a hundred years ago, and you can end up with a disaster if your remodeler or contractor knows only modern techniques. Ask any prospective remodeler if he is familiar with balloon or ribbon framing and how much work he has done on older houses. Then ask to see the work. It is critical that you work with a knowledgeable, reputable carpenter or craftsman.

Before you launch into a renovation project, ask yourself whether the dwelling is worth rehabbing. Determining this requires thoroughly inspecting the building, preferably with an expert (contractor, engineer, or architect), and then weighing the cost of repairs against the estimated value of the finished product. A dwelling that was well built in the beginning can last for centuries. If you find that the home's foundation, floors, walls, and roof framing are structurally sound, chances are good that the house is worth rehabbing.

Finally, you should know that rehabbing may qualify you for some extra tax breaks. Under the Tax Reform Act of 1976, owners of income-producing property listed in the National Register of Historic Places or located within a historic district listed in the National Register are eligible to take certain tax deductions for rehab costs. The law provides for amortization, over five years, of money spent on a certified rehabilitation of a certified historic structure. So if you rehab a house and rent part of it out, you'll qualify for these tax benefits.

Houses within historic districts or listed in the National Register may also qualify for federal grants or other aids. Your state historic preservation officer should be able to tell you whether a house is listed in the register or is in a historic district. He is responsible for nominating sites to the National Register and may be able to direct you to eligible candidates. You can also dig into your local library and historical society archives to find out a house's history, origins, and importance, and then follow the steps that will get it enrolled in the register.

You might also wish to join the National Trust for Historic Preservation, which has a number of free booklets on federal programs and incentives for historic preservations and guides on how to save older structures. Write to the National Trust at 748 Jackson, N.W., Washington, D. C. 20006.

Many municipalities also provide long-term tax abatements for houses in rehabbed areas or tax exemptions for the cost of rehabbing. You should keep accurate records on all the remodeling and refurbishing costs, which can be used to reduce your capital gains when you sell. By all means, check with your tax accountant to find out how undertaking a rehab will affect your filing.

5

Shopping the Sunbelt and Western Boomtowns

Fed up with battling bitter winters with their endless snowstorms and the high energy costs, many individuals and companies are migrating to the southern and western cities with more temperate climates. Indeed, the Census Bureau projects that between now and the year 2000, populations in the South and West will grow twice as fast as the rest of the country. If present trends continue, Florida will be the fastest-growing state, followed by Arizona, Nevada, and Colorado. California and Texas will also be among the big gainers, adding at least 2.4 million citizens each. Hundreds of thousands of Americans are expected to abandon the older industrial north-central and midwestern states.

Native Chicagoan Jeremy, a twenty-seven-year-old tax accountant who decided to look for work in Phoenix, San Diego, and Dallas, explained, "The weather has gone from a wind chill of forty below to twenty-two inches of snow. It's a major task to get around the streets, and getting stuck in the snow is depressing. If you want that kind of weather, you can move to Alaska."

Companies and individuals alike are losing money in the northern climes. Productivity is lowered when it takes employees six hours to commute to work through the snow. Energy bills—both for home heating and car transportation—are outrageous, as are the ongoing expenses for maintenance and repairs necessitated by ice, snow, and wind damage.

The lure of these warm and thriving western and southern states includes excellent career opportunities, abundant year-round recreational facilities, fine cultural entertainment, and frequently, lower living costs and higher wages. Many single persons are flocking to these cities, where they have the chance to grow with an expanding community and economy. Each of these boomtowns pulsates with its own rhythm of excitement and energy.

In most Sunbelt cities, there is a wide range of housing available—both for the younger singles and the empty nesters and retirees. Builders cater to these specific markets. Because of the year-round building season and lack of both unions and no-growth moratoriums in many of these states, housing is less expensive than in the northern states. Of course, maintenance is also less costly.

To give you an idea of the expansion and opportunity in these flourishing areas, here is a brief rundown on some business trends and activities:

- Between 1970 and 1980, the population grew rapidly in the West and South, but almost stood still in other regions of the country. The Northeast has virtually stopped growing and the north and central regions have increased by less than 3 percent since 1970.
- The technology center of the United States, formerly located in the Boston area, has shifted to the "Silicon Valley," between Palo Alto and San Jose, California. The area around Los Angeles also has many high-technology firms.
- Other technology- and energy-related firms are settling near Phoenix and Tucson; around Dallas, Austin, San Antonio, and Houston; and in some parts of Florida.
- In San Diego, companies are hiring at a rapid pace, particularly in the electronics and aerospace fields.
- Office and plant construction is spurting ahead in most Sunbelt cities. Business construction is especially brisk in San Francisco and Oakland.
- Downtown construction is surging in Houston, one of the fastest-growing cities in the country. During the last couple years of the seventies, Houston led the nation in housing construction.
- San Antonio and the Dallas-Fort Worth Metroplex, the new corporate headquarters of American Airlines, are rapidly remodeling and expanding their downtowns.
- Houston and Dallas-Fort Worth are expected to remain the top two metropolitan areas for new housing starts in the immediate future, with four others in the top ten coming from California.
- Oklahoma City is aburst with construction activity.
- New buildings are going up all over Louisville, where plans are underway for an $84 million cultural, retail, and office complex.
- Rocky Mountain communities are reaping the benefits of the intensifying search for energy, and the increase in airplane construction is stimulating growth in the West.
- The energy boom is strongest in Casper, Wyoming, another of the fastest-growing cities. Oil, uranium, and coal developments are fueling expansion— creating thousands of jobs. Jobs in Casper's construction industry grew a phenomenal 50 percent between 1978 and 1979.
- The search for energy is also keeping Albuquerque's economy surging ahead.
- To the north, airplane production keeps the economy of Seattle, the home of the Boeing Company, humming.
- Retail, trade, tourism, and home building are prospering in Las Vegas.
- Southern educational institutions have improved so much that business managers have rejected the long-held idea that academic wisdom resides in the North—a further stimulus to corporate expansion in the Sunbelt.
- The migration of both people and companies has triggered the need for more service-oriented operations—department stores, supermarkets, restaurants, recreational outlets, financial institutions, health-care facilities—creating many more jobs in the process.

As you can see, the robust economies of these areas offer ample challenge and potential for the ambitious single individual. Before packing up and joining the exodus, however, there are a few factors you should carefully check out about any southern or western city you consider.

Cost of Living

Even though you may have a line on a great job, you should first find out what the cost of living is in your prospective city. In many of these boomtowns, wages are higher than in northern cities, while the costs of goods and services, including food, housing, transportation, clothing, personal and medical care, as well as income and property taxes, are lower.

For example, Houston, Austin, Dallas, Atlanta, Nashville, Orlando, and Bakersfield are ranked among the ten lowest in the yearly cost of living averages for forty metropolitan areas.

But you want to make sure that the influx of people doesn't drive up demand to the extent that prices suddenly soar out of sight.

Taxes

Definitely inquire about property taxes as well as state and local income taxes. Find out what the property tax base is and how houses are assessed in respect to their value.

The southern and western states presently have some of the lowest property taxes. In fact, a recent Census Bureau study, comparing typical taxes paid on single-family houses in cities around the country, found the lightest taxes are in the South. Overall, U.S. property taxes averaged 1.8 percent, or $900 on a $50,000 house, at the end of the seventies. Of thirty-three cities with taxes under one percent, all but six were in the South. City taxes in the Midwest averaged near the U.S. median. Western cities' taxes averaged between those in the Midwest and the South. Hardly any western cities had a tax rate above 2.5 percent, and nearly all were less than 1.5 percent. California's rate, of course, was reduced by Proposition 13 to one percent of 1975 values.

Larger cities, with more than 100,000 population, generally have a lower tax rate than cities of 50,000 to 100,000 size—1.6 percent compared with 1.9 percent. The steepest taxes on real estate are found in the northeastern states, where the average tax on a $50,000 home was 4 percent in fourteen of the cities sampled by the Census Bureau.

Bear in mind, though, that as increasing population demands more community services, taxes may rise. Although the tax-expenditure limits movement has become a potent force, the realities of those limitations can have some horrifying consequences for first-time buyers. Proposition 13 (the legislative initiative to lower property taxes) did slash tax bills an average 57 percent in California, but some cities are now being forced to charge local "user fees" to maintain sanitation services and keep hospitals open. New service fees have been levied for such facilities as swimming pools, tennis courts, and museums.

So far, in forty states outside California, tax cuts amounting to some 3.5 billion dollars have been passed or are on the legislative agenda, according to the Tax Foundation, a private, non-profit group. In addition, at least twenty states are looking at new limitations on future state and local spending and taxes.

Already new or larger homestead exemptions have been voted in Wyoming and Mississippi. States are also looking at ways to hold down spending. Utah, for instance, has adopted overall limits on state and local spending. Arizona, Hawaii, and Texas are among other states that have put spending limits on the books. Texas now has some of the lowest tax rates in the nation, with no state or local income taxes. Alabama, Louisiana, and New Mexico are among states with the lowest property taxes.

It's become apparent, however, that cutting the tax rate with no substitute or alternate revenue resources can create more problems than it solves. If you're buying in any state that has enacted a Proposition 13–type initiative or is considering one, keep these facts in mind. The home-building industry has been hard hit in California because municipalities no longer have the funds available to extend sewer systems and water lines for new subdivisions. As a result, new home buyers often pay an additional $2,000 fee for services the builder and municipality must shoulder.

You may want to avoid states altogether where there are pending tax cap initiatives, if they mean higher costs for the home buyer. Although taxes are frozen or reduced for existing home owners when Proposition 13–type initiatives go into effect, houses are usually reassessed when sold, so the buyer doesn't really reap the full benefits of the tax cut.

You should inquire whether a prospective community levies an "occupation tax." Authorized by the California Supreme Court in 1978, this tax imposes a 1 percent employee license fee on gross earnings for "the privilege of engaging in or following any business, trade, occupation, or profession as an employee." The tax is withheld from the employee's paycheck.

Make sure you ask about any pending tax increases, initiatives, or proposals for changes in the rate structure, before relocating.

Home Prices, Appreciation, and Availability

First you need to know whether housing is available for newcomers. Some cities have expanded so rapidly that housing starts haven't been able to keep pace with the demand. That's often driven up the prices to preposterous proportions. Recent figures show that the fastest-growing areas in the Sunbelt have been experiencing the greatest price jumps.

On the brighter side, in many areas in the South, new homes are less expensive than comparable new homes in the North. That is because major housing manufacturers construct large developments on a high production, cost-efficient basis. They build year-round with non-union labor, unfettered by no-growth moratoriums or the inability to get in water and sewer lines.

Some western regions, notably in California and Colorado, have experienced considerable difficulty with growth restrictions. You should investigate what the building situation is by contacting consumer housing organizations, the local home-builders' association, the Chamber of Commerce, or the municipal planning and zoning commission.

You should also inquire among real-estate agents or acquaintances in the city about housing options, prices, and rehabilitation projects. In Atlanta, for example, incoming singles would find that a like-minded group of individuals has joined forces to revitalize a deteriorated mid-town section. They have created a comfortable and compatible community of singles who enjoy a similar life-style.

Many builders in the Sunbelt and western cities cater to the younger singles with town-house and condo complexes, offering a full range of amenities—swimming pools, tennis courts, party rooms, and so on. Realizing that these are quality-oriented buyers, the builders also provide town homes, zero-lot-line, and patio homes, with such innovations as vaulted ceilings, skylights, lofts, and clerestory and greenhouse windows.

In places where land costs are extremely high, such as southern California, mid-rise condominiums are geared to the twenty-five-to-thirty-five-year-old singles market. Basically, these units offer high-quality apartments with equity. Condo conversions, proceeding at a rapid pace in Houston, Denver, and Los Angeles, have also proven popular with singles. Condos and town houses are expected to comprise 50 percent of all new dwellings throughout California in the eighties. This is apt to be the trend in other Sunbelt and western communities, as builders cater to singles who seek a relaxed life-style and want to avoid time-consuming maintenance.

Don't jump right into the purchase of a town house or condo, however, without a thorough investigation of the market. You want to make sure you get the best buy for your money, and in some places you can get a detached house for less than a condo or town house. For example, new detached homes recently sold in Orlando in the $40,000 to $50,000 range. In those areas where major housing manufacturers build for the young Sunbelt emigres, there are some excellent selections and buys in subdivision housing.

One of the nation's largest home builders, Fox & Jacobs, targets its model homes in Texas and Oklahoma to first-time buyers with moderate incomes. F&J produces three lines of homes, ranging from the most modest model in the low $50,000 bracket up to the more elaborate model in the $70,000 category. F&J, which maintains its low prices through factory-line assembly of each home's components, offers about twenty different floor plans, with such standard features as two bathrooms, three or four bedrooms, air conditioning, carpeting, a fireplace, kitchen appliances, and a landscaped lot. The firm further holds down costs by acquiring low-priced, undeveloped farmland on the outskirts of metropolitan markets and installing its own subdivisions. Although owners have complained about the sameness and lower quality of these component homes, they do offer the first-time buyer equity in some of the nation's fastest-growing markets, where real estate appreciates rapidly.

Fox & Jacobs has concentrated its developments in Houston, Fort Worth, and Dallas until recently, but is now expanding into Oklahoma.

U.S. Homes, another major Sunbelt manufacturer, markets affordable homes for first-time buyers in the twenty-five-to-forty-four age bracket. The company closed out 1979 with models at an average selling price of $50,000—considerably lower than the national average for a new home. Florida, Nevada, and Arizona have been the strongest markets for U.S. Homes, which also operates in eight other states. And, the company may soon move into California, South Carolina, Washington, Oklahoma, and New Mexico.

To combat the high prices that force out many first-time single buyers, U.S. Homes plans to build more attached housing, such as two-to-three story garden condominiums, at an average cost of $40,000. In 1979, the company began building three-story condos one block from Houston's Astrodome and intends to sell those units for an average $39,000.

The economics of manufactured houses make them an affordable and reasonably attractive option, if you are willing to accept the tractlike standard for an equity investment. Appreciation on real estate in the southern and western markets is rapid—ranging between 20 and 30 percent annually in many areas. Thus, you can always move up later to a home better suited to your desires and tastes.

There is also an abundance of mobile home communities in the warmer states. Many of them are set up on a condominium basis, whereby you buy your home, rent the lot, and share the expenses for mutually used facilities. These communities are often architecturally designed, and the homes are hard to distinguish from standard, site-built houses. Many of these adult-only mobile home parks for retirees provide an assortment of recreational and civic activities.

Throughout the West and South, you will find predominantly planned communities or planned unit developments (PUDs), as municipal officials and home buyers and owners alike eschew the suburban sprawl of earlier eras.

Financing

In most prospering Sunbelt communities, mortgage money has been available, albeit sometimes at a premium, throughout the past decade. That availability, however, is subject to the fluctuations of the economy, as well as local usury rates. Major builders usually make sure that there will be money for their buyers by prearrangement with local financial institutions. And those developers catering to the young singles market have frequently pioneered the introduction of alternative mortgage instruments into their communities (more on this subject in Chapter 8 "Bargain for the Best Financial Package"). These instruments enable buyers with limited cash resources and moderate incomes to buy their homes with lower down payments on repayment schedules often geared to their salaries.

Retirement Communities

Many retired persons find living in the Sunbelt more comfortable and economical. Over the years, a number of retirement communities have been developed to accommodate these persons. Sun City, outside Phoenix, is perhaps the most well known of these communities. With a population close to 50,000, Sun City has been sold out, and Sun City West, a new self-sustained community, is under construction. The backlog of orders is in the thousands.

Before investing in a home in one of these communities, you should inquire about all the particulars, giving special attention to those details discussed in Chapters 4 through 9. Visit the community, get the background on its financial solvency, and talk with a number of residents. Find out if they are pleased with their homes and the services provided. Also, inquire whether all promises regarding facilities and maintenance have been met.

Before putting down any money, you should have your attorney go over all of the details. It's probably also advisable to see your tax accountant about how the purchase will affect your taxes and estate planning.

Before investing, you should contemplate at length whether you desire a move away from your home, especially if you have lifelong friends and family there. You will be leaving behind familiar doctors, dentists, attorneys, bankers, and other professionals knowledgeable of your needs. For a single person, this can be a drastic change—to leave behind all the conveniences and familiarities taken for granted over the years.

Don't allow yourself to be beguiled by trappings and a fast-talking salesman, as Matilda and Irene did. The two former school teachers, during a visit to a friend at an Arizona retirement community, were totally entranced by the relaxed life-style and the activities arranged for the residents. They were literally charmed into signing an agreement and put down some money.

They then returned to their native Rockford, Illinois, sold their three-story Victorian house—for much less that they should have because it was a mid-winter buyer's market. And they moved to their new home. Unfortunately, all of their sunny expectations were not met. Matilda couldn't find a cardiologist she felt could handle her problems nearly as well as her doctor back home.

Although at first the women enjoyed the games and prearranged entertainment of their new community, after a while they wearied of those diversions and longed for their friends back in Illinois. They even found themselves missing the snowfalls and crisp winter days and regretted horribly their precipitous action. Eventually, they gave up their retirement home and returned to Rockford. But home will never be the same, they report, because in the process they forfeited their house of twenty-five years, which they loved dearly.

Beware the Dangers of Buying Land in the Sunbelt

Miami-based Cavanaugh Communities Corp., a land development firm, has been ordered by the Federal Trade Commission (FTC) to tell prospective customers that some of its homesites in Florida and Arizona may be roadless, susceptible to flooding, or worthless as an investment. The company is charged with allegedly misrepresenting the value, investment potential, and extent of development of lots, and with failing to disclose hidden costs accompanying the purchase of a lot. Under a negotiated settlement with the FTC, the company is not required to make refunds to buyers. However, buyers can stop payments and sue the firm.

GAC Corp., once the largest land sales and development company in the country, is being reorganized under federal bankruptcy laws. An exhaustive investigation revealed the firm had sold uninhabitable Florida land as homesites. Many of the unsuspecting buyers bought undeveloped land that is frequently flooded.

Despite repeated warnings, consumers continue to buy land in the Sunbelt sight unseen and keep up payments on it—to the tune of billions of dollars—for years. Over the past two years, HUD's Office of Interstate Land Sales Registration (OILSR), acting on more than four thousand complaints, has suspended 225 developers.

"Thousands of consumers have already lost money on purchases of land that is uninhabitable or has little or no investment value. Thousands more will lose all or a substantial part of their investments, if they are able to sell their land at all. For some, the loss represents the bulk of their savings," reports Jeffrey Harris, assistant director of marketing abuses for the FTC.

Lest you become the victim of one of these unscrupulous operations or salespersons, you should have some knowledge of interstate land sales and the laws. The Interstate Land Sales Full Disclosure Act covers all transactions involving land in a development of fifty or more lots that is sold in interstate commerce *if* the land is not located within a municipality or county that has minimum subdivision standards in force. (If you are unsure whether the land is located in a municipality or county with such standards, inquire at the local planning and zoning office.)

Under this federal law, you have the right:

- To receive a property report forty-eight hours prior to the time of your signing a contract or agreement to buy. Read and compare the property report with what you were told and what your contract says. Inspect the land, and compare it with the property report. If the property is not what it was represented to be, you may be able to take action. See your attorney immediately.

- To cancel any contract or agreement and get your money back, if you can prove that you did not receive a property report forty-eight hours prior to signing the agreement or did not receive the report at all.

To avoid being defrauded or sold uninhabitable land, there are a few other precautions you should take:

- If you are contemplating an interstate land purchase, ask for copies of the property report, contract, and other pertinent documents. Take them home, read them carefully, and have your attorney go over them before signing anything. If you are not allowed to leave with these documents before signing, just leave.
- Check the contract for your rights to get out of the deal. These rights usually are conditional upon your making a personal inspection of the land with a certain time period.
- Do not assume that anything you are told about the lot or development is true. Go over the contract with your attorney to find the truth.
- Take your time. If you're told that the lot you want won't be there tomorrow, don't worry. Even if that's true, there are many other lots in other developments.
- Do not assume that because the development is registered with the U.S. Department of Housing and Urban Development (HUD) that the government has inspected, investigated, or appraised, or in any way endorses the land. *It has not and does not.*

For further information, send for a copy of "Before Buying Land . . . Get the Facts," Office of Interstate Land Sales, U.S. Department of Housing and Urban Development, Washington, D.C. 20410. You can also obtain a copy of "Buying Lots from Developers," for fifty cents from the Superintendent of Documents, Government Printing Office, Washington, D.C. 20420.

If you believe you have been defrauded, or if the land or developer's obligations have been misrepresented, you should notify your attorney immediately and HUD's Office of Interstate Land Sales at the above address.

Further Sources of Information

Most Sunbelt and western boomtowns have magazines targeted at newcomers and prospective home buyers. These publications contain a wealth of valuable information, and you should obtain one on your prospective city and read it thoroughly. Most of these magazines provide enlarged maps of the metropolitan area and designate exact locations of housing developments in the suburbs. You'll find ample pictures and floor plans of homes in the various subdivisions, since builders and developers are the main advertisers. Therefore, do not expect to find any negative comments or reports on questionable activities of any builders or other principals in the real-estate industry.

These magazines often include elaborate layouts on newly planned unit developments, condo and town-house complexes, stating prices and availability. They also feature communities catering to singles and retirees. Some publications regularly insert a new house directory, giving the location and type, prices, and sizes of homes in various developments. A few of these guides also assist readers in their relocation efforts.

Says Gary Campbell of the *Southern California Guide to Homes for Sale,* "Readers can write to us telling us the type of homes in which they're interested and we'll send their inquiries on to the appropriate builders who will mail them additional literature."

The *Greater Atlanta Home Buyer Directory* contains a section of postage-paid coupons that the reader can mail to various real-estate brokers and builders stating their preferences and requesting more information.

Living magazine, a product of Baker Publications, Inc., of Dallas, has individual editions published in Dallas, Austin, Houston, San Antonio, Denver, Phoenix, and West Florida. In addition to the relocation information in the magazines, the firm has established relocation centers in Houston and Dallas, where newcomers can pick up maps and get a rundown on the new developments and housing and apartment markets. The centers are staffed with trained professionals in real estate, although no selling or promotion of any products occurs on the premises.

The local real-estate magazines for any city can give you an idea of the style of houses available in your price range. Home styles in the South and West often differ significantly from those in the Midwest and Northeast. However, you'll not find much, if any, material about existing houses in these publications. But you will find the names of a number of real-estate firms that are advertisers and can be contacted for information on existing homes.

These newcomers' guides also often provide data on taxes and accounts of all community facilities—recreation, health, churches, fire protection, schools—in the various suburbs. They usually advise how and where to apply for a driver's license, how to register your vehicles, as well as how to register to vote.

The *Living* magazines tend to be most consumer oriented, giving extensive backgrounds on each city—municipal government, historical notes, major industries, population and area data, climate, voting procedures, tax structures, cost of living comparisons, outdoor activities, entertainment, and medical facilities. Each *Living* magazine has a complete map system showing all new housing developments in the suburbs. New detached homes, condos, town homes, and patio homes, as well as apartment developments and their names are listed and price-coded alongside the maps. Going a step further than some of the other publications, *Living* offers guides to dining and dinner theaters and schedules of upcoming music, art, theater, and sports engagements.

Most of these regional real-estate publications are distributed free through Chambers of Commerce, major hotels and motels, at banks and savings-and-loan associations, at airports, rental car locations, real-estate offices, model homes, and customer service offices in major department stores. Many are also available through subscription. To obtain names and addresses of the publications in your prospective city, write the local Chamber of Commerce.

Also inquire whether the city has other magazines that would give you a greater feel for the real-estate market and the community. For example, Dallas has *D* magazine, and in Atlanta there is *Atlanta* magazine. These publications, covering a spectrum of subjects and features, can give you some important insights into the ambiance and political climate of a new community.

You can also write to state development commissions or tourism commissions informing them of your intention to relocate in their states, and they should send you a packet of information with material on areas of particular interest to you.

6

How to Evaluate the Quality of Your Prospective Home

This chapter will provide some very specific standards that you should use to evaluate each house you seriously consider. These standards will determine the value and livability of your home and are the measures the lender will use to determine how much to loan on the house or whether to give you the mortgage at all.

Energy Efficiency

"If disposable income continues to shrink as energy costs rise sharply, defaults on conventional home mortgages could zoom to five percent from a current national average of one percent," warns Peter Back, acting director of the residential and commercial building division of the Department of Energy (DOE).

Already, monthly heating and utility bills in some parts of the country are as much as or more than mortgage payments. Research by the federal government indicates that home energy costs will rise an average 13 percent a year in the early eighties.

"If you get stuck with an energy hog, it will be hard to sell, because the clock is running out on homes like that," Back predicts.

The U.S. League of Savings Associations reports that a home's energy efficiency has become increasingly important in establishing its value. The league notes that many lending institutions now consider energy costs in their home appraisals. Some lenders even require homes to meet certain minimum energy standards to qualify for loans.

In fact, an energy-efficient home is worth from 5 to 9 percent more at the time of resale than a similar, but less energy-efficient house, according to a recent survey of 160 real-estate brokers and eighty appraisers in twenty-two U.S. cities. Two-thirds of the brokers surveyed said that a well-insulated house was worth more than a similar house that was poorly insulated. The average improvement in value noted by the brokers was 9 percent. Appraisers indicated that an energy-efficient house averaged 5 percent more in value.

One-third of the brokers and appraisers said that an energy-efficient home is easier to finance, and the majority stated that lenders are definitely taking a greater interest in the energy efficiency of homes.

Before signing an offer to buy on any home, you should get as much information as you can about its annual energy costs—and then assume they'll be higher in the future. You should ask to see all copies of the past year's utility bills.

Specifically, you want to find out what kind of heating and cooling systems the house has and how efficient they are. You'll want to know how well the house is insulated and whether the windows and doors have weather stripping and caulking around them. You should also find out whether the house has storm windows and storm doors. A number of factors determine the energy efficiency of any house—the type of home, its location, the age and efficiency of its utilities and appliances, to name a few.

To help you calculate the energy efficiency of various homes you consider, National Homes Corporation has developed an energy performance rating system you can use. The "Energy Performance Rating" booklet, available through National Homes' 1,400 builder/dealers, gives point values for thirteen basic components of the home including the ceiling, wall, and floor insulation; windows; doors; infiltration; heating system; fireplace; air conditioner; duct system; clock thermostat or individual room controls; water-saving fixtures and solar-assisted hot water. The booklet, available in five editions—one for each of the nation's climatic zones—provides checklists for seven types of homes.

The EPR formula consists of adding up the energy values for the different components and using a multiplier. The higher the rating, the more energy efficient the home. This system applies to all homes, not just those built by National.

If there is not a National Homes builder/dealer near you, you can obtain a copy of the booklet by writing to Fred Harless, National Homes Corp., Box 250, Lafayette, Indiana 47902.

In addition, there are several inexpensive mail-order booklets that provide sound information on how to evaluate a home's energy efficiency and how to improve its rating. These books can be ordered from the following sources:

- *In the Bank . . . or Up the Chimney* (price $1.70), Superintendent of Documents, U.S. Government Printing Office, Washington, D.C. 20402.
- *Making the Most of Your Energy Dollars* (price 70 cents), Consumer Information Center, Pueblo, Colorado 81009.
- *How to Save Money by Insulating Your Home* (price 30 cents), Mineral Insulation Manufacturers Association, 382 Springfield Avenue, Summit, New Jersey 07901.

A more expensive ($8), but excellent book that discusses energy efficiency, with a section on solar energy, is *The McGraw-Hill Home Book*, which can be obtained at most bookstores. A guide for the just-moved, this book provides advice on home improvement and decorating projects, and includes a section, "The Whole House Energy Inspection," that explains the different types of insulation and the R-values required in different systems of the home to ensure maximum energy efficiency.

Since there is much misinformation and confusion about what constitutes valid energy upgrades, you should obtain some basic information about energy-efficient standards before contracting for any insulation or other work or buying expensive supplies for do-it-yourself projects. There are many rip-off artists taking the money of naive home owners who think they are getting a good deal. If you do hire a contractor, make certain he is an established businessperson, and check his credentials with the Better Business Bureau.

You should also check on whether your state has an energy code. By the mid-eighties, most states will have their own codes, and you may find that your state energy department has already developed energy performance standards for homes. The federal government is now in the process of implementing the Building Energy Performance Standards (BEPS), regulations that will require most new residential and commercial buildings be constructed to use a limited amount of energy.

Tax Incentives for Energy Upgrades

The National Energy Act provides tax credits of up to $300 for home owners who insulate their homes or install other energy-conserving equipment. It gives a maximum tax credit of $2,000 to those who install solar heating, wind energy, or geothermal equipment. Your state may offer additional tax incentives for energy improvements.

Solar Energy

Solar energy is, indeed, a technology that has come of age. Some builders in the Sunbelt now offer solar hot-water systems as standard options in their new homes. And the National Association of Home Builders, which represents 117,000 builders, has called for an industry-wide effort to make cost-effective solar energy available throughout the nation.

Unfortunately, there are many unscrupulous operators in the solar business. Before investing in any solar equipment, you should carefully check the credentials of the company and make certain that it has specialists who know how to *install the equipment properly.* You should also check for warranties.

For more information on passive solar energy, you can write to the Small Homes Council-Building Research Council, One East St. Mary's Road, Champaign, Illinois 61802. This organization, which for years has explored and tested innovations in residential dwellings with its staff of professionals, is an excellent source of information on every facet of home construction, energy, or technical data. You can write to the council for brochures on most subjects or with particular questions pertaining to problems you experience with your home.

For further information on solar energy, contact the National Solar Heating and Cooling Information Center, P.O. Box 1607, Rockville, Maryland 20850. The center, operated under the auspices of HUD and DOE, acts as the national clearinghouse for information on solar developments and has an ample supply of literature. Your state energy department may also have a division or specialist on solar energy.

For a list of solar manufacturers and their components, you can send for *The Solar Engineering Master Catalog and Product Index*. It can be ordered for $15 from Solar Engineering Publishers, Inc., 8435 N. Stemmons Freeway, Suite 880, Dallas, Texas 75247 or by calling 800-648-5311.

Underground Houses

In recent years, underground houses have been rediscovered as a means to survive the energy crunch. Earth-sheltered houses come in a variety of forms—some are built into the sides of hills, others are constructed partially underground. Their main feature, however, is the use of soil for insulation.

Architect John Barnard, who pioneered in the construction of underground homes in Massachusetts, says, "The underground concept is eminently practical for suburban communities—single-family homes, apartments, or commercial buildings. Such communities would resemble a park rather than the urban sprawl that blights much of the country."

Before you go burrowing into the ground, there are a few facts you will need to investigate. First, if there's a high water table where you live, it may be impossible to go underground. Second, if you're within municipal boundaries, the house may not meet code standards, so check with city building and zoning officials. Third, you may have difficulty getting financing for an underground house, since this is a relatively new concept for residential dwellings, and the lender may view it as a risky venture. Above-ground building principles, which have been tested and established over the years, simply don't apply or adapt equally to underground structures.

For more information, write the American Underground Association, Department of Civil and Mineral Engineering, University of Minnesota, Minneapolis, Minnesota 55455.

Compact Houses

Builders, who for years have built large four- and five-bedroom houses, are now finding that many persons prefer smaller, compact houses that don't cost an arm and a leg to heat and cool or maintain. In recent years, most houses were designed to accommodate the typical family with 2.6 children, and small homes under a thousand square feet were not even allowed in many communities.

With the changing population trends and life-styles, builders, zoning officials, and bankers are beginning to cater to single buyers with more modest, scaled-down homes. You may find that working with the right builder you can construct a compact, energy-efficient house for less than you can buy a home that would be less energy efficient and less adaptable to your needs.

Architect Alex Wade, a designer of small homes, says, "Over half the people in America are denied access to the housing market. Detached houses are invariably designed for families. Single people who do not have or do not plan to have children find that the housing industry has traditionally turned its back on them."

In his book, *30 Energy-Efficient Houses You Can Build*, Wade describes principles to follow in designing your own compact, low-cost, energy-conservative home. Wade advises building only as much house as you need and not wasting space on unnecessarily expansive foyers and the like. Going up a story or two can save space and money, as can incorporating an open plan that allows a good flow of air. The less square footage you have, the less you'll have to heat, cool, and light and the fewer windows you'll need to seal to stop weather infiltration.

Floor Plans Analysis

"Nobody has to agree with the kind of house you buy except you, but you better be sure that you're getting what you want and need and what will be appropriate for your life-style," advises Natalie, a single woman buying her second home.

Analyze each house you go through and try to decide what makes you like the home. Don't allow gadgetry or superficialities to overwhelm you. If you find yourself attracted to a house because of such details as an automatic garage-door opener or a bathroom-to-basement clothes chute, think again! Consider the house without those items, which can always be added later.

It's the floor plan that to a great extent determines how well a house will fulfill your needs. Try to get a set of plans and study the room arrangements. How well do they fit the way you'll use the house?

- If your hobby is photography, is there space and running water for a darkroom?
- If your hobby is carpentry, is there space and are there electrical outlets for a workroom and tools?
- Does the house have adequate storage—closets, as well as space for sports equipment, luggage, and your other collectibles?
- Will your furniture fit easily into the rooms?
- Is the layout convenient?

One single-again woman, who raised her family in a large, two-story Cape Cod house, contends singles don't need that much space. "It's a bother to keep that much house cleaned, heated, cooled, and maintained," says Jesse, who sold her Cape Cod home and bought a fifties' ranch-style house. In her "new" home, of less than a thousand square feet, the rooms are all on one floor, close together, and getting around the house doesn't require a lot of extra steps or running up and down stairs.

"That's especially important," she adds, "for older persons who have arthritis or heart ailments."

A survey of first-time buyers by Walker and Lee Inc., one of the nation's largest real-estate firms, reveals that singles prefer modest one-story homes with a living room, dining room, kitchen, two bedrooms, and one-and-a-half baths. This is the basic house that so many people bought in the fifties and builders are successfully marketing again today. The survey also found that many single buyers happily settle for the less expensive, stripped-down model without a fireplace, dishwasher, garbage disposal, and carpeting.

Don't buy more space than you need, since your ability to survive in your house over the next several years may well depend on your ability to heat it. If you intend to live in the house alone, you don't need a two-story or split-level—the type of houses put up by the hundreds during the sixties. They were designed for families and zoned with separate areas for children and parents, who wanted their own privacy.

Jesse reports she's had great fun revamping her "modern bungalow," as she calls it. Since she enjoys entertaining and likes open spaces, she ripped out the walls dividing the kitchen, dining room, and living room, and she refinished the wooden floors. She now has that entire area in which friends can mingle at gatherings. She converted closets into storage components for her stereo system and television and installed bookshelves and a handsome bar. Out of two small bedrooms she made one large one with a walk-out deck.

Then she tackled the kitchen, tearing out unnecessary cupboards and installing a cabinet for her microwave oven and pull-outs for other frequently used appliances, such as her food processer and toaster. She also built a breakfast nook into one corner of the kitchen.

The possibilities for these smaller homes are limitless. One can install greenhouse windows to draw in more sunlight and create an even more open feeling or add sliding glass doors and decks to extend living areas.

The formality of a family-type home is often inconvenient for the relaxed, single life-style. It's handier to have space in the kitchen to grab a quick breakfast or dinner by yourself, rather than to always cart meals into the dining room. Keep your needs in mind as you evalute the layout of each home. And don't get yourself boxed into something that requires traipsing through the living room each time you want to get to the bedroom or bathroom.

Here are the criteria you should use in analyzing the layout of each home. Remember, these factors will also determine the resale value of your home.

Zoning

Every house can be divided into three basic zones: the working, living, and sleeping zones. The garage, entryway (or mudroom), the kitchen, and the laundry room usually comprise the working zone, which is apt to be the noisiest area of the house. It's convenient to have these rooms grouped together—it makes hauling in groceries much easier and provides you a place to rid yourself of coats and boots during inclement weather.

The living zone is generally the dining, living, and breakfast rooms. Both the living and working zones are usually buffered from the sleeping zones or bedrooms by hallways and closets. Other buffers you should look for are stairways and floor-to-ceiling built-ins, such as bookshelves or storage units. Although these details may not seem important to you now, they could be eminently important to eventual buyers—especially a couple or single person with a child.

Traffic Patterns

Optimally, you will choose a house with a traffic pattern suited to your activities. A garage-to-mudroom-to-kitchen route is ideal, because there are no wasted steps, and the mudroom takes the brunt of dirty footprints and wet boots and coats. This arrangement also makes carting in groceries and carrying out garbage much simpler—you don't have to haul them through the dining room or living room.

It's ideal to have traffic lanes going directly from the main entrance to the living, sleeping, and working zones. That way, guests don't have to cut through the kitchen to get to the living room. You should be able to get to the bedrooms without walking through the kitchen, or living or dining rooms. If you have a housemate, it's particularly handy to have traffic systems geared to privacy. Then, if you're entertaining in the living room, your housemate—whether renter or partner—can go directly to the bedroom without interrupting your activities.

It's always best to have a kitchen that dead-ends so you don't have to walk through it to get to the other main rooms. Also, you should go through the kitchen with the doors of the refrigerator, oven, dishwasher and cupboards all open to make sure they won't interfere with your flow as you're cooking. Make certain you check drawer and door openings for clearance. The workflow in the kitchen should be a natural process—from the refrigerator to the sink to the cooking area—and should not require any extra steps.

Siting

Finally, you want to make certain that your home is effectively sited on its lot. The land around most houses is divided into three zones—public, service, and private. The public zone is usually the front lawn; the service zone consists of the sidewalks, driveway, clothes-drying, and trash-disposal areas. You want to devote as little space as possible to public and service zones so most of your land can be used for the private area, where you relax.

Ideally, the house should set forward on the lot, with small spaces to the sides. The garage should serve as a buffer from the street and against cold, northern winds. With a small front yard, you have less walk and drive to maintain or shovel in winter.

Don't find yourself enslaved by a massive lawn as Meredith did. When she first saw her home-to-be—a large ranch house on an expansive lot— Meredith thought it was beautiful.

After one summer she ruefully reports, "I wish I'd thought twice about all the yard work that was going to be necessary. I'm tired and ache for two days after I mow the lawn. Then I still have the shrubs to prune and weeds to pull. It never ends."

If your home is close to neighbors, it's best to have windowless walls on those sides to increase your privacy. Your living room and dining room and any large windows should overlook the most attractive parts of your lot and landscape.

Taxes

First, you want to find out how much the property taxes are and when they are due. The owner or real-estate agent should supply that information. However, if you're still shopping around, you can check the property tax base for various neighborhoods and the taxes for a particular piece of property at the county tax assessor's office. You should also inquire at that office when the last rate and assessment increase occurred and when the next assessment will be made. Make sure you find out whether the property is reassessed when it's sold. If so, the taxes automatically go up.

For example, although Proposition 13 rolled back real-estate assessments to 1975 levels in California, when homes are sold they are reassessed and taxed at one percent of their market value. Stewart, who bought a San Francisco home shortly after the passage of Proposition 13, feels he really bore the brunt of that initiative. The rolled-back tax bill on his $95,000 home was $450, but when he took title and the property was reassessed, the annual taxes jumped to $955.

If you're purchasing property in a state or area that has either just passed or is considering a tax cap or spending-limitations initiative, you should find out what the ramifications of those measures will be for home owners and buyers. Often, these initiatives result in additional service fees being levied against property owners. In some areas of California, buyers of new homes must pay an additional $2,000 fee for services (the installation of sewer, water lines, roads) that the municipality can no longer afford to fund. (For a further discussion of Proposition 13–type initiatives, see "Taxes," Chapter 5, page 63).

In general, larger cities with more than a hundred thousand population have a lower tax rate than smaller cities of fifty to a hundred thousand. Taxes are usually higher in new subdivisions, where special assessments are likely to be levied to finance such facilities as parks, sidewalks, schools, or a new hospital. Also, suburban locations have smaller tax bases due to their lack of established industry, which means you pay higher taxes to subsidize community facilities. As you're inquiring about property tax rates, keep in mind any home-owners' association fees you'll have to pay.

You should find out what services the property taxes finance. Usually, they go for such items as road construction and maintenance, the water and sewage systems, garbage collection, recreational and educational facilities, pollution control, and fire and police protection. But be sure to find out if the imposition of any spending limits has necessitated extra assessments for those services.

You should also check:

- Whether there are any impending bond issues or referenda that will raise your taxes.
- If there is a major property reevaluation slated in the near future.
- Whether you can expect to be socked with an additional bill for special assessments.
- What the tax district boundaries are. It's possible that a house across the street from the one you're considering is in a different district and taxed considerably less.
- Whether the municipality levies an "occupation tax" or any other kind of special tax.
- What the homestead exemption is for the property you are considering.

Neighborhood Checklist

Presuming that you have found a locale that seems suitable to your present life-style and needs, and perhaps even have a specific house in mind, then you should systematically check out the neighborhood before committing yourself to a purchase. The quality of the neighborhood will determine the soundness of your investment—affecting the value of the house and your ability to get the loan you want.

Consider each neighborhood in terms of comfort, convenience, and cost. As you look, it's a good idea to take along a tablet and jot down your impressions of each neighborhood based on these factors. Also, note any questions you might have for the real-estate broker, owner, or local officials.

Neighborhood Stability

Security is one of the prime concerns of the live-alone person. You want a stable neighborhood where you won't have to worry about your own safety or that of your home when you're away.

Therefore, one of the first things you should check are the burglary and vandalism rates in the neighborhood. The local police department can fill you in on this score. Visit also with residents, inquiring whether there have been any recent break-ins or incidences of personal attacks.

If you're shopping in an older neighborhood, look closely at the condition of homes. Are they well maintained and are the yards mowed and uncluttered? The obvious signs of a declining neighborhood are deteriorating houses. Avoid buying in a neighborhood where properties are not kept up. Not only will that hurt the resale value of your home, but it's also an indication of irresponsible residents.

If you're buying in an older neighborhood that is being recycled, you need to be especially careful. Unless you're a real pioneer, you may not want to be the first one to locate in the neighborhood. The trick is to invest when there's a firm grass-roots commitment to renovate the neighborhood, but before speculators get in and start buying up property and driving up the prices.

Watch for these trends:

- Are there many For Sale signs in the neighborhood? If so, that may be an indication the area is starting to deteriorate.
- Are the majority of homes owned by their residents, rather than rented? Extensive rental housing usually indicates a transient, less stable neighborhood and may be another sign of present or impending decline.
- Are there many businesses or commercial establishments in the area? If they're increasing in number, the neighborhood is becoming commercial and residential property may already be depreciating.
- Are roads being expanded into major thoroughfares, a further sign of commercialization and decline of residential values?

Don't get stuck like Harrison did. When duplexes were going like hotcakes, he bought one on the southeast side of town, within the city limits. He planned to live in the duplex, renting out the upstairs, until it had appreciated enough that he could sell it and purchase a larger duplex on the more affluent and expanding west side. Unfortunately, after five years, Harrison is still waiting for the appreciation to occur. In the meantime, he's seen gas stations and quick-shops go up all around him. Although it's been on the market for one year, he can't sell the property for a price that would enable him to move up to a larger duplex in the neighborhood he desires.

Utilities

Make sure you find out about the adequacy and rates of local utilities. Area residents can advise you whether the service is satisfactory. Inquire at the utility company about rates.

Give particular attention to future plans of the utility company. Has it applied for permission to build a nuclear power plant or other generating facility that could jeopardize the value, as well as safety, of the neighborhood? If you're in the outlying suburb of a metropolitan area, the utility company may be proposing major electrical power installations to supply the city.

Zoning and Building Regulations

Optimally, you want a neighborhood zoned strictly for residential dwellings, without any heavy commercial/industrial areas nearby. If there are undeveloped sections of land in the vicinity, check the zoning restrictions carefully. You don't want to invest in a new suburban home and then discover a large shopping mall and major thoroughfare are in the works just one block away.

You should find out whether the building code allows you to add on a room or build a garage. Also, investigate whether there are regulations or restrictive covenants for the community that would prevent you from keeping boats or recreational vehicles in your yard or operating a small business in your home. Some planned unit developments (PUDs) have restrictive covenants prohibiting pets. Your real-estate agent or builder should be able to advise you about such local regulations. However, the local building and zoning enforcement officials are the final authorities on such matters.

Here are a few other items you should check on with local zoning officials and area residents:

- Are community zoning regulations strictly enforced? Or are variances frequently granted to powerful business interests?
- Is there a planning board or commission that oversees orderly community growth? If no such body exists, how is community expansion planned?
- Ask to see a planning map for your neighborhood. It should indicate plans for new construction, highways, and major thoroughfares that would change the flow of traffic and put your home within a stone's throw of a busy road.

Community Services

Investigate diligently the quality and proximity of community services—fire and police protection, medical and shopping facilities, public transportation systems, and garbage collection. You'll want to know the exact distance and reputation of the local fire station, as these factors can affect your insurance rates.

Because of the high gasoline costs, you should find out whether there's a reliable mass transit system. If you're in an outlying suburb, are there community car pools that can get you into the city if needed? Are supermarkets and drug stores within walking distance?

What about recreational facilities? Are there bike paths or jogging paths, nearby tennis courts or golf courses? If such activities are important to you, you'll want them easily accessible. If you or a housemate have regular need of medical attention, you should inquire about local hospitals or other facilities you'll require.

City planning officials and your prospective neighbors should be able to give you answers about these services.

Neighbors

Finally, you should try to learn a bit about the residents of the neighborhood. Are there other single people in the area, or are they all couples with growing families? If you're seeking peace and quiet, you don't want to buy in a neighborhood where you'll come home every night to a gang of kids playing next door. Knock on a few doors, introduce yourself, and try to get a feel for the area. If you're greeted in a friendly manner, that's an indication of goodwill that should prove reassuring. Ask about the residents' professions and interests.

If you're buying with a friend, avoid locating in an intolerant neighborhood where you would constantly feel like outsiders. Cold rebuffs can wear on one over a period of time, and you don't need that type of aggravation.

Visit with the residents immediately surrounding your prospective home and discreetly inquire about the other neighbors. Such inquiries can prevent you from inheriting a couple who fights all night long or a batch of rowdy teenagers two feet from your bedroom window. Don't be shy about asking how well the owners have maintained your prospective home and about its general condition.

Although this whole process may seem like a lot of unnecessary and time-consuming work, it can assure you a compatible match with your new neighborhood. And it can keep you out of an area where you're despised because you're single and free to come and go as you please or where your neighbors chronically complain about your beautiful new wind chimes and darling new schnauzer, when basically what they resent is your life-style and ability to take off each weekend for the beach.

Schools

For pointers on how to evaluate the quality of the school system in a neighborhood, see Chapter 13, "Suggestions for the Single Parent."

Inspection Checklist

Because of the large number of defects found in both new and used houses, it is vital that you make a thorough structural inspection of your prospective home. Optimally, this inspection should be conducted before you sign an offer to buy or any other documents. If that cannot be arranged, then the offer should be tendered subject to an inspection, with the right to withdraw your offer if serious flaws are uncovered.

This checklist will enable you to make a systematic inspection of all components of the home. You should note the condition of the various items you inspect and get estimates of any needed repairs to use as negotiating points on the sales price. If you don't have a basic knowledge of house structure, it's advisable to hire a professional inspector who can expertly evaluate the house. You can also call the city building code inspection department and request that an inspector come out and check all the components of the home to make sure it meets code standards. The city inspector will do this free of charge, although you may not be able to arrange for the inspection as rapidly as if you hire a private inspector.

Arrange with your real-estate agent to conduct your inspection during the day when the owner is away. Wear old clothes you don't mind getting dirty and take along a tablet, pencil, flashlight, binoculars, thermometer, tape measure, pliers, level, screwdriver, knife, and any other equipment you plan to use. As you're evaluating the house, also consider how much maintenance it will require and whether you will have the time and money to handle the necessary upkeep.

It's usually advisable to bypass houses with such serious flaws as badly rotted wood, untreated termite infestation, or major defects in the plumbing, wiring, or heating systems.

There are several high-priority items you should check first to determine whether the house will be a good investment. Inspect the basement or crawl space for leaks, wetness, and structural soundness. Examine the roof and attic for severe damage or weakened condition. Check the foundation for serious cracks and all of the mechanical systems to make sure they're in good working order. These items usually are the most costly to repair if they have serious deficiencies.

Basement

Floor

Is the floor level? Most basement floors slope slightly to the floor drain so water runs off. Severe sloping, however, can cause pocketing of water, and drainage will be a problem. Also, you won't be able to put down finished flooring.

Check for floor cracks or evidence of sagging. Small cracks aren't a problem, but large cracks may have to be cut out and repaired. You can expect to find cracks in most older houses, but the cracking should have stopped as the house settled. Floor cracks and sagging are signs of extreme foundation settlement and should be checked by a professional. A severely cracked basement floor also may be a sign of intense water pressure underneath. Make sure there is a working floor drain.

Walls

Are the walls straight or do they lean? Are there vertical cracks that widen as they travel up the wall? If so, the foundation may be sinking, and the condition should be checked by a home inspector or masonry contractor. New houses often have some horizontal cracks and bulges in the walls. Large cracks, however, may be a sign of weak walls. Have them checked by an expert, and make sure you get a written warranty from the builder.

Leakage and Flooding

Piles of magazines, boxes, and furniture sitting on the floor usually indicate the floor is dry. Beware if the basement floor and walls have been freshly painted and objects are stored off the floor. To determine whether there has been flooding, look under the furnace for telltale rust stains. Also look for water stains on the walls and baseboards. Soft and darkened baseboards generally are a sign of chronic dampness. Whitish markings on the joints of the floor tiles indicate continued dampness and repeated floodings. If water leaks into the basement, you probably can't stop it without expensive repairs. You won't be able to use the basement as a finished room or for floor storage.

Insulation

If the walls and band joists are insulated, less energy will be required to heat the basement. Is there insulation in the basement ceiling? If the basement is normally unheated, then insulation in the ceiling will reduce energy costs throughout the rest of the house.

Crawl Space

Check this area very carefully, as it's a place where you can detect evidence of structural damage that will affect the home's value. Are the beams and joists decaying? Look especially for decay where the floor joists meet the concrete walls.

A vapor barrier should cover the crawl space floor to keep out moisture. Is the floor dry enough to use for storage? Are there closable screen vents to provide ventilation? These vents are usually kept closed, but should be there so you can open them to dry out the crawl space if it gets wet.

Is the crawl space properly insulated? There are two ways to insulate crawl spaces. One is to insulate the walls and band joists. If these parts are insulated, then the pipes and heating ducts won't need to be insulated because the crawl space will be kept warm in the winter and pipes won't freeze. The other method is to insulate the ceiling and put a vapor barrier on the warm side of the insulation toward the floor. In this case, pipes and ducts must be insulated. The most efficient method is where both walls and ceiling are insulated.

While you are still in the basement or crawl space there are several other items you should inspect.

Sump Pump

In areas where there aren't storm sewers or where the storm sewer depth is higher than that of the basement or crawl space floor, a sump pump is necessary to collect water and pump it away from the house. Turn the sump pump on to make sure it works, and check its age and condition. If it's old and decrepit looking, it may need replacing and you should get estimates on the cost.

Beams and Joists

Do beams and/or joists sag? If so, the floor above may sag and creak and the walls may be cracked. Ask a carpenter how the situation can be remedied and how much it will cost. Get several bids, however, before contracting for major repairs.

Are beams and joists decaying? Check for decay at the points of contact with the concrete—where the floor joists are supported on concrete walls—by jabbing the beams and joists with a knife. If the wood is decaying, it may break across the grain and fall out.

Are there large cracks or splits which weaken the wood and do the floors bounce when you walk across them? This may be a sign of weakened wood or it may indicate that undersized joists were used. If so, undersized lumber was probably used in other parts of the house—an indication of cost-cutting and substandard construction. If you suspect the builder tried to cut too many corners, look elsewhere.

Termite Infestation

If you're in an area where termites are common, ask the owner for a certificate of termite treatment. If the house hasn't been treated, you should inspect for termites. (Often as a condition of sale, the owner must have a termite inspection to prove the house is free of infestation. If the inspection turns up evidence of termites, the owner should pay for the treatment.) If it turns out that termite damage is extensive, look for another house.

You can tell if the house recently has been treated for termites by looking for small holes drilled in the basement floor next to the wall. Check for termite shields in the basement or crawl space. Inspect for evidence of termites by looking for the mud tubes through which they travel up to the wood. Look at joist ends on the wall plate upon which the joist rests. Also look for mud tubes under porches and stoops on the outside of the foundation just above the ground level. Examine windowsills near the ground for termite damage.

Foundation and House Exterior

After you've inspected the basement or crawl space, you should go outside and look over the foundation and the exterior condition of the house.

Drainage Around the Foundation

Does the ground slope away from the house so water doesn't stand around foundation walls? The ground six feet around the house should slope downward at least six inches. If it doesn't you can expect a wet basement or sinking foundation. This is critical in a new house. If there is not a proper grade away from the house, a few truckloads of groundfill may solve the problem. Get a cost estimate.

Do entryways slope down and away from the house? Are the porches sloped away from the house so water doesn't collect along the foundation?

If a neighbor's lot drains onto the property, it could flow toward the foundation and cause a wet basement. If the house is in a low-lying area—lower than surrounding properties—you can expect water in the basement after a heavy rainfall. It may cost several thousand dollars to install an adequate drainage system. If the house is in a valley, ask nearby home owners if they have leaky basements. It may be a chronic condition that can only be remedied by installing a sump pump.

Foundation Walls

Walk around the house and check for cracks in the foundation walls. You can expect to find some small cracks, but cracks of one-quarter inch or more may indicate unusual settling of the foundation. In such instances, have a building contractor or house inspector examine the situation.

Look for loose masonry and area wells around basement windows. Do basement windows have well-fitted screens with storm sashes, and do they lock securely?

Exterior Walls

Most outside walls are either frame or masonry and your location primarily will determine what you'll find.

SIDING. Several common types of siding are aluminum, plywood, shingles, and clapboards. Many new houses are covered with hardboard, aluminum, or plywood siding. Check the siding for splits, loose nails, and nail pops (nails showing through the wood).

Is the paint worn off or very thin? If there is blistering or peeling paint, make sure you find out what the cause is and whether it can be corrected. Peeling can be caused by condensation from excessive moisture trapped in the walls (sometimes condensation problems cannot be cured), a poor paint job, or low-quality paint.

Is there evidence of mildew or fungus? If the house is in an extremely humid climate, the paint should be fortified with a mildewcide booster.

Check metal siding for dents, worn places in the paint finish, and discoloration.

Is there flashing where siding and another exterior surface join? There should be flashing under all material changes to waterproof the underlying surfaces and joints.

MASONRY WALLS. Masonry walls may be masonry stone, concrete block, brick, or artificial stone. Masonry walls offer the advantages of greater fire and sound resistance, less exterior maintenance and greater solidity and durability.

Check for missing mortar and cracks in the mortar joints. Repointing the mortar is expensive, and you should consult a brick mason if much work needs to be done. Is the brick stained or are there white stains below windowsills? Check with a paint store for a recommendation on how to remove these stains.

STUCCO WALLS. Stucco, common in California and the Southwest, is a coat of cement plaster applied over sheathing or solid masonry. Check for cracks in the stucco. If the stucco is well bonded to the supporting surface you can usually repair cracks with patching cement applied with a caulking gun. If the stucco is loose, it will have to be removed and the surface will have to be replastered. Get an estimate from a masonry or plastering contractor.

INSECTS. Check carefully to see whether beetles or ants have bored their way into the siding. The telltale sign on wood-sided houses is sawdust. Get an estimate on the extent of the damage from an exterminator.

TRIM. Trim should be in good condition and well caulked. Check soffits, fascia boards, and wood around the windows and doors for cracking, rotting, and warping. Wood trim should be neat and tight, not curved or crooked with any gaps or peeling paint. Do the ends of trim show signs of discoloration or decay? Do fascia boards under the gutters need replacing due to decay?

WINDOWS. Are the windowsills and trim painted to protect them from water or are they peeling and flaking? Are windowsills sloped so water drains away from them? Is there evidence of termite damage on the sills? Check for weather stripping around the windows. Putty around the window panels should be solid and unbroken to prevent drafts.

Are there storm windows and screens? Are they wood or metal? Wooden storm windows require maintenance and probably will have to be put up and taken down each year. Metal ones are self-storing and can be left up year-round. Make sure storm windows are properly installed and open and close smoothly. Storm windows can substantially reduce your heating and cooling bills, and if the house doesn't have them plan on several hundred dollars for installation.

Outside Doors

Are they solid or hollow? Knocking on the door will tell you whether it's solid. Solid doors provide more security and better insulation.

Door sills should be raised above the entrance piece platform to prevent snow and rain from blowing under the door and keep rain from delaminating the wood. The door should be sealed at the bottom and water should drain away from it.

Check for storm doors, which will reduce heat loss by about 50 percent. Also, look for weather stripping. Any cracks around the door will have to be caulked.

Are there lights at all doors? Do all the doors have dead-bolt locks for maximum security? It's advantageous to have peepholes in all exterior doors. Is there glass around or in the doors that might easily be broken to gain entrance? If there are sliding glass doors, do they have extra security devices? If not, consult a locksmith about installing some burglar-proof equipment.

Gutters and Downspouts

Are gutters sagging, rusting, or peeling? Do they need repainting or replacing? Are they clogged with leaves from nearby trees? Are the joints open and leaking? Check the woodwork below for water damage.

Roof

There are several types of roofs, but most are covered with asphalt shingles. Use your binoculars to check for worn, loose, or missing shingles. Look also for loss of granules or blistering—if there is a severe loss of granules, plan on replacing the roof within a year. Find out when the house was last roofed. A new roof can be applied over one existing roof, but not over two, because of the weight and because nails cannot hold a third reshingling. Asphalt shingles last about fifteen to twenty years. Get estimates from a few roofing contractors if it appears the roof needs repair or replacement.

Slate shingle roofs of high quality last for about a hundred years. Check for chipped or discolored shingles, and if they are badly damaged, get a roofing contractor's estimate.

Flat, built-up roofs, made of layers of asphalt or tar, felt, and stone granules, pose special risks. Water often puddles on these roofs and may seep down into the house. Check for leaks at the seams between overlapping metal plates and the roof edges. Look also for tears, absences of gravel, and blistering. If you have any questions, contact a roofing contractor.

Also check the roof for flashing—at the edges, intersections between chimney and roof, at vent stacks and in valleys. Make sure the flashing isn't broken or cracked—one piece of metal should tightly overlap another piece of metal.

Chimney

Is the chimney plumb and the brickwork in good condition or does the chimny need rebuilding? Look for signs of patching and puttying and check the chimney flashing. If repairs are needed get a professional estimate, as brick work can be very expensive.

Grounds

While you're still outside, you should check out the condition of the ground surrounding the house and the landscaping.

Yard and Landscaping

Are there trees and shrubs on the lot? Shade trees, properly placed, can be a real asset, adding to the appearance of the property and reducing air-conditioning bills. Make sure trees and shrubs are healthy and disease-free. Having them removed can be very expensive. Likewise, it can be costly to landscape the yard yourself. How close are the trees to the house? If they're closer than thirty feet, leaves may clog gutters, and falling branches can be a problem.

What is the condition of the lawn? If it's full of weeds and crabgrass, it will take time and money to remove them. If you buy a new house before the lawn has been planted, make sure you have an agreement with the builder about who is responsible for the landscaping and lawn. If the builder doesn't provide enough topsoil, the lawn may erode.

Is the yard level or sunken? Sunken lawns may indicate a broken storm or sanitary sewer or a broken tile drain, which will have to be repaired.

Electrical Outlets and Lighting

Are there weatherproofed convenience outlets near where you'll need them? Do they have Ground Fault Current Interrupters (GFIs) to prevent shock in the event of electrical equipment malfunctioning? Most new houses have GFIs.

Are all entries as well as pathways to other buildings, parking places, and patios well lighted?

Is there a television antenna? Is there a cable television franchise which will wire the house?

Driveway, Sidewalks, Patio

Is the drive paved or gravel? Paving a driveway or repairing a poorly paved drive will be expensive. Is the concrete in any areas deteriorating? Is it cracked, crumbling, or tilting—an indication of settling? If walks, patio, or drive are near large trees, root growth may disrupt the concrete. Broken concrete must be replaced. Water should drain away from the sidewalk, patio, and drive.

Carport or Garage

Is the garage attached or detached? If it's detached, how close is it to the house? How many cars does it hold? Are there electrical outlets in the garage and is it adequately lighted for use as a workshop or for other projects? Is there storage room for bikes, lawn furniture, and other items in the garage or carport?

Try the garage doors to make sure they open easily without sticking. Are there locks on garage doors? Automatic door openers? Make sure doors are not sagging or rotting. If they need replacing, get an estimate.

Check the condition of the garage's siding and roofing, looking for the same things you did when you inspected the house's exterior. Make sure the garage has gutters to prevent wood rot. Check also for termites and evidence of rotting at the base. Does the garage floor slope downward so water and snow from cars drain away from the garage?

Sewage System and Septic Tank

If there are no storm and sanitary sewers, future assessments for them could cost several thousand dollars. If the home has a septic tank, determine its location and check for odors or soggy ground around the tank. A lot of thick grass around the leaching area is an indication of poor absorption which may cause odors during heavy rains or wet periods. If there's evidence of recent digging around the septic tank, the drainage system may be faulty and the tank may have to be dug up and reinstalled—a costly proposition.

House Interior

Now go back inside the house, and starting in the attic, make a thorough inspection of the structural condition of the interior.

Attic

Is the attic adequately insulated? There should be a minimum six inches of insulation, but ten inches is preferable. In an unfinished attic, you can see the insulation lying between the floor joists. (In a finished attic, you'll have to look under the floor.) Check the knee walls or rafters for insulation. Are air-conditioning ducts insulated, and do they have a vapor barrier on the outside of the insulation?

Is the attic properly ventilated? Check for ventilating louvers at the ridge, underneath the soffits, or at the ends. Make sure insulation isn't blocking the vent openings. Without adequate ventilation, condensation occurs in the winter, and water drips down onto the wood and insulation, causing them to rot. Do exhaust fans empty into the attic? Exhaust fans from the kitchen and bathrooms should be vented to the outside, or you run the risk of grease accumulation and fire or moisture condensation and rotting in the attic.

Are there signs of leaks, rotting wood, or dry rot? Look for watermarks on the bottom of the roof sheathing. Inspect rafters and roof sheathing for signs of dry rot, mold, decay, or other deterioration. Get estimates from a reliable contractor on needed repair work.

What's the condition of wiring and plumbing pipes in the attic? Do wire splices fit correctly into metal junction boxes? Check flashing around the plumbing stack vent which releases gases from the sewer system. If you can see daylight where the vent goes through the roof, the flashing needs repairing.

Is the attic accessible for storage, or could it later be expanded to provide more living space?

Floors

Are surfaces worn, and does the floor need replacing? Check for wear in front of the range, at the kitchen sink, at doorways, entries, and other places that get a lot of use. Get estimates for replacement costs on any bad flooring. Refinishing a hardwood floor calls for professional help.

To determine whether a hard surface floor is level, set a marble in the middle of the room. If the marble rolls to one side, the floor isn't level, which means the house has probably settled or poor materials were used. If the floors are severely uneven, furniture placed on them will rock.

Check the condition of the carpeting. If you're buying a new home, examine the quality of the carpet. If it's cheap, you might have to replace it within a few years. Check the pile density, the backing, and the padding. If these items seem inadequate, consult a carpet layer. Walk over all carpeted areas several times, listening for a clapping or rumbling, which indicates the subfloor isn't securely attached to the floor joists.

If the floors shake when you walk across them, the floor joists may be too small and the floor may need additional support beams and posts to stiffen the system. Consult a carpenter.

Walls and Ceilings

Look for cracks in the dry wall or plaster. Some cracks are to be expected; but if the cracks are large or there are many of them, have a carpenter examine the situation. He can tell you the cause of the cracks, how serious they are, and how much it will cost to repair them.

Dry-wall panel joints should be invisible. It's an indication of substandard work if they're not. Look for nail pops—not uncommon in older houses. Usually you can fix them yourself, but if you're unsure about your abilities, consult a carpenter.

Look for leaking water and water stains on the walls and ceiling, especially below the bathroom. If the situation appears serious, consult a professional.

Is the paint cracked or peeling? If you're looking at an older house where the paint is in bad shape, get an estimate on how much it would cost to repaint. The walls may have to be scraped and sanded, which can be expensive.

Are the walls insulated? Older homes may not have insulated walls. Check by removing the cover plate of a switch or receptacle and look for insulation. If there isn't any, get estimates of how much it will cost to insulate. Also, check for air leaks through wall switches, receptacles, wallboards, and shoemolds by holding your hand up to them and feeling for a draft.

Interior Windows

You'll find windows in a variety of styles and sizes. All windows should provide adequate lighting, ventilation, and energy loss prevention. Windows in the main living areas should face south, providing a sunny exposure. Other windows should be shielded from the sun's strong easterly and westerly rays.

To be energy efficient, all windows must have tight seals against their frames. You'll get the best insulation from double- or triple-glazed windows with a buffering air space between windowpanes to prevent excessive heat gain in the summer and heat loss in the winter. Hold your hand up to the window and feel for air seepage. Examine all windows for weather stripping—the key to a tight, energy-efficient window.

Open and close all windows to see how well they operate. Depending on the house, you may find more than one style of window. Check to see if the house has fold-in storm windows and if they operate properly. Open and close all self-storing storm windows, examining them for warping and ease of movement. Neither the windows nor storms should rattle in the wind if they are properly installed and snug.

DOUBLE-HUNG WINDOWS. This is the most common type. Check to make sure the window casings are in good shape. Open and close each window and look for signs of weathering, such as cracked and peeling paint and splits in the wood. Make sure none of the windows is painted shut—a common problem in older homes and a lot of work to fix. Check for cracked windowpanes, and make sure both the upper and lower sashes open and close freely.

CASEMENT WINDOWS. These windows open vertically with a crank or lever. Check the condition of casements. Are they well painted to retard rust and corrosion? Aluminum casements don't need to be painted. However, casements with aluminum or steel frames often get cold in the winter so heat loss and condensation are problems. Make sure the gears work properly and there's a good seal when the window is closed. If parts of the frame are rotted and the windows are in bad shape, they may need replacement. New casements can be very expensive so get estimates.

SLIDING WINDOWS. These are easy to operate and usually have few maintenance problems. Check to make sure they open and close easily and that the runners aren't rusted or damaged. Sliding windows should fit tightly to prevent heat loss. The best ones come from the factory with weather stripping.

AWNING WINDOWS. Such windows swing up and open horizontally and operate by means of a lever or crank. Make sure the hardware is in good shape.

JALOUSIE WINDOWS. Most common in warm, southern climates, jalousie windows are made of overlapping glass slats. Make sure the crank mechanisms operate properly and the windows open and close smoothly.

Interior Doors

Open and close all doors, checking for sticking or rubbing. Make sure the doors are hung straight in their frames. Doors should be large enough so that you can easily get your furniture inside rooms. All interior doors should be at least 32 inches wide and 80 inches high or higher.

Sliding, bifold, or jackknife doors should open without sticking and close easily. If not, they may need an adjustment. If the doors were installed in a poorly fitted frame they may be expensive to fix.

Trim

Check the condition of the baseboards, the window and door casings, and the trim around the ceilings. Make sure you examine the trim around registers and radiators, doors and windows, and appliances, where moisture, dryness, or exposure to sun may have caused damage. If the woodwork is painted and there are many chipped, flaking, or dirty spots, you'll have to repaint. If the woodwork is stained and/or varnished and in poor condition, it will have to be refinished—a time-consuming task.

Fireplace

A properly working, well-installed fireplace can be a real asset to a house; a malfunctioning one can be a real hazard. Many homes have sustained extensive damages from substandard and improperly installed metal prefabricated fireplaces and wood-burning stoves. If you have doubts about the quality of the fireplace or its installation, call the local fire chief and ask if there have been any problems reported with fireplaces installed by the builder of your home. You can also ask the local building inspector for an opinion on the brand of the fireplace or stove and the workmanship. Check the fireplace carefully to make sure all bricks or stonework are in good shape. The hearth should extend at least 12 inches on either side of the firebox opening and 18 inches in front to provide safety from flying sparks.

Examine the area surrounding the fireplace for soot or dark discolorations. Are there smoke stains on the ceiling in front of the fireplace? If you can, start a fire and watch for smoking and a proper draw of smoke up the flue. Smoking is caused by any number of factors: an obstructed flue, a too-low or poorly operating damper, downdrafts, or poor design of the fireplace. The home may be too tightly sealed to provide an adequate draw, and you may have to open a window. Check to see whether the fireplace has a vent brick, and make sure it isn't obstructed by leaves, grass, or ashes. If you can't figure out what the problem is, have an expert inspect the fireplace. Consult the Yellow Pages for fireplace repair services or have an experienced contractor examine it.

Look up into the chimney and check the damper. To guarantee a good draw when the fire is burning, the damper should be located about 8 inches above the top of the firebox opening. The damper should be free of excessive soot and debris, and the damper opening should be at least 90 percent of the size of the flue.

Make sure the flue is clear and open. Birds' nests, accumulated soot, debris, or a clogged chimney top will cause the flue to quit functioning and present a possible fire hazard. Also, make sure the flue is not overloaded— the fireplace should not share its flue with the hot-water heater, kitchen range, or other appliances. In fact, many building codes prohibit such sharing.

Make sure the chimney is in good shape and of the proper height. Check for cracked or missing bricks inside the chimney. Has the mortar fallen away between bricks in spots? Is there a chimney cap and is it in good condition? The chimney should be at least 2 feet higher than anything else within 10 feet, including the roof and nearby trees. If it's not, you can expect downdrafts when the wind blows from certain directions.

If you want a fireplace mainly for the heat, it's best to have one built in the middle of a room with interior walls surrounding the chimney. A chimney on the side or end of the house with three exposed sides loses a great deal of heat. If you're buying a new house, you may wish to have one of the newer fireplaces, which is ducted throughout the house for heating.

Bathrooms

Because repairing or remodeling a bathroom can be very expensive, you should examine each one in the house carefully.

Begin by checking the condition of the fixtures. Do they leak or need replacement? Is the bathtub porcelain, fiberglass, or plastic? Check porcelain tubs and sinks for chips and permanent stains. Examine fiberglass tubs for mars or fibers coming out. Check plastic tube for scarring.

Check for leaky faucets or drains. Turn the water on to see if the tub and sink fill rapidly and empty quickly and quietly. If there are rust-colored stains where faucets drip, the water may have a high mineral content. If so, the house may need a water softener or the existing one may not be working properly. Get an estimate on this item.

Check the toilet by flushing it several times to see whether it works efficiently without gurgling or running.

Examine the ceiling directly below the bathroom for stains, crumbling plaster, or evidence of recent repainting—signs of leaky bathroom fixtures.

Look over the plumbing around the sink and toilet for drips or wetness. If the floor is damp around the toilet, it may be caused by a cracked bowl, tank, or loose pipe fitting. Or there may be a loose seal at the floor flange.

Splash water on the walls around the tub, and then check the ceiling below for signs of leaks. If there are leaks, the caulking around the tub or the grout between tiles probably needs replacing.

To find out if the tub drain leaks, aim water from the tub faucet directly into the drain opening. Let the water run for fifteen minutes, and then check the ceiling below for dampness.

To determine whether water pressure is adequate throughout the system, turn on all the faucets and flush the toilet at the same time. If the flow of water from the faucet slows to a trickle, there's a pressure problem that will be expensive to fix. Typical causes are old galvanized pipes that are full of rust or an undersized main line running into the house. Have two or more plumbers check the pipes and give you estimates.

Are the bathroom walls and floor in good condition? Look for spots where water has seeped beneath the flooring. Check around the tub, toilet, walls, and sink for deterioration. If the floor is ceramic, you may need only a few replacement tiles and some regrouting.

Are the walls clean and free from mold and mildew? If the walls are tiled, check the grouting. Look for cracked or loose tiles and see if water has seeped behind the tiles. You may have to retile part or all of the wall.

If the walls are painted or wallpapered, will they have to be redecorated? Check the paint on the bathroom window frame. Is it cracked or peeling and has moisture damaged the window frame?

Does the bathroom have an exhaust fan ducted to the outside? Many building codes require fans in windowless bathrooms. Is the lighting adequate? Fluorescent lighting is not desirable because it's the wrong color for makeup application.

Make sure there are enough electrical outlets for hairdryer, curling iron, razor, and other appliances. For safety, all outlets should be protected by a Ground Fault Current Interrupter (GFI).

Kitchen

Since the kitchen is usually the most expensive room to remodel, make sure it's large enough and suited to your needs. In the best-designed kitchens, one should be able to work in a 22-foot triangular path between the sink, stove, and refrigerator. A U-shaped kitchen is considered the most efficient. Before buying a home with a kitchen that needs major remodeling, consult a professional kitchen designer or contractor for an estimate.

Make sure there's enough counter space next to the refrigerator, as well as on both sides of the sink and stove. Check the countertops for chips, cuts, scratches, and worn spots. Are there enough wall and base cabinets? Make sure all cabinet doors open and shut easily and that all drawers slide open and shut smoothly. Will the cabinets need repainting or some of the hardware need replacing?

Do the appliances come with the home? If so, examine the range, oven, broiler, refrigerator, dishwasher, garbage disposal, compactor, and freezer for age, cleanliness, and appearance. Does everything work satisfactorily? Listen for rattles or other odd noises in the disposal and dishwasher. Try each burner on the range. See if the oven door leaks heat. Is there a hood over the rangetop, and if so, where is it vented? It should be vented directly to the outside.

If any appliances are over ten years old, they'll probably need to be replaced soon. If the appliances are fairly new, find out if their warranties are still good. If appliances don't come with the house, is there enough space to install your own appliances? If you need to buy appliances, have you allotted funds for them in your home-buying budget?

Check the sink for chips, scratches, and stains. Do the faucets leak, and how's the water pressure? Check pipes beneath the sink for leaks and corrosion.

Is the kitchen well lit? It's best to have task lighting over work areas and a light over the sink.

Are there enough circuits for all the appliances? Do kitchen appliances share a circuit with other rooms in the house? Turn everything in the kitchen on at once to see if the electrical capacity is adequate. Are outlets conveniently located so several small appliances can be plugged in without moving them around?

Laundry Facilities

Do the washer and dryer come with the house? If so, examine them carefully. Is the dryer properly vented to the outside? If there is no laundry room, is there space to install one? Is there access to plumbing and to a 220-volt grounded outlet for installing your washer and dryer? Is the floor solid enough to absorb vibrations without making a lot of noise?

Mechanical Systems

Give special attention to the mechanical systems—plumbing, electricity, heating and cooling, and security. They can be very costly to repair if substantial work is needed.

Electrical System

First, find out if there's enough power for your needs. Check the service panel (it will be either a breaker or fuse-type panel) to see the amount of service reaching the house. It should be marked on the service box. If not, have an electrician tell you what the rating is. Older homes are often equipped with as little as 30 amps—not nearly enough power for the demands of today's appliances. Houses built in the late forties and early fifties usually are equipped with 60-amp service, which is insufficient for present needs. In most homes, 100 amps is the minimum amount you will require. However, 150-amp service is much better, and 200 amps is best. Most new homes have 150 amps or more.

One way of checking the house's power is to turn on all the lights and then turn on a major appliance, such as the air conditioner or stove. If the lights dim, there's a problem with the home's service capacity. Have an electrician examine the system and give you an estimate for needed updates.

You also may need an electrician to tell you whether the wiring is in good shape throughout the house. Is the wiring copper or aluminum? Copper is better, but because of copper shortages many homes built over the past decade have aluminum wiring, which requires repair or replacement. Make sure the branch circuits running to the various rooms are wired with the correct gauge wire.

The best wiring system for a home is a three-wire, 120/240-volt system—one that consists of two 120-volt circuits plus a common neutral wire. Every home should have a 220-volt entry. If the house doesn't have 220-volt service, have an electrician give you an estimate on how much it will cost to install.

What kind of service panel box is there? Fuses are inconvenient and less desirable than circuit breakers. There should be GFIs on the service panel. If there aren't, each one will cost about $50 to install. Count the number of circuits on the panel. Is there a directory that tells where each circuit goes? Are there spares for future circuits in case you add onto the house or install major new appliances?

Plumbing System

Check the condition of pipes carefully to make sure they carry water to the various fixtures without leaking, making noise, reducing the pressure, or imparting any color or taste to the water. Look for signs of sloppy workmanship or the use of poor-quality pipes and fixtures.

Find out whether the pipes are copper, brass, plastic, galvanized steel, or galvanized iron. Copper and brass traditionally were the best materials, but plastic has gained wide acceptance and is now used in many new homes. If you don't know what the pipes are, see if they attract a magnet. If they do, they're galvanized steel or iron. Galvanized steel is easily attacked by corrosive water; galvanized wrought iron is more resistant to corrosion.

Check to see whether some of the old iron or steel pipes have been replaced with copper sections. This is an indication that other parts of the piping may soon need to be replaced.

If the house has galvanized piping that is over twenty-five years old, it may have to be replaced, which could cost $1,000 or more. To determine the condition of the piping, turn on all the faucets in the house and then check to see whether the flow slows to a trickle anywhere. Be sure to check fixtures on the second floor when you do this test. If the flow slows substantially, rust and corrosion are probably blocking the system. Get repair estimates from a few plumbers.

Poor water pressure can also be a sign of inadequate main line service.

Check the dimension of the pipe leading into the water meter. Galvanized piping should be one to 1¼ inches in diameter; copper piping should be ¾ to one inch in diameter.

Are there shutoff valves near all plumbing fixtures and appliances, as well as a main shutoff at the meter? Make sure you find out where the main shutoff is, and check under sinks, near toilets, and behind access panels near tubs and showers for the other shutoffs.

Noisy pipes are not only an irritation, but may be a sign of problems. Find out whether the problem can be cured by installing an air chamber. Get bids from a few plumbers.

If the home you're considering has a well, inspect it carefully. It's advisable to have the quality of the water tested by the state laboratory or county health officer. Find out whether the water supply is adequate or whether you will have to install special water storage equipment. Make sure the pump and pressure storage tank are in good working order. Test them by running water for about fifteen minutes from several spigots. If there are fluctuations in pressure or the water gets cloudy, the well may be inadequate.

Check the condition of the water heater. Find out whether it's a gas, oil, or electric heater and how fast it reheats the water. The recovery rate should be stamped on the heater nameplate. What's the capacity of the water heater? A thirty- or forty-gallon heater will adequately serve two persons. Make sure it's properly vented.

Check the heater for leaks, rust spots, and banging or rattling—a sign of mineral buildup inside. Most good heaters last at least ten years. You can determine the age from the plumber's installation tag. If a large family lived in the house or if the heater ran constantly on its highest setting, it may be due for replacement.

Heating System

Find out whether it's a gas, electric, or oil system and how old it is. Find out exactly when the furnace was installed. Older homes with original furnaces and systems over twenty years old will probably soon require replacement.

If the furnace has been patched in a number of places, it's probably falling apart. If there are add-on features, such as a humidifier or electronic air filter, make sure they work.

Do all thermostats in the house register properly? Place a thermometer next to the thermostat to find out. Check how long it takes to heat the house by turning the heat up high and watching the time. Listen for banging and other noises after you turn up the furnace. If it's extremely noisy or takes a long time to heat up, the system should be examined by a heating contractor.

If the furnace is a hot-air system, check around registers for soot, a possible indication of a flaw in the combustion system. Does the blower operate quietly? Are there noises when the fan is on? If it's an oil furnace, check for oil spots on the floor, tank, and around the fittings. Look inside the furnace with a flashlight. Heavy soot is an indication of poor combustion. If it's a gas furnace, check whether the burners are clogged.

Check to see whether the filters are extremely dirty. If so, they probably haven't been changed regularly and the system will have to be cleaned out by a heating contractor.

If the system is hot water or steam heating, it's advisable to have a professional check out the condition of the boiler. Make sure all the controls and wiring mechanisms function correctly. Do pipes bang and hiss or are there water leaks around shutoff valves at the radiators? Steam or hot-water heat provides steady, draft-free heat, but add-on services such as air conditioning, humidifying, and filtering are more difficult than with warm-air systems.

Most new houses have electric heating systems, which are more efficient, but also more expensive. If it's an electric warm-air system, make sure the blower works properly. If it's a wall, baseboard, or panel system, make sure it's sufficient to keep the house warm when it gets extremely cold.

Finally, make sure you get records of the past year's heating and cooling bills. If the seller doesn't have these records, ask the local utility company to provide you this information. Also, find out who services the heating system, and check with the serviceperson about the condition of the furnace and other equipment.

Cooling System

Does the house have central air conditioning, a feature which will increase its resale value? Is the air conditioning combined with the furnace or separate? Air-conditioning ducts should be high on the walls, and heating ducts should be located near the baseboards for optimal performance. Check whether the compressor/condenser operates quietly.

Heat Pumps

Heat pumps are practical in temperate parts of the country. In colder climates, auxiliary heaters are needed with heat pumps to provide enough heat when it gets cold. If the house has a unit that was installed before 1972, you can anticipate problems, especially with the compressor.

Security System

Proper security is important for your peace of mind, so you should make sure that the home has adequate safety equipment. Electric, gas, and water meters should be outside the house to eliminate the need for strangers to enter the house to read them.

Do all windows, including basement windows, have security locks? Do all the exterior doors have a peephole, or is there an intercom system? Do the doors have dead-bolt locks? An additional safety feature is a door chain that permits the door to be opened a crack to talk with a stranger before deciding to let the person in. Most professional thieves will get into a house regardless of the kind of locks and other precautions. However, many burglars are not professionals, and good hardware with locks that are difficult to pick will act as strong deterrents. An automatic burglar alarm system connected to the police station provides maximum burglary protection and would be advisable if you have a valuable jewelry, antique, or picture collection. A system that sounds an alarm on the premises may scare away prowlers before they have a chance to take anything. These systems are expensive to install if the house doesn't already have one.

Before moving into your home you should change all of the locks, even if it is a brand-new home.

Finally, make sure there are functioning smoke detectors on every floor. They should sound if you hold a match up to them. There should also be fire extinguishers on every floor. Check their condition.

7

Protect Yourself: Understand the Real-Estate Game

"It's like going through a divorce. Once you get into the process of buying a home, it takes over and you just kind of get caught up in the undertow. You wonder which decisions you're supposed to be making at what time, who you should rely on, and when to do each thing."

That's how the senior editor of a national shelter publication summed up her feelings about her home purchase, and she deals with the housing industry on a daily basis.

Psychologists report that real-estate transactions are among the most stressful of human experiences. Single buyers often become so nervous or emotionally distressed that they are unable to grasp the complexities of the transaction, become confused by the terminology, and forget important information. Single persons, a newly emerging segment in the real-estate market, face some special obstacles.

In the first place, you are going through the process alone. In the second place, many real-estate agents and other professionals aren't fully in tune with the single person's needs. An agent accustomed to dealing with families may insist on showing you split-levels out in the suburbs when what you really need is a condo in town. Assuming that you don't have as much to spend as a family, the professional may not give you the full service to which you're entitled. Moreover, it's estimated that single buyers who don't thoroughly understand the details of the purchase process may lose as much as $1 billion per year in illegal or unnecessary fees paid to sellers of real-estate services.

To help you avoid these pitfalls, this chapter will discuss the professionals with whom you will deal and the services they should perform for you. You will learn the steps of the real-estate process, as well as how to select and when to consult the various professionals and how much you can expect to pay them. Costly schemes, such as kickbacks and interlocking relationships between lenders, attorneys, appraisers, real-estate agents, and other real-estate providers for which you must be on guard, will be described.

Caution and diligence can prevent you from becoming a victim like Carl, who disgustedly reports, "Today houses are not sold for the people who live in them, but for everybody else involved in the process. To me it's black marketeering."

Single persons tend to be more vulnerable, so it is imperative that you proceed with the doctrine of *caveat emptor*—let the buyer beware. Don't sign anything unless you know exactly what it is. Just remember that with the proper knowledge and some advance planning, you can rationally make all the necessary decisions to get the home you want.

The Real-Estate Agent*

A reliable professional agent can be your greatest asset in your search for a home. On the other hand, a dishonest or unprincipled agent interested only in his commission can be your greatest liability. Your best bet is to get referrals from other single friends. You want a broker who will be sensitive to your needs as a single person. Working with a single broker is one course to consider.

Jan, who has a large clientele of single and single-again persons, says she generally has to educate them about the pre-purchase considerations they should make. Usually, her orientation begins with a visit to her own home, designed around her needs as a single working person. A remodeled 1950s ranch house, her home has only one bedroom (plus a guest area downstairs) and an open floor plan for maximum convenience and entertaining efficiency. For a busy, single person, it's helpful to have a compact house all on one floor, she notes. It saves steps and time, yet she has the illusion of great spaciousness because of her open plan, along with bedroom and living-room entries onto a backyard deck.

It's awfully easy to be sold instead of serviced by a broker, and you want to make sure you get one who will really search for a home suited to your needs. If you've got a tight budget, you want an agent who will hang in there with you and go that extra measure to scout out the affordable options.

There are a few guidelines that can help you select a dedicated, sincere agent. Definitely choose a full-time agent, and avoid the part-timers who don't know the market or business as well. The more professional brokerage firms require their people to be full-time. Choose an agent familiar with the area where you want to live. This can probably best be accomplished by getting referrals from friends who have bought in that area. It's usually advisable to avoid referrals from employers who are apt to be offended if the relationship doesn't work out, as well as from lenders or other professionals who may have a vested interest. They know by making the referral they'll get the business, but that may work to your disadvantage.

Ask a prospective broker for his credentials—how long he's been in the

*The terms "real-estate agent" and "real-estate broker" are often used interchangeably. In fact, a real-estate agent is a salesperson licensed to sell real estate. The agent is an independent contractor operating under the license and supervision of a broker, who is responsible and liable for the agent's actions. To be licensed as a broker, one must undergo more extensive training, usually work as an agent for a given number of years, and then pass a test administered by the state real-estate commission. The broker, who is also properly referred to as an agent, can open his own firm and has generally been in the business longer than the real-estate salesperson.

business and what his volume was last year. You want an experienced broker who has good contacts and can *help* you shop for financing and other services. Membership in the National Association of Realtors (NAR) or National Association of Realtists is often the mark of a seasoned pro. These two groups have professional standards and codes of ethics their members pledge to observe, and they provide ongoing training and information to the industry. Of course, an agent may not belong to either and still be skillful and knowledgeable. Agents are licensed in all fifty states, although the standards for licensing vary widely.

If the real-estate market is very tight and houses are moving fast, you might gain an edge by working with an agent affiliated with a large firm. If the firm lists a house that meets your needs precisely, you can get first crack at it before it goes onto the multiple listing. The multiple listing is a cooperative arrangement among brokers that gives one agent access to lists of all the houses currently on the market in a given community.

It is always advisable to work through a brokerage firm with a solid service reputation. Many real-estate franchises—e.g., Century 21, Gallery of Homes, Electronic Realty Associates (ERA), Better Homes and Gardens— claim they offer better services than non-affiliated brokerages. This isn't necessarily true. In fact, it's often the case that firms on the downslide affiliate, figuring that the brand-name identification will bring in more business. If business is down, it's usually because the agents aren't working hard enough. The main service that franchises can offer is assistance for persons relocating to another city (see "How to Handle a Relocation," page 111).

Ask a prospective agent whether his company has a mortgage pool for its buyers. If the firm has arranged for a block of money with a lending institution, you'll be sure of getting financing for your purchase. Also ask the agent whether he'll agree to any expert inspections you wish to have made prior to the purchase, and advise him that you'll want your attorney to review the *offer to buy*.* A respectable agent shouldn't balk at either of those points. One who dismisses those measures as unnecessary probably doesn't have your best interests in mind. Find out how the broker's firm handles defects that show up in the house either prior to *closing* or within a short period following the purchase.

A good agent should reassure you that he'll work with you and the seller to resolve any difficulties. Ask the agent how familiar he is with house construction and what courses he has taken in this area. Many agents claim to know house structure in and out. Yet their buyers tell stories of roofs that collapsed and of holes in walls discovered after they've moved in. The agent is charged with making a thorough inspection of the home for any defects or shortcomings. Unfortunately, many agents know very little about house construction and are incapable of conducting comprehensive inspections.

Above all, remember that the agent is *never* the buyer's representative. The agent's first loyalty is to the seller, from whom he earns his commission,

---

*This term is explained more fully in Chapter 8.

even though you, the buyer, pay for it indirectly through the sales price. This dual role can put the agent in a tenuous position at times, and that is why it's extremely important for you to have an ethical agent who takes his responsibilities seriously, both to the seller and to you.

There are certain basic services a good agent should perform for you. First, he should discuss with you your income, assets, needs, and preferences. On the basis of those factors, the agent should tell you how much house you will be able to finance (as explained in Chapter 3, page 8) and should then make a sincere effort to locate some homes suited to your means and requirements. The agent should also explain to you the steps of the real-estate transaction and the documents involved. You may, however, have to ask the agent for this explanation. It is your obligation to be frank and honest with the agent and his obligation to pre-screen prospective homes and show you only those that fit your specifications.

"Buyers are liars," comments one broker with a large singles clientele. Not because they lie purposely, he hastens to add, but because they usually have not exposed themselves to the market enough to know what they really do want and need. If you follow the shopping guides suggested in the previous chapters, you will not fall into this buyer/liar category, because you will have already done your homework. Thus when you engage an agent, you will not be wasting his time, and in return you can demand the same from him.

Make sure the agent really shops for you and doesn't merely show you his own listings in order to get a full commission. (When an agent sells you a house listed by another agent, he splits the fee with that agent. The standard commission is 6 to 7 percent of the sale's price.)

When an agent shows you a house, he is responsible for giving you a full tour—inside and out—of the house and pointing out the good points as well as the deficiencies. Under the law, the agent is presumed to be an expert and is required to inspect the house for defects. If the basement wall is cracked or the roof leaks, the agent should learn about these problems and inform you of them. If the agent in any way knowingly misrepresents the condition of the house or withholds information that would affect your decision, he is liable and can be sued. However, an agent is not responsible for conditions he can't detect, such as pipes enclosed within the walls, or for conditions the seller fails to point out. The agent is responsible for disclosing all defects that a reasonable inspection would uncover.

If you have any doubts about the house, you should have an expert inspect it. If it turns out the seller has either misrepresented the condition of the house or concealed defects, that's fraud, for which you have legal recourse. If after occupying, you run into problems, you should first go back to the agent. A good agent will contact the seller and advise him to repair the defect or face the possibility of a lawsuit.

To illustrate: Sally bought a pre-World War I bungalow in an older section of town. There were stains on the living room ceiling from a leak in the roof, which the seller claimed he had fixed. Following the first heavy rainfall, Sally heard a constant dripping above the living room. She called the broker, who came over and discovered that the seller's method of fixing the leak had been to put a bucket under it. The broker immediately called the seller who agreed to pay for the repairs.

You should question the agent thoroughly about any prospect, and he should reply with positive statements of fact. If he tries to evade or sidestep direct answers to your questions, if he rushes or pressures you in any way, stop him *at once*. Tell him that you want a full, honest answer that will enable you to make a rational decision and that only when you are fully satisfied that you have all the necessary information will you make a decision. If the seller is present when you look at the house, ask him as many questions as you can about the condition of the house. If you don't ask, he is not obligated to tell you anything.

The sincere professional will want you to feel that you are making the right decision, because his future business will depend on your satisfaction and referrals. Therefore, he should be willing to take you back to the property several times so you can reinspect it. He should inform you about the taxes, the zoning, any restrictions or easements, the building codes, the neighborhood, available transportation, shopping and medical facilities, and the resalability of the house. If he doesn't know the answer to a question, he should tell you so and promise to get the answer and call you.

The Offer to Buy

Once you decide on a particular house, the agent is responsible for drawing up the offer to buy (also called offer to purchase, or sales agreement). This instrument, a legal and binding contract, states how much you will pay for the house, provided that certain conditions are met. It is called different things in different states, and the provisions contained in this document vary, depending on local practice. Your attorney should review this document before you sign it. Brokers often say it's unnecessary for an attorney to see the offer and warn that in the time it takes for you to get that done, you can lose the house to another buyer. If you trust the agent implicitly and time is truly of the essence, you might sign prior to having your attorney review the offer, but he should see it before the transaction is closed.

It is up to you to decide how much you will offer for a house. The agent can be sued by the seller, whom he legally represents, for advising you what to bid. However, the agent should have educated you well enough about market rates that you will know what is a reasonable offer for a given home or you can get an appraiser's opinion. The agent can tell you what comparable homes in the same neighborhood have sold for or you can check comparable sales yourself at the county registry of deeds.

When you sign the offer, you will put down your earnest money as an indication of your sincere intent. This money, usually ranging between $250 and $1,000, should be held in the broker's trust or escrow account until the closing. (At the closing, you and the seller exchange final papers, you pay the balance to the seller, and the transaction is concluded.) For your protection, the offer should be made subject to certain provisions being met.

They include:

- That you are able to arrange suitable financing. The offer should state that the purchase is contingent upon your getting X amount of money at X interest with X down over X amount of years.
- That the property be conveyed to you with a free and clear title. It's critically important that you receive the property free of any encumbrances or liens.
- That the property be conveyed to you in its present condition. This protects you from any subsequent damage to the property, for which the seller is responsible, prior to the closing.
- That the seller warrants he has no notice or knowledge of pending public improvements that will result in special assessments or notice of any government-required or court-ordered repairs, alterations, or corrections of existing conditions. The seller should also warrant that he has no knowledge of any structural or mechanical defects.
- That a structural inspection be conducted, if you feel this is necessary, to determine whether the house is in satisfactory condition and meets the conditions represented by the seller. It is very important that this contingency be written into the offer, because the standard sales agreement contains a provision whereby the buyer acknowledges he has inspected the house and waives any future inspection rights. So even if a major defect would be uncovered later, you and your attorney could have problems getting a satisfactory remedy if you had signed this standard form. Although many brokers and sellers may balk at the insertion of an inspection clause, and the broker may warn you that the seller won't accept an offer with such terms, stick to your guns. The broker is obligated to put it in if you insist. If the seller has misrepresented nothing, he shouldn't mind.
- That the house is appraised for the amount offered. The lender will require an appraisal of the property for his loan purposes. If the appraisal is below the amount offered, you may want to lower your offer. You don't want to be locked into paying more for the property than the lender believes it's worth, because you'll be required to come up with more cash.
- That the offer states which amenities will be included in the sale, such as drapes, carpet, water heater, and appliances (i.e., stove, refrigerator, washer and dryer). It also should state whether ceiling lamps and other fixtures will stay. Make sure you and the seller agree on exactly what will remain and write it into the offer.
- That a termite inspection be made on the house, paid for by the seller and approved by the buyer. The offer should stipulate that if there is evidence of termites or other pests, the seller will remedy this condition prior to closing. (In many cases, the seller will have this inspection made before putting the house on the market, and you will see the report prior to making the offer. In some northern states where there are no termite problems, this might not be a standard provision, and you should ask your agent about this.)
- That the offer state the date of occupancy. If you are unable to occupy by that date, the offer legally becomes null and void.
- That the offer state when the closing will occur and who will pay which closing costs.

- That if the lender charges "points" to make the loan, the offer stipulates who will pay the points or how they are to be split between buyer and seller. Make sure you get this provision into the offer, as it can save you a lot of money.
- That if you presently own a home that you are attempting to sell, the offer is made contingent upon the sale of that house at a certain price by a certain date. Then you won't get stuck paying for two mortgages.
- That the expiration date of the offer is stated. This gives the seller so many days to accept or reject your offer. If he doesn't sign it within that period, the offer becomes null and void.
- That the offer also state how much you are bidding on the house and contains a legal description of the property.

You should receive a copy of the offer. And you should pay particular attention to the manner in which the agent drafts the offer and his willingness to include your stipulations. This is the point at which an unethical agent often shows his colors. If he's misrepresented anything to either party, it's apt to turn up now. Ask as many questions as you wish, and if you feel the need, call your attorney. Don't sign an offer that you don't fully understand or about which you have any hesitation.

The agent will carry your offer to the seller. By this point, you should have done or should hastily be doing some shopping around for financing terms and closing services (see Chapters 8 and 9). The agent may also help you arrange the financing and closing. Often, he will know where you can get the best terms—a competent agent has good contacts with local lenders and knows their rates. The agent may also refer you to a title insurance company, escrow company, and insurance agent. For example, one large West Coast brokerage firm offers what it calls "total real estate service." The firm has a subsidiary escrow company, mortgage banking company, and insurance agency, as well as a referral service for persons relocating.

The California Insurance Commissioner's office, however, has discovered that referrals by brokers to affiliated title, mortgage, and escrow companies sometimes result in kickbacks and higher prices to the consumer. If you find youself being strongly "steered" by the broker to certain providers of other services, the chances are good you'll pay a higher price there. You owe it to yourself to shop around.

On the other hand, a reputable agent who really shops for you can provide time-saving assistance. In any case, the only way you'll know what reasonable rates are for the various services is by making some independent inquiries. If money is tight and the agent arranges for your loan through a mortgage pool held by his firm, you may pay slightly more than the prevailing rates, but then that's a service and there's always a cost for a service performed.

If for some reason the appraisal required by the lender comes in lower than the price you've offered, then it's up to the agent to work out the difference. Again, this is where it's critical that you have an honest, ethical broker. A lazy agent might just tell you to come up with the additional cash if you want the house.

A conscientious agent should pursue several courses. First, he can go to the lender and show him that sales prices of comparable houses in the same neighborhood are at the amount you're offering and attempt to get the lender to agree to a higher appraisal. He can ask the seller to come down in his price if this seems reasonable, or he can negotiate a compromise between you and the seller.

An agent's job is extremely complicated because of all the factors involved in the real-estate transaction, the liabilities, and the varying market conditions. The importance of working with an experienced, ethical agent simply can't be stressed enough. He can make your transaction a smooth, understandable, and satisfactory one. Select your agent with great care.

How to Handle a Relocation

If you're relocating, as a single person you're an easy mark for an unprincipled agent wanting to turn over a fast commission. Therefore, it's critical that you get sound, professional advice on the real estate and lending practices in the area where you are relocating. Prior to making your relocation decision, you should investigate the cost of living, housing prices, and other conditions of the proposed area to make sure you find them tolerable. Proper advance planning can save you endless amounts of grief.

Barbara, a thirty-eight-year-old executive relocating from Atlanta to Iowa, in her anxiety to get into her new job and get settled, hurried through the house-hunting and purchase process. The result: Within two weeks of occupying her house, she paid $2,000 in repair bills for undisclosed defects, was nearly hospitalized from poisoning of carbon monoxide emitted from a faulty furnace, and is now involved in costly litigation with the sellers. She hates the house and can't wait to get rid of it.

Barbara's experience provides a classic case of *don'ts* for any single person relocating. When hired for her job, she spent one day looking at houses and then returned to Atlanta with the multiple-listing book to study the style of houses and determine what she liked and could afford. Barbara, who had previously purchased two houses in Georgia and was living in a 1,800-square-foot, four-bedroom home with a swimming pool, discovered that the houses in Iowa half that size cost twice as much. She decided she wanted a ranch house with a fireplace and attached garage because of the severe Iowa winters.

Two weeks later, she returned to Iowa and spent two days looking for a house. On Saturday night, she signed an offer of $55,000 for a one-and-a-half story, three-bedroom house with no fireplace and a detached garage. In retrospect, she said, she doubted her decision from the moment she signed the offer.

The agent deliberately did not make the offer subject to specific financing provisions, leaving that portion of the offer blank, and then pressured Barbara to sign it, telling her, "This is just the way we do things here, don't worry."

He did not explain to her the Iowa real-estate process nor any of the documents or costs she would encounter. Barbara questioned the owners about the condition of the house, and they reported everything to be in good working order. So Barbara wrote out an earnest money check of $1,000 and returned to Atlanta.

"My real-estate broker in Atlanta, who was excellent about handling details, referred me to the real-estate company in Iowa. So I was expecting that broker to take care of me and answer my questions and be concerned about what I wanted," Barbara later said. "And it's quite obvious he wasn't and I was probably very stupid. I don't feel as if the broker took care of anything. All he did was tell me what time to be at the bank to give them my money."

When she arrived in Iowa one month later to begin work, Barbara discovered that she was not living in the city where she was working. The agent had "failed" to point out that her new house was in an incorporated suburb, subject to higher taxes than the main city. She arrived in town on the weekend, and the closing was scheduled for Monday morning. She called the agent and asked when she could make a final inspection of the house to learn about how the appliances worked and recheck its condition before concluding the transaction. He told her she didn't need to make a final inspection, that was not the practice in Iowa.

The agent at no point offered to shop for financing for Barbara, who mistakenly allowed her new employer to arrange for the loan at his bank. The morning of the closing, the interest rate went up one-quarter percent. Barbara, who had not received the legally required estimate of her settlement costs, walked into the closing totally cold and alone to face a loan officer she had never met before. She then discovered there was no termite bond on the house, no title insurance, and no attorney present. She was stunned, because in her previous purchases in Georgia, both seller and buyer, as well as their respective attorneys and agents, attended the closing.

Moreover, the lender failed to include in the mortgage papers an insurance escrow for homeowner's coverage that Barbara had requested. The lender misspelled her name on the documents and then informed her after she had written out a $13,000 check (the balance of the down payment) that she would not receive the deed that day. The lender told her the deed first had to be sent to the courthouse for recordation and then would be mailed to her. Therefore, when she closed, Barbara didn't have proof of ownership or insurance on the house, which is a gross breach of practice and poses a considerable risk to both owner and lender. Underwriting procedures of practically all lenders require proof of insurance before they are allowed to close a loan.

"I thought it was very sloppy the way the whole loan process was handled," Barbara said. "In the first place, no one informed me which closing costs I would be paying. In Atlanta, the lawyer goes over this list of fees at the closing and the real-estate broker negotiates which fees the seller pays and which the buyer pays. That was never done, and the broker really took me because he never explained anything.

"I would never have gone to that closing if I'd known in advance what was going to happen. I do feel that as a single woman I was extremely vulnerable at that point."

Barbara added that because of her new employer's high-level connections at the bank, she was afraid to delay or halt the process. In addition, the pressure of getting her daughter into school, getting established, hassling with the movers, and fighting the fears that she had made a terrible decision overwhelmed her. She said that she uncharacteristically acquiesced and went along with the process, failing to ask whether there was a prepayment penalty or escalation clause in the mortgage.

Barbara spent the first week in her house battling a flood in the kitchen, where the pipes under the sink disintegrated from corrosion. She lost practically all water pressure, and when the plumbers came, they informed her the whole house needed new pipes. Her cats almost died, and she and her daughter became violently ill from the carbon monoxide emitted from the furnace, which she had to replace at a cost of $1,000. In the offer to buy, the sellers had warranted that all heating and plumbing equipment was "in normal and acceptable working order." Both the sellers and the agent expressed "distress" when Barbara informed them of the situation. Neither party, however, offered any remedies. So Barbara, struggling to get on top of a new executive position, is now in the costly and harrowing process of suing the sellers.

"After all I've been through with that house, I'm ready to pack up and just go back home," Barbara concluded.

You can avoid such a plight. In the first place, if you're interviewing for a new job or being transferred, ask what relocation services the company provides. It costs between $15,000 and $20,000 to relocate an employee, and companies regularly pick up these tabs for families. Unfortunately, many single employees have not gotten the same benefits. Apparently, employers think the single person, unhampered by the details of resettling a spouse and children, doesn't need or deserve the same assistance. That's ludicrous.

Personnel experts estimate that the typical transferee or new employee spends about four months in the many activities connected with a relocation, and one certainly doesn't need the added anguish of a difficult real-estate transaction. Most major companies today reimburse employees for house-hunting trips, temporary living quarters at new locations, and shipment of household goods. Because of the increasing incidence of transfers, those firms with offices in various cities often hire relocation management companies to facilitate moves.

The relocation companies provide counseling and home-hunting services. They have experts trained to find out what a person's needs are, to educate the individual about what he can expect in the new location, and to advise him how to proceed with the real-estate transaction.

The experts discuss cost-of-living differentials, home prices, and answer any questions for the transferee. Most of these relocation experts show slide presentations of various neighborhoods in the new location. They also provide detailed information on taxes, financing, and moving. Once you decide on a particular area, you are referred to a real-estate agent there by the relocation consultants.

These agents are monitored to assure they service you in every way. So if you have complaints, you can go back to the relocation consultants, and they're obligated to iron out any difficulties. Also, when a relocation company handles the moving, a further source of inconvenience and potential problems is eliminated. Moving companies, which are constantly being investigated for various abuses, are evaluated closely by the relocation experts, who make certain every effort is made to maintain schedules and handle your goods carefully.

Many employers, either through their own personnel offices or relocation management firms, will help the transferee sell his present home. If you have difficulty selling your house, they'll do it for you or they'll buy the house from you at market rate and then resell it. That way you have the capital to purchase a new home. Some firms will arrange "equity bridge loans," to help you finance a new home while you're still trying to sell your present one.

Many companies also reimburse new employees and transferees for brokerage commissions, closing costs, duplicate house-carrying expenses, loss on sale below fair market values, and additional income-tax liability. To get employees to agree to relocate, many employers now pay cost-of-living differentials and that portion of the home price that exceeds what the employee would pay in his present location. As a further enticement to reluctant employees, corporations may also arrange for low-interest mortgages and frequently pay for home inspections.

If you're taking a new job or transferring, find out which services your company offers and advise them which services you'll need. Do not allow yourself to be discriminated against as a single person. Chances are, if you don't ask for the services, they won't be offered.

As Warren, an accountant who was transferred to another city by his multinational corporation, notes, "The big companies won't tell you the things they will or won't pay for. You must tell your boss-to-be what you want, or it won't be offered and you won't get it. You have to beat them by intimidation—refuse to relocate if they won't meet your conditions."

If you have to handle your own relocation, there are several avenues of assistance to explore. Of course, your first step should be to find out the cost of living and home prices in your new site. That type of information should be available from the Chamber of Commerce, which may also suggest additional sources of information for newcomers. If there is a real-estate magazine published in the city, get a copy of it. Most major cities have some type of real-estate publication that contains a guide to the area and discusses various new developments. Some of these publications even offer relocation assistance. One California-based magazine will forward any inquiries you have to builders and developers who will follow up by sending you information.

Living magazine, which is published in seven southern and western metropolitan areas, has established Home and Apartment Information Centers in Dallas and Houston. These centers, staffed with experts on local real estate, provide free services to newcomers. The centers are equipped with large maps of the metro areas, and the staff provides detailed information about various communities.

Some of the major relocation companies also offer counseling and home-finding services on an individual basis. You can check for these companies in the Yellow Pages or at the Chamber of Commerce. The member of a national real-estate franchise in your present location can obtain information for you about housing in your prospective area and refer you to a broker there. Some large real-estate firms with offices across the state or in several states can also provide you information on a new location and help in relocating. Contact your local Board of Realtors for a referral to a local firm with offices in your new site.

Remember, however, that whatever route you go, all the guidelines suggested in this book regarding brokers, other professionals, and shopping still apply. If you place the responsibility for your relocation completely in someone else's hands, you'll pay for it, either immediately or in the long run. You should establish for yourself a checklist of things that you need to find out and must do in order to facilitate your relocation. Making a major move can, in itself, be a traumatic event; don't compound it by becoming involved in a precipitous or unwise real-estate transaction. Above all, you should find out about the real-estate procedures in your new area and the approximate costs, so you can shop knowledgeably and bargain wisely.

Some costs of relocating and closing fees involved in a relocation purchase are tax deductible. You should visit with your tax accountant about which costs you are eligible to deduct.

The Attorney

Because real-estate transactions are becoming increasingly complicated, it is important that you have an attorney knowledgeable in local real-estate practices to assist you with several aspects of the purchase. Many buyers do not consult attorneys, and if most brokers had their way, none of them would. The fact is, having your own attorney review certain documents and oversee the transaction can save you a lot of money and grief.

You should not rely on the lender's or the seller's attorney, as a number of single buyers have misguidedly done at the urging of the real-estate agent and seller. You should consult an attorney who handles real-estate transactions on a regular basis. If you don't know such an attorney, ask around among acquaintances or call the local lawyer referral service and ask for the names of several attorneys specializing in real estate. Then call the attorneys, tell them what you're planning to buy—condo, co-op, detached house—and ask for estimates of their fees to assist you. You need not pay an arm and a leg for the attorney.

One young attorney who handles most transactions involving single

buyers for his firm says his fee usually runs between $30 and $50. For the
peace of mind it can buy, that's cheap. And don't be embarrassed about
asking an attorney for a fee estimate. Because of greater consumer awareness
regarding legal matters, attorneys often get such inquiries.

Ask each prospective attorney if he charges on a flat or pro-rata basis.
Inquire whether he'll break down his fees by the various legal tasks he
performs for you, such as title search, examining the offer to buy or sales
contract, preparation of the deed, and attending or conducting the closing.

These preliminary inquiries can guide you to a solid, independent
lawyer, who will serve exclusively as your agent. The main thing you want to
avoid is an attorney with tie-ins to title companies, lenders, or other
professionals. It's acceptable for attorneys to suggest the services of other
parties on whom they rely, and it's up to you to make sure the fees you
pay for those services are at the prevailing rates for your area.

You should also be aware that an experienced paraprofessional working
with an attorney may be able to handle many of your needs for a lesser cost.
Although paraprofessionals are not heavily involved in real estate today,
there's a good chance they may play a greater role in these transactions in the
future.

If you're considering a house being sold by the owner, a good attorney
can guide you through the process for a lot less than you would pay if a
broker were involved. In such a case, since you will rely on the lawyer for
advice every step of the way, his fee might amount to $400 or $500. But that
sure beats $4,000—approximately what you'd pay for the real-estate agent's
7 percent commission on a $57,000 home. When there's an agent involved,
the buyer always pays for his commission indirectly in the increased price of
the house. On the other hand, you probably will have more negotiating
power with an owner selling his house.

Although exactly what services the attorney performs vary according to
local real-estate practices, these are basically the things your attorney should
do:

- Examine the offer to buy (also called binder or sales contract) before you sign
  it. The attorney will make sure that all the provisions necessary to protect your
  rights are included in this document, which is the legal and binding contract
  governing the entire purchase process. Remember, once you put down your
  earnest money and sign the offer, you are obligated. If you don't follow
  through with the deal, you forfeit your deposit and could be sued for failing to
  uphold the contract. If, for example, the agent doesn't make the offer subject
  to your getting financing at terms affordable to you, and you, in fact, can't
  arrange the loan, you forfeit everything.

    Your attorney can make sure that provision is in the offer and stipulate
  that unless certain conditions are met, the offer is voided and your earnest
  money is returned to you.

    One metropolitan attorney with a large single clientele warns that most
  buyers don't come to her until after they sign the offer. Then, she says, it's too
  late, because the offer excludes from the purchase all kinds of fixtures and

appliances that the seller verbally promised would be included with the house.

The offer is a highly individual document, which must be tailored to your specific needs. You should go over it with your attorney to make certain all your requirements are met. If unusual circumstances arise, he'll know how to handle them to assure your legal protection.

- Conduct the title search and examine the abstract (legal history of the property) to make sure you receive the property free and clear of any encumbrances. In many states, abstract, or title, companies conduct title searches. Usually the lender's attorney will examine the title, a service for which you pay. However, it's still advisable to have your own attorney review the title to make sure there are no legal claims on the property.

In some cases, the lender will let your attorney do the title work for him and you, especially if he knows the lawyer. So you don't pay for the same service twice, ask the lender about this possibility. In fact, some states are considering legislation prohibiting the lender from requiring his attorney and not the borrower's to perform the title search. Federal Trade Commission officials contend that the practice of using a lender-designated attorney is "anticompetitive and inflates prices" to the buyer, who should be free to shop for his own attorney.

- Recommend the kind of deed you should have—a general warranty deed is most common—and see that it is properly recorded.
- Recommend how you should take title to the house, and arrange for passage of the property through a will in the event of your death. If you are buying with another person or persons, it is extremely important how you hold the property—through joint tenancy, tenancy in common, or a partnership—and that you have a contractual agreement regarding the property. (More on this in Chapter 11, "Special Tips for Single Persons Buying Together," page 201.)
- Advise you of your position as a property owner regarding federal estate laws and state inheritance laws. You may also wish to consult a tax accountant if you are making a sizable investment.
- Review any other documents, such as home warranties, involved in the purchase.
- Advise you regarding the legal obligation of the real-estate agent, seller, home inspector, or other professional involved in the process. If you have questions about the actions or statements of other parties, your attorney will answer them. Moreover, if these other principals are aware that you have an attorney, they are more apt to make every effort to accommodate you.
- Review the closing costs and perhaps attend the closing. In some areas it's routine for attorneys to be present at the closing, and in some cases the lender's attorney conducts the closing. In other areas, attorneys never attend the closing—it depends on local practice.
- Assist you with any post-purchase problems, although you will probably pay an additional fee unless these matters are routine follow-up. (In some areas, the local bar associations have exerted their influence to ensure that attorneys *always*, albeit unnecessarily, perform certain functions in the real-estate transaction. If this is the case where you live, there's really not much you can do about it. As a consumer, however, you should be aware of this fact, and you can express your dissatisfaction to elected officials. Buying a house is expensive enough without an extra party getting an automatic cut.)

The Appraisal

Since your ability to get a loan on a given property is determined by the appraisal, there are several aspects about it you should understand. First, you should know that the lender will require an appraisal of the property to determine its fair market value and will base the loan on that value. Second, you should know that you can hire your own appraiser to evaluate the property and give you an estimate of its worth, upon which you will base your bid. If you're unfamiliar with the housing market and don't know what constitutes a reasonable bid, it can be good strategy to hire an independent appraiser. He can save you a lot of money if you use his estimate to negotiate a lower price.

For example: David decided to invest in a beachfront condominium. He said he didn't want to waste a lot of time looking around and consequently signed an offer to buy of $80,000 for one of the first units he saw. In his zeal, the broker wrote no contingencies into the offer. The independent fee appraiser hired by the lender determined the condo's market value to be $69,000. The other two-bedroom condos in the building were selling for about $65,000—a fact the broker didn't point out and about which David didn't ask. The appraiser later commented that had David contacted him prior to signing the offer, he would have advised him the condo was overpriced based on comparable sales, and David could have bargained for a much lower price.

The appraisal *required* by the lender is performed after you have signed an offer to buy and applied for your loan. This appraisal, conducted by an employee of the lending institution or an independent fee-appraiser, is strictly for the lender's self-protection. He wants to make sure the property is worth what you're offering for it, so that if you default on the loan he can recoup his investment in a resale.

You will pay for the lender's appraisal, which is often cursorily performed and based on arbitrary factors. Often, the appraiser is told what the offer is and may just drive by the house to confirm that in the given neighborhood a house that size will bring that much. And for this "windshield appraisal" you pay about $75 to $100 to the lender in your closing costs. If the appraiser doesn't think the house would get in a resale what you're offering for it, he'll appraise it for a lower amount. His interest lies with the lender, whom he'll protect at every point, which means appraisals tend to be overly conservative, often to the buyer's disadvantage.

If your lender is going to package your mortgage with others for sale into the secondary market (the case if you're dealing with a mortgage banking company), then often a more thorough appraisal is required. If the mortgage is to be sold through the Federal Home Loan Mortgage Corporation (FHLMC, also called Freddie Mac) or the Federal National Mortgage Association (FNMA, also called Fannie Mae), then the lender must use an appraisal form called the Residential Appraisal Report, which is required by those agencies. The appraiser must sign a statement verifying that he has personally inspected the property, inside and out, and not knowingly withheld any significant information regarding structural condition or sales of comparable properties. This is an extremely thorough appraisal, if properly performed. You can ask your lender if your mortgage will be sold in the secondary market and, if so, through which agency. Then if you aren't allowed to see the appraisal, you will at least have a fair idea of what it should have covered. Appraisals on loans held by the lender may not cover as many factors as the appraisals on loans sold into the secondary market.

If the lender's appraisal is several thousand dollars less than what you've offered, you either have to come up with the additional cash for the down payment, get the seller to lower his price, or forfeit the house, unless the lender will accept an independent second appraisal. For instance, assume that you bid $58,000 on a twenty-year-old house and apply for an 80 percent loan based on that price. The lender sends out his appraiser, who comes back with an estimated value of $55,000. That means the lender will only loan you $44,000 instead of $46,400, and you'll have to come up with the additional $2,400 for the down payment.

One experienced real-estate broker says lender's appraisers are notorious for underestimating the value of homes with any unusual or outstanding characteristics. Often, they don't acknowledge those features that make the house unique and, instead, downgrade it for its very assets.

So what can you do?

First, ask to see the appraisal. You are paying for it, and you should be allowed to see it (under *common law,* if you pay for something, you can see it), although this isn't always the case. Many lenders, fearful that remarks made on the appraisal regarding the house could subject them to lawsuits, simply refuse to show the appraisal to the buyer or the broker. In other cases, based on years of custom, the lender refuses to show the appraisal. However, if you are getting an FHA- or VA-backed loan, the lender must show you the appraisal. Most likely you'll either strike a compromise with the seller or forfeit the house.

Federal regulatory agencies have proposed enactment of legislation requiring the lender to give the buyer a copy of the appraisal. Up until this point, lenders' lobbying efforts have squelched that proposal. If you encounter difficulties on this score, you should inform both your state and federally elected legislators and your attorney.*

Assuming that you are allowed to see the appraisal, study it to determine why it came in lower than what you're offering. If it appears that a thorough appraisal was not performed, you can challenge it. This is not the point at which to get militant, however. Make a reasonable counter-proposal that the lender accept the estimate of an independent certified fee-appraiser hired by you. A good, concerned broker should assist you in this effort.

If you have already had an appraisal, the lender may accept this estimate. You might want to consult your attorney about the best course to take. He should know how to handle such matters in your community. You

---

*If you're denied a loan because of a low appraisal, you can ask the lender to refund any appraisal fee you've paid.

should also know that sometimes the lender will use for his documentation the appraisal you have performed at the outset and upon which you base your bid. Ask any lender you contact for a mortgage loan about this possibility, and be prepared to tell him who your appraiser is. It may be that the appraiser you hire is one used on a regular basis by the lender.

Here are the things that a competent, certified appraiser will do in determining the value of the property:

- Consider the value of the land itself and the cost of reproducing the house as it now exists.
- Look at surrounding property values, basing his estimate in part on what similar houses in the neighborhood have recently sold for.
- Consider the tax structure of the community and the area's traffic patterns.
- Indicate on the appraisal whether, in his opinion, the community is stable, appreciating, or declining.
- Note the zoning of the area and its makeup—whether it's mostly detached houses or a mixture of apartments, duplexes, condos, and commercial establishments. He should indicate whether this makeup is apt to remain stable or is prone to change in the near future.
- Check the current legal ownership of the house to make sure it's in order, and check for any easement records and special zoning regulations.
- Note the appearance of the neighborhood: Do residents maintain their property well, thus creating a market appeal for the entire community?
- Check the distance and availability of city services, such as police and fire protection, and indicate the convenience of shopping and recreational facilities.
- Check for structural soundness, and examine the overall condition of the house's major components, such as foundation, walls, basement, roof, heating, plumbing, and so on. He should also analyze the interior for livability and comfort.

The thorough appraiser will look over all major systems of the house and should detect any *obvious* problems. For example, if there are apparent defects in the roof that will require costly repairs, he should note that on his report. Optimally, the appraiser's report prevents the buyer from getting into a situation where he immediately faces expensive repairs. In practice, this isn't often the case with a lender's appraisal. If a defective roof is discovered, the lender may not tell the buyer, because he fears the seller will sue him for overstating the seriousness of the condition, which really can only be determined by a professional roofer. It all gets quite complicated, but always boils down to money. If you question the condition of the house, you should hire a professional inspector to give you an in-depth report on its structural integrity.

If you are buying a condominium, cooperative, or dwelling in a planned unit development (PUD), the appraisal form and procedures used are slightly different than those for a detached dwelling.

Before you run out and hire an appraiser, you should know that all Realtors (members of the National Association of Realtors) are supposedly trained to conduct a competitive market analysis. This analysis, based on the Realtor's research of sales on surrounding properties, should indicate the approximate value of the house you're considering. You can ask to see this analysis and use it as a guide for determining what to offer. You can also check the sales price of surrounding comparable houses at your court house, where the deeds are recorded. Your agent can tell you which office keeps those records.

If you decide it's necessary to have your own appraisal, you should hire an appraiser certified by one of the four major appraisal organizations with established codes of ethics and standards of professional conduct for their members. These organizations and their national headquarters are: the American Institute of Real Estate Appraisers, Chicago; the Society of Real Estate Appraisers, Chicago; the American Society of Appraisers, Washington, D. C.; and the National Association of Independent Fee Appraisers, St. Louis. If you can't find a local appraiser affiliated with one of these organizations, you can contact the area office or national headquarters for a referral. Only a few states now license appraisers, and there are few regulations covering their qualifications, so your best bet is to get an appraiser who has a current certification by one of the professional organizations. Ask to see his credentials.

Although fees vary, you'll probably pay from $95 to $175 for an appraiser you hire. For houses in the $100,000-plus bracket, appraisal fees may run as high as $300 to $400.

The Home Inspection

If you don't know how to evaluate thoroughly the condition of a prospective home from basement to roof top, including the furnace, water heater, electrical system, and plumbing, you owe it to yourself to have a professional inspection. In just one year, buyers of existing homes paid roughly $750 million to repair undisclosed defects. Because of poor construction and cost-cutting measures, new dwellings are often riddled with defects (see "Defective Housing," page 35). No home is perfect, and many factors can cause trouble—age, inferior materials, poor craftsmanship, inadequate maintenance, severe weather.

In this era of fast real-estate transactions, these problems often are not brought to the buyer's attention. Consequently, the buyer invests all his available cash in the purchase, then faces unanticipated and costly repairs upon occupancy.

Lee, for example, scraped together all his assets to invest in a four-family house and thought he had a great buy. He managed to finance it with a low-interest, FHA-insured loan. Unfortunately, Lee allowed his real-estate agent and attorney to talk him out of a professional home inspection. It would cost too much, they advised, and while he was waiting to get the inspection, some other buyer would grab the house because it was such a deal.

As it turned out, the FHA inspector failed to conduct a thorough examination, and Lee wound up literally with a large pile of sawdust supported by a bunch of termites holding hands. After taking possession, Lee discovered that the house had a sub-basement spanned by a termite-infested, fifty-foot girder that was about to crumble. Lee's predicament also underscores the single buyer's need to remain constantly vigilant about the relationships between providers of real-estate services. Single buyers are more vulnerable to these schemes.

In this case, the agent and the attorney, who was brought into the deal by the agent, discouraged the inspection because the agent would have lost his sizable commission had Lee discovered the house's true condition and refused to buy. The two were very shrewd—the lawyer advised the agent not to make any definite misstatements of facts to avoid liability, so the agent just didn't mention the sub-basement.

Optimally, you should have the inspection performed prior to signing the offer to buy or sales contract. Since this isn't always possible, you should make the offer contingent upon a professional inspection. This clause, which should be written into the offer by your attorney, should stipulate that the offer is contingent upon receipt of a structural, mechanical, and electrical inspection of the house and a written *condition report*. If you know which inspection firm or inspector will conduct the inspection, that name should be included, and the fact that the inspection will be conducted within seven days (or a reasonable period determined by you, your attorney, and the seller) of the signing of the offer.

The contingency should stipulate that if the inspection reveals any major structural, mechanical, or electrical defects (you and your attorney should assign dollar amounts to what constitutes "major"), the seller will have the option of making the necessary repairs, renegotiating the sales price, or declaring the offer null and void. This clause should also specify that if the seller doesn't exercise any of these options, you have the right to declare the offer null and void and obtain a full refund of your earnest money.

Note that *you* are responsible for getting this contingency into the offer or sales agreement. In many areas, the standard offer or sales contract states that the buyer acknowledges he has inspected the property once he has looked it over and *waives* any further inspection rights. If you sign a document with such a provision, you will not be able to require a professional inspection. *Read the sales agreement carefully before you sign it!*

A good real-estate agent concerned about protecting you will willingly include a contingency for a professional inspection in the offer. If the agent objects and you want an inspection, stand firm.

One agent who dug into her own pocket to pay for a defective air conditioner on a property she sold a single woman in November says, "I tell people buying older homes that as far as I know the plumbing, wiring, and so on is in good condition, but I'm not an expert. I advise them to hire someone to come in and look at those systems, because I really feel bad when something goes wrong on a house I've sold."

What the Inspection Covers

A good inspector should make a thorough evaluation of the central heating and the central cooling systems, the interior electrical and plumbing systems, the roof and exterior of the structure, the interior walls, ceilings, floors, windows and doors, the attic, the foundation, basement, and slab structures. In addition, the inspector will look over each room and its permanent fixtures, and he'll check to make sure the dwelling is adequately ventilated and insulated and that it's free of termites. Before hiring an inspector, you should find out exactly what he will do. Many professional inspection firms will ask you to sign a contract or work order, which spells out what the inspector will do and will not do.

You should accompany the inspector as he goes through the house, which will take several hours if he conducts a thorough inspection. The inspector should point out the good and bad features of the house, as well as the defects and potential problems. He can tell you what repairs to anticipate, and he may give you estimated costs for repairs or advise you to get bids, *which you should do immediately.*

If you're planning to buy the house, you should learn as much about it as you can, since you'll be dealing with those problems as long as you live there. Most inspectors will provide you a preliminary on-the-spot written report right after the inspection and a formal, typed report within a few days.

Says Joseph McNeill, technical director of AMC Home Inspection & Warranty Service, "We advise buyers to go out and get quotes on repairs and they usually wait. Then they nearly have a heart attack when they find out how much the repairs will cost. The worst thing a home buyer can do is not check things ahead of time, because when the tradesmen get there to do the work, the buyer is a dead duck. Tradesmen are very expensive."

A professional inspector should provide you an unbiased report on the condition of the dwelling. He should not offer repair services nor steer you to any tradesmen. To do so is a conflict of interest and a breach of professional ethics. Above all, avoid inspectors who find flaws and then offer to repair them at a discount rate.

Some inspection companies offer warranties on their inspections. Basically, these warranties specify that if any substantial, undisclosed defects occur with any of the inspected components during the term of the warranty (usually one year), the home buyer can require the inspection firm to pick up the tab for the repairs. Generally, the warranty will stipulate minimum and maximum price limits on the repairs to be made. You pay an additional fee for the warranty and before buying it you should consult your attorney and make sure it complies with state and federal statutes.

You can expect to pay somewhere between $100 and $200 for a professional inspection, though rates vary considerably depending on location and practice. Often the fees are pegged to the price of the house. One experienced architect/inspector, who requests the home buyer to accompany him, gives on-the-spot, verbal reports and charges only $35. Ask any inspector what he will charge and how he sets his fees.

How to Choose an Inspector

The home-inspection industry is still in its infancy, and there are no national regulations governing inspectors, though a few states are considering licensing procedures. The leader in setting standards for the industry is the American Society of Home Inspectors (ASHI), a professional organization that has established a stringent code of ethics and conduct for its members. The ASHI code requires that the home buyer's rights always be upheld and bars membership to persons who are involved in the sale of real estate or the recommendation of service companies or contractors to repair defects. In addition, ASHI had developed a set of standards for home inspections to which its members adhere.

Your best ensurance of quality service is to have an ASHI member perform your inspection. If you are unable to locate an ASHI-affiliated inspector in your area, you can contact the national office at 175 Fifth Avenue, New York, New York 10010. There are ASHI members in most major cities and corporate centers. Home inspectors in a few states, notably California and Texas, have established their own affiliated organizations.

If you're in an area where there are no ASHI members, you should find out how long a prospective inspector has been in business, what kind of insurance he carries, and what liability he assumes for his report. You should choose a firm that carries errors-and-omissions insurance, has licensed engineers and architects on its staff, and has a tested training program for its employees. Your attorney may be able to assist you in your selection.

If there are no known inspectors in your community, you can contact an architect or engineer to conduct the inspection and call in a heating and cooling specialist and other mechanical expert if needed. You can also call the code inspection division of your city building department and request to have an inspector examine all the conditions of the house to determine whether they meet city code standards. This is a free service, and therefore, you likely won't get as rapid a response as you do with a paid inspector. The city can't order the seller to bring the house up to code standards, but at least you'll know its shortcomings.

Whoever you select, you should *always* accompany the inspector, as he can provide you much valuable information and education regarding your prospective home.

The Home Warranty

Home warranties, also called home-protection plans, have suddenly become the hottest new tool in the real-estate trade. Builders began offering warranties on their new homes in the early seventies in an effort to stave off federal regulations. Now a number of title companies, insurance companies, and independent firms are getting into the act by offering home-protection plans on existing houses.

Home-Protection Plans for Existing Homes

The number of protection plans literally mushroomed overnight once real-estate agents discovered that the plans helped sell homes. These existing home warranties, although not marketed directly by the broker, are generally sold through him. Usually the way it works is that the agent will recommend to the seller that he buy a home-protection plan to make the home more attractive to a prospective buyer.

So by the time you, the buyer, see the house, it's already under some warranty. Although the seller purchases the warranty, you pay for it indirectly in the sales price. It's up to you to examine the plan and determine how much protection it actually gives you. This section will provide a short primer on these various programs, which, to date, have not proven to be the great consumer service they're billed as.

First, you should know that the National Association of Realtors (NAR) evaluates and approves home-protection plans offered by many of the major warranty-companies. Noting that the Realtor must divulge any *known* defects in a house, NAR maintains that these programs protect the home buyer against the nasty shocks of unknown defects. In fact, NAR urges its members to use home-protection plans, pointing out that "the concept can relieve the Realtor of significant exposure to legal liability for misrepresentation and non-disclosures by his agents. In an increasingly litigious environment, this is a significant benefit."

So who is the real beneficiary of these programs? According to that statement from the NAR Home-Protection Program Guide, these programs provide a loophole for the agent who is charged with inspecting the property for defects. Ask yourself whether you want to pay a sizable agent's commission and then an additional $200–$300 for a warranty program to protect the agent from liability. If the agent does his job properly, he shouldn't have to worry about liability.

The companies authorized to offer NAR-approved warranties must demonstrate certain standards of financial responsibility and the ability to promptly handle claims to a NAR review board. Because of the number of unsound and illegal warranty companies that have folded, leaving their policyholders hanging, NAR does screen companies and require them to meet reasonable performance specifications.

There are two basic types of warranty programs for existing homes: the inspection program and the non-inspection program. With either type of program, buyers usually get twenty-four-hour complaint service and are promised a response within forty-eight hours from a network of independent repairmen.

Under the NAR-approved inspection program, the warranty company must inspect seven major components of the house and warrant their condition for one year. Those components include the central heating and central air conditioning systems, the interior plumbing system (including the hot-water heater), the electrical system, the structural soundness of the exterior and interior walls, floors, ceilings, and the foundation, basement, and roof. The cost of this program is about $300, *with a $50 deductible for each repair call.*

Under the NAR-approved, non-inspection program, four major components of the house are warranted sight unseen for one year. They are the central heating and central air-conditioning systems, the interior plumbing system (including the hot-water heater), and the electrical system. Most firms also warrant the built-in appliances and for an extra charge will cover additional structural and mechanical components. These NAR-approved non-inspection programs offer one-year breakdown protection for $225 to $275, *with a deductible ranging from $25 to $50 for each repair call.* For coverage of additional components, the cost can be much higher.

These non-inspection programs, based solely on actuarial data, are predicated on the fact, says NAR, "that a substantial number of home buyers are less interested in knowing the condition of the various mechanical systems and the components of a property they desire than they are in being assured that such systems and components will be repaired or replaced if they fail."

The buyer less interested in disclosure than performance risks some serious hazards. Holly, for example, bought a fifty-year-old house that was under a one-year, non-inspection warranty. As she was holding a house-warming party, a fuse blew. When a friend checked the fuse box, she discovered the house only had 30-amp service, which presented a severe fire hazard (most houses today have service of 100 amps). Her house could have burned down before Holly ever discovered that fact, which a thorough inspection would have disclosed. Moreover, her protection plan wouldn't have reimbursed her one cent for fire damage.

A top official of the American Society of Home Inspectors warns: "Non-inspection programs are not a good deal. All of them have limitations and confine protection to a few major items, but there are many components that make up a home. What these firms are selling is an insurance policy based on the law of averages.

"Most of them have a high deductible, often $100, and if they guarantee appliances, there's a $100 deductible for each repair call. Not many repairs would run over $100; therefore, the home buyer ends up footing the bill. Most of these firms also have it written into their contracts that they can omit any item from the warranty. With the non-inspection programs, the broker pre-screens the house and can see that faulty items are omitted. With the inspection programs, if they see a problem, they just omit that system."

Another serious question regarding home warranty companies is who regulates them: the state real-estate commission or the state insurance commission? They are unregulated in most states where this issue hasn't been resolved. In Connecticut, the state insurance commissioner ruled that all home warranty programs violated the law. That ruling stated that in order to sell warranties, firms had to be accepted, approved, and licensed by the state insurance commissioner. California recently passed a law that's apt to be the model for other states. It requires warranty companies to maintain a minimum net worth on a sliding scale related to policy volume outstanding and to make regular reports to the state insurance commissioner.

So before you accept a home warranty, check with the state insurance commissioner's office to make sure it's legal. And have your attorney review it carefully to make certain you still have legal recourse in the event of substantial undisclosed defects not covered by the policy. If you suspect major defects with a prospective home, your best protection is to have an independent professional inspect it. It is incumbent upon you as a buyer to know what you're getting into.

One California broker, who has handled a number of warranties for which the buyer and the seller split the price, complains that the policies often exclude coverage for the very things against which the buyer needs protection. They cover all the mechanical systems, she notes, but not all the structural components.

"The way you run into trouble here is with roofs. Most roofs on older homes are twenty-five years old, and if there is a heavy rainfall, suddenly you need a new roof. The protection plan doesn't cover that. Also, you see a lot of additions for which the owners didn't get building permits and code approvals. None of these additions are covered by the protection plans, and if repairs are necessary, the buyer pays for them."

The home warranty, however, can also be a significant benefit to the single buyer. Carol, who stretched her budget to the limit to afford her home, obtained a one-year maintenance warranty as part of the purchase package. She bought the house in the winter and didn't check out the air conditioner prior to the closing. During the first siege of hot weather, the compressor on the air conditioner blew out.

"Having the warranty was a real godsend," she said. "It paid the $1,000 repair bill in full. Without the warranty, I would have just sweated out the summer, because it would have been impossible for me to come up with that amount of money."

A number of real-estate franchises, such as ERA, Century 21, and Better Homes and Gardens, also make home warranties available to sellers. Some independent firms sell warranties to the buyer. In either case, before buying a warranty or a home with one, make sure you check these items:

- Exactly what the program covers and what the deductibles are.
- When coverage begins, the duration of coverage, and whether there is a renewal option.
- What you do in case of a complaint, and what promises the warrantor makes regarding service.
- Whether it complies with the Magnuson-Moss Warranty Act, and other state and federal statutes. Your attorney or the consumer protection division of your state attorney general's office can help you with these points.
- Read the warranty thoroughly before signing or accepting it and have your attorney look it over. Take up any questions with your real-estate agent and attorney.
- Find out whether it reimburses you for costs incurred in securing alternative living quarters if a covered defect renders your home uninhabitable.

- How long the warranty firm has been in business, its reputation and financial stability. Check with your Better Business Bureau.

Warranties on New Homes

Because of the increasing number of complaints about shoddy construction, many builders are now cleaning up their acts and offering written warranties on their homes. They have, in fact, been warned by the Federal Trade Commission to police their own industry or face hard-hitting national regulations. Only one state, New Jersey, now requires builders to provide warranties on their new homes.

If you buy a new house with federally backed financing—FHA, VA, or FmHA—the builder is required to provide you a written warranty. If you experience difficulties in getting the builder to remedy any items covered under the warranty, you can go back to the federal agency, which should take the issue up with the builder.

Most reputable builders offer written warranties, and if you're buying a new house, you should read the warranty and find out exactly what it covers, over what period the coverage is effective, and how it will protect you. A good warranty should protect you in case of major structural or mechanical defects. You should ask the builder how he will remedy any problems, and visit with owners of his other homes regarding his follow-up.

Most states have enacted implied warranty laws, making the seller of a new home liable for defects in materials and workmanship. Unfortunately, federal and state warranty requirements fail to address two important issues. First, the builder may put you through a long and costly court battle before making good on a legitimate claim. Second, government requirements don't address the problems of builders who go out of business or are financially incapable of paying a large claim. Because of the perennial swings in the home-building industry, this is a very serious problem.

Under the threat of federal legislation, the National Association of Home Builders took the lead in addressing these issues by developing the Home Owners Warranty (HOW) program.

HOW handles the problems of the builder's unwillingness or inability to pay on claims by: 1) providing a dispute resolution system in compliance with the Magnuson-Moss Warranty Act, and 2) providing an independent insurance company that underwrites all claims after the second year and any claims against an unwilling or insolvent builder.

The FTC has expressed satisfaction with HOW, which is the only warranty that provides a procedure for settling complaints out of court. Under it, the disgruntled buyer or builder can submit the case to a local HOW council for conciliation. If this procedure fails, the local HOW council appoints a neutral conciliator to investigate the problem and clarify the issue so the parties can reach an agreement. If that fails, the conflict can be submitted to the American Arbitration Association by either party and at no cost to the consumer.

HOW provides a one-year warranty against defects in materials and workmanship, a two-year warranty against defects in major mechanical systems, and a ten-year warranty against major structural defects. To participate in the HOW program, builders must meet HOW's standards of technical competence, financial soundness, and fair dealing with consumers. To obtain the names of builders offering HOW, contact your local homebuilders' association. The cost of HOW coverage is $2 per thousand of the home's selling price. On a house of $50,000, the fee would be $100. The builder pays for the coverage, but passes the cost along to you.

The greatest weakness of HOW and all other builder's warranties is that they're available only at the builder's option. If you are unable to get HOW coverage, you should buy a home with a minimum one-year, written warranty. Read it carefully and have your attorney review the document before accepting it.

The national Magnuson-Moss Warranty Act requires all warranties to be written in easily understandable language instead of incomprehensible legalese. The act also mandates that the home buyer be given the chance to read the terms of the warranty before the sale is closed, and those terms must include a clear explanation of the coverage period of the warranty.

Ultimately, your guarantee of quality and follow-up rests on the integrity of the builder. Should you experience severe problems with a defective house or a builder failing to live up to his guarantee, notify the FTC's Bureau of Consumer Protection, Sixth and Pennsylvania Avenue, N.W., Washington, D.C. 20580, and the consumer protection division of your state attorney general's office.

The Insurance

Right before and right after you buy your home, you're apt to have purveyors of all sorts of insurance calling you up at all hours, both at home and at work. These salespeople get your name from any number of sources—the lender, the broker, court records. And they invariably zero in on single buyers, with a line of double-talk about why you need this or that coverage.

In fact, there are certain types of insurance you will need and other coverage that the lender may require, depending on the practices where you live. Here, then, is a rundown of the policies needed to protect your investment, the additional types of coverage required and offered, and the schemes to avoid. Bear in mind that insurance needs vary, and so what you purchase will depend on your specific situation.

Home-Owner's Insurance

Before your loan can be closed, most lenders will insist that you have home-owner's insurance (also called hazard insurance) on your dwelling. This coverage protects the home and its contents from certain specified perils, such as fire, lightning, theft, and vandalism. There are three basic types of home-owner's coverage: *basic,* which covers the most common perils; *broad,* which covers additional perils; and *comprehensive,* which covers all perils except flood, earthquake, war, nuclear attack, and others specified in your policy. In addition, there are variations on these packages tailored to various needs.

Property coverage for all home-owner's packages insures: 1) the dwelling and its attached structures; 2) appurtenant structures, such as detached garages, for 10 percent of the dwelling's coverage; 3) personal property, including all household contents and personal belongings, usually for 50 percent of the policy's face value; and 4) additional living expenses, such as for lodging or restaurants following a fire or other damage, for up to 20 percent of the face value. Most home-owner's packages also provide liability coverage in case of major injury or property damage lawsuits, medical payments for others' injuries, and payments for minor damage to others' property.

It's very important you understand that most home-owners' policies cover personal property only up to a percentage—usually 50 percent—of the insured value of the house itself. For instance, if you insure your home for $40,000, then its contents are insured for $20,000. Coverage is automatic only for those articles included in the basic policy (those items are called "unscheduled" personal property). You may need a floater in your policy to provide additional protection for "scheduled" items, such as expensive camera equipment, artwork, antiques, or jewelry.

Before you buy any policy, you should carefully go over the details of the exceptions, restrictions, and limits of the coverage, and ask your agent about any floaters or endorsements you should add to assure adequate protection. If you're in California, for example, you may need a floater for earthquake protection. Your agent also can help you determine which deductibles to take on your policy. You may be able to lower your premium appreciably by taking a high deductible.

The mistake many single home buyers make is leaving the details of insurance to the last minute. Consequently, they don't have time to shop for an agent or a policy and usually wind up working with an agent affiliated with the broker or recommended by the lender and making an uninformed decision on their coverage. If you presently have an insurance agent whom you trust, visit with him about the coverage you will need as a home owner and its cost. If you don't have an agent, ask a friend who owns a home to recommend a reputable agent. It's advisable to get quotes from several agents.

If you're buying an older house in an older neighborhood and you encounter difficulty getting insurance, you should contact your local HUD office and your attorney. Insurers have frequently discriminated against dwellings in older areas. Refer to the section on "Rehabilitation Housing," page 57, for the names of organizations that can help you if you encounter insurance red-lining. You can also take any complaints about discrimination to your state insurance commissioner.

If your property is in a designated flood plain (which the broker is required to disclose), you will need flood insurance, which is not available in a basic home-owner's policy. Without this coverage, however, you will not be able to get a loan. If your community has qualified for the sale of flood insurance under the National Flood Insurance Program, you should be able to get this coverage from any insurance agent licensed within your state. Make sure the agent explains to you how this program works.

How Much Coverage Will You Need?

Insurance coverage is based on what it takes to actually replace a dwelling and the structures attached to it—its "replacement value" or how much it would cost to rebuild the house today. Insurers require that the property be insured for a minimum of 80 percent of the replacement value in order for you to be reimbursed the full cost of property damages or losses. Some companies are now increasing their minimums to 90 and even 100 percent. If you want to be entirely safe, insure your home for 100 percent of its replacement cost, the amount it will cost to rebuild if it's completely destroyed by a tornado or fire. If you have a $100,000 house which is demolished by a tornado and you have only 80 percent coverage, you'll only be able to recover $80,000 from your insurance company.

Do not confuse replacement value with market value or the price you pay for your property. In some places, particularly California, where land is terribly expensive and prices drastically inflated, the replacement value of a home may be *less than* the market value or sales price. Where it is standard practice for the lender and insurance agent to negotiate the amount of insurance required, they will ask you to insure the property based on the sales price. Usually the broker will go along with that quote. *However,* you can and should negotiate for insurance based on the replacement value.

One professional woman who paid $125,000 for her older Los Angeles home discovered that the insurance company inspection pegged the replacement value at $95,000. She insisted on insurance coverage for that amount to save a chunk on her premium and the lender required her to make a written request to that effect. She did, and got insurance for the lower amount. *It is up to you to negotiate for the insurance and usually no one will warn you about this difference between replacement value and market value.*

Because of the rapid inflation in housing, it is *critical* that you keep your policy updated. Today, almost every insurer provides some means of automatic increases in coverage to keep pace with escalating costs. Be sure you understand how these clauses work before you buy a policy with one. Because these escalation clauses often fail to keep up with inflation, it's also a good idea to have your property appraised each year and upgrade your coverage accordingly. You should also have an appraisal following any major improvements that increase the value of your property. If your coverage falls below 80 percent of replacement value and you have a fire or other damage, you'll foot a big tab for the repairs.

How Much Will You Pay for Coverage?

Brokers often use a rule-of-thumb formula to figure the amount you will pay for home-owner's insurance. They multiply the amount of your loan by .0003 to determine what your *monthly* premium will be. However, rates vary greatly depending on area. As you're getting quotes from various insurance agents, you should realize that several factors determine the amount of the premium.

Foremost, of course, is the value of the home and the type of coverage. The proximity of your home to police and fire protection and the efficiency and dependability of those facilities will also affect the rate you pay. Location makes a big difference in calculating premiums. If you're in what the insurer considers a high-risk neighborhood, you're apt to pay more. (Check with your local HUD office about the availability of Federal Crime Insurance, which enables individuals in areas where the cost or availability of crime insurance is a problem to buy affordable coverage against robbery losses.) The insurer will also take into consideration the age of your home, usually requiring a higher premium for older homes. Some insurers, however, give discounts for such home improvements as the installation of a smoke detector or burglar alarm system.

The type of construction will also be considered. Fire-resistant materials, such as brick or stone, warrant a lower premium than wood. And, of course, the loss experience of the insurer—the amount the company has spent settling claims—also affects the rate.

Above all, you should be concerned with service. After you've shopped for an agent and learned the details of the policies available to you, check out the service record of the company. Does it respond immediately in the event of a loss? Have the agent explain to you what procedures to follow if you suffer a loss.

Finally, you should know that the lender may require you to escrow your insurance premium. That is, when you take out a mortgage loan, the lender may insist that part of each monthly payment goes for the insurance premium to make certain that the coverage doesn't lapse. This is a common procedure when your down payment is less than 20 percent, but also depends on local practice.

Title Insurance

Although title practices vary greatly, lenders in all states but Iowa require the purchase of title insurance before they will close your loan. It's important, however, for you to distinguish between the two types of title insurance policies.

One is the *mortgage title policy,* required by the lender to protect his investment against claims on the title based on flaws in the property's ownership record. This mortgage title policy assures the lender that his mortgage is a valid lien on the real estate. You will pay the premium for this policy, as well as for the title search, which outlines the history of the property and defines the items that require action to clear the title. The lender requires insurance in the amount of the mortgage. The *average* fee for the mortgage title policy is $2.50 per $1,000 of value. Thus, on a $40,000 mortgage, you'll pay $100 for the policy.

You are not covered by the lender's policy. The mortgage title policy will pay off the lender's investment, but the title insurance company could sue you to recover the money it paid the lender. So if you want protection for yourself, you must buy an *owner's title policy*. Then you will have a written guarantee that an insurance company will defend your title in all legal actions or proceedings alleging title defects. So if forged deeds, releases, wills, or liens turn up later, your title insurance will pay the expense for ironing out the difficulties and any litigation. For example, after six months in her house, Joan was faced with an expensive street-paving lien missed in the title search. Her insurance paid off the lien.

Before you buy your own title policy, however, you should know that most titles are valid. If your attorney conducts a proper title search and determines the title is valid, that should provide you adequate protection. One attorney contends that his study of title insurance shows that the loss rate by consumers is considerably less than the rates paid in for the purchase of title policies. In fact, the industry's loss experience is miniscule, with the average title company spending only 5 to 6 percent of pretax operating income for losses and loss adjustment expenses.

In California, where title companies conduct the title search through title plants and often conduct closings, one broker complains, "Regardless of the extent to which the company goes to conduct the title search, the rate is always the same. The buyers don't bargain and the title companies are getting rich fast—it's a real racket."

Beth paid $339 for the mortgage title insurance and her owner's policy when she closed the loan on her $67,000 town house in a Washington, D.C. suburb. On the other hand, the mortgage title premium and owner's policy on Art's $68,500 San Diego house was $382.10, plus a $10 service fee to the title company.

The title insurance premium is a one-time cost, levied at the time of the closing. In some areas, the cost for the mortgage title policy is split between the buyer and the seller. And in a few areas, local practice requires the seller to buy the policy, although the cost is always passed along to you. The rub, however, is that each time the property changes hands, a new policy must be taken out. In markets where property moves quickly (home owners sell and move about every eight years according to national figures), the title companies are cleaning up. Better that you should buy stock in a title company than buy a house!

You should know that there is such a thing as a *reissue rate*, which can reduce your premium. For example, if a title policy was issued within the previous two years on the property you're buying, then the title only needs to be updated from that last title search. Most title companies give discount or reissue rates in such cases. Unfortunately, no one is apt to inform you of this, so you must specifically ask when the property last exchanged hands and when the last title search was performed. Although practices vary among title companies, some insurers offer discounts if the current policy was written within the last ten years.

Also, if you decide to purchase an owner's policy, request it at the same time that the mortgage title policy is taken out so that both policies can be written on the basis of a single title search, examination, and underwriting process to reduce the cost to you. This so-called *simultaneous issuance* can save you a substantial amount of money. The average rate for an owner's title policy is $3.50 per $1,000 of the purchase price of the house. Thus, on a $50,000 house, you'll pay $175. (If there are problems on the title that complicate the search, the title company may assess you an additional fee.) With simultaneous issuance, you may pay $175 for your policy and only $7.50 for the mortgage title policy.

Most owner's title policies contain inflation riders, which increase the amount of coverage so much per year to keep pace with the rising value of your house. Make sure this rider is included in any owner's policy you buy.

One of the first things you should have your real estate agent and your attorney explain to you are the title practices in your area. Then you will have the opportunity to shop for your own title services. Usually, the single buyer knows nothing about title practices, and the agent or the lender applies for title insurance for him. Incidents have recently surfaced of tie-ins between brokerage firms, attorneys, lenders, escrow companies, and title companies. You invariably pay for these interlocking relationships and should be alerted about them early in the purchase process.

You should also know that the Federal Trade Commission (FTC) advocates that buyers be allowed to shop around for their own attorneys to do title searches rather than be forced to use lawyers chosen by lending institutions. FTC officials believe that requiring buyers to use attorneys designated by lenders "constitutes an unfair trade practice" and creates unnecessary expenses for the buyer. Officials note that lenders can insure that the borrower's attorney has properly prepared the title documents by simply having their own attorneys review them. If you encounter difficulties on this point with your lender, advise him of the FTC position and suggest he allow your attorney to handle the title documentation.

In some states, notably California, where attorneys are rarely involved in home sales, the title companies perform the title searches. Many title companies pool their efforts to establish "title plants," which maintain detailed computer records on the histories of all properties within their areas. This enables the companies to quickly and easily perform title searches, which should result in reduced consumer costs.

Unfortunately, rates of title insurers are often not regulated. One official of HUD, which is now investigating title company practices, reports that title companies are only nominally regulated by state insurance commissioners. Because they never go in for rate reviews, the official adds, the title companies "are mostly unregulated."* A few states, however, have

*Title insurance has often been attacked by critics who feel the cost—based on the price of the house and not on the risk involved—is too high. One of the problems is that title companies use a whole series of legal price-fixing arrangements, such as organizations that file uniform insurance rates with state insurance commissions. Furthermore, these insurance companies are not subject to antitrust laws.

done something about this. In Texas, rates are now set by the insurance commissioner, who required title companies to lower the fees they were charging.

A good real-estate agent should investigate title insurance rates and types of services available from the various companies in your area. He then can recommend companies with good service reputations and the lowest rates. If you have questions regarding the title company or any title procedures, ask your agent for explanations. If you have complaints, take them to your attorney and the state insurance commissioner's office.

If you live in Iowa, your title examination will be conducted by an attorney designated by the lender, and your own attorney should also review the title opinion. Iowa does not allow title companies to operate offices within its borders, and abstract companies usually perform the title searches.

Title procedures and land recordation systems are under review nationwide. Alternatives to the present complicated and costly system are being explored and may soon be implemented in various areas. Also, some state bar associations are challenging title companies, claiming they are improperly performing legal services. These challenges may result in tighter regulation of title companies.

Reputable title companies, where they are an established part of the real-estate transaction, may provide protection and services to expedite your purchase. You should, however, *shop* for title services. The American Land Title Association, 1828 L Street, N.W., Washington, D. C. 20036, can provide you the names of established title companies where you live.

Mortgage Insurance

If you put less than 20 percent down on your loan, the lender may require you to buy *private mortgage insurance* (PMI). This insurance, available from a private mortgage insurance firm, insures the lender against default on the low down-payment loan. For example, if you put down only 10 percent and get a 90 percent loan, the lender wants this insurance to cover his additional risk (most conventional loans are 80 percent).

Use of private mortgage insurance has been expanded to meet the needs of the young, single home buyer with a limited amount to put down. PMI costs one percent of the loan amount for the first year and one-quarter of one percent every year after that. Usually, once the loan is amortized to 80 percent, the lender will drop the requirement for this coverage. The first year's premium is paid at the time of the closing.

If you're getting an FHA-backed loan, you will be required to pay mortgage insurance at a rate of one-half of one percent of the loan amount annually. After the loan has been amortized over a period of years, some lenders no longer require you to carry mortgage insurance. However, the lender may require you to carry it for the term of the loan—it depends on local custom.

Mortgage Life Insurance

Some lenders may also require mortgage life insurance, which is life insurance that will pay off the mortgage if you die. If you have no other life insurance and want your property passed along to a relative or other person, this may be a good investment. If you're already adequately covered, you should visit with your personal insurance agent about the necessity for this coverage. Individual circumstances should govern the decision to buy this kind of policy.

Two unrelated women who bought a duplex together, for example, decided to take out mortgage life policies on each other. They owned the property jointly, but each woman lived in her own side of the duplex. Neither had a sufficient income to carry the mortgage. Therefore, the only way they could assure that in the event of the death of one the other could keep the property was by purchasing mortgage life policies.

If you buy mortgage life coverage, make sure that the money from the policy doesn't automatically pay off the house instead of going to the survivor who may decide to sell the property.

Warning

There is a routine scam used on single buyers by mortgage insurance salespeople, who usually obtain the buyers' names from mortgage bankers. Linda explains how it works:

"I was contacted by a man who claimed to work for the mortgage banking company that was handling my loan. He called just as I was expecting the final loan papers to be mailed, and he said there were things he wanted to discuss with me relative to the loan to prepare me for the closing and before the final signing.

"He came to where I worked and we talked in the lobby. He started trying to sell me a decreasing term mortgage insurance policy and urged me to sign the papers by telling me that I could get out of it within ten days of signing.

"I said I wasn't interested, but what really bothered me was the fact that he misrepresented himself and claimed to be an employee of the mortgage company when, in fact, he was an insurance salesman. I was also distressed by the fact that the mortgage company had so freely given out my name and wondered what other information they had given out and to whom. I later discovered the salesman's insurance company was a subsidiary of the mortgage banking company, and that's how he made the claim he was with the bank."

Linda, who said she felt particularly vulnerable as a single woman buying a home for the first time, warns other single buyers to put up a wall of resistance if there is anything they don't understand. Since you're bound to get offers for everything from various types of insurance to home improvements, make sure you get detailed explanations before you sign anything. If you know the offer is for something you don't need, tell the purveyor to buzz off. The real-estate industry is rife with rip-off artists: Don't allow yourself to be a victim.

The Other "Experts"

Once you decide to buy a home, relatives and friends usually have loads of well-intended advice. In most cases, however, they know little about the intricacies of the real-estate process or home construction. It's fine to accept their leads on prospective homes, but relying on them for more in-depth help can spell disaster.

For instance, Jackie depended upon her brother to conduct her home inspection and bought the house with his approval.

"He's always been so good about helping me out, and he seemed to know what he was talking about," she said.

One month after moving in, Jackie paid a plumber $4,000 to install all new pipes, including a line out to the main in the street and a new water meter. A week later, one of the bedroom ceilings caved in. So much for brotherly advice!

8

Bargain for the Best Financial Package

In time of runaway inflation, high interest rates, and tight money markets, it can be exceedingly hard to obtain mortgage financing. For the single buyer, who many lenders still consider less stable and reliable than a married couple, it may be even more difficult. Therefore, it's extremely important for you to understand the basic steps of the financial transaction, as well as the underlying factors that determine whether you will get a loan.

For example, the relationships between your attorney, broker, lender, and even your boss may influence your ability to get a loan. It's quite common for attorneys, real-estate brokers, developers, and other prominent business persons to be directors on the boards of local lending institutions. Or your attorney, broker, or builder may keep substantial sums invested in the trust departments of local banks. When money is really tight, referrals from these types of individuals can get you your loan.

As twenty-four-year-old Larry, who bought a $45,000 house right after taking his first job with a major law firm in his town, noted, "Getting financing is amazingly easy if you have connections."

You do owe it to yourself, however, to do some independent shopping to see what rates and loans are available. This chapter will advise you of the various financing methods and the new alternative mortgages being created to aid single buyers with limited budgets. You will learn how to bargain for the lowest sales price and how to select a financial package tailored to your economic situation. This chapter will also explain the numerous money sources you can check and will prepare you to conduct your financial transaction in an efficient, businesslike manner.

Lending procedures are based on local practice and vary greatly from city to city and state to state. For that reason, it's impossible to describe exactly what practices you'll find in your area. The discussions of the financial transaction in this book will familiarize you with the routine, and then it's up to you to learn the specifics that apply where you live. Above all, try to remain unemotional, and make your decisions logically!

Bargaining for the Sales Price

The seller always asks more than he expects to get and anticipates that the buyer will try to negotiate a lower price. Your job is to find out as much about the property as you can to use as bargaining points and then bid the seller's rock-bottom price. Most first-time single buyers give in too easily to the initial demand made by the seller or the broker, either because they are unfamiliar with the financial procedures or because they are too intimidated to bargain.

Celia, a department head at a community college in a mid-sized city, illustrates this point perfectly. Forty-three-year-old Celia, who had previously rented several homes, bought her first house—a three-bedroom ranch—for $42,500. The only other bid on the house—$42,000—was from a couple who was having great difficulty raising money for the down payment. The sellers were extremely anxious to unload the house, since they were already making payments on their new home. Unquestionably, Celia could have bought the house for $42,001—even her lender later confirmed that—and possibly much less. So why did she pay $42,500?

"I really felt like the high forties would not have been terribly unreasonable for this house," she said. "My friend suggested offering $42,500, and so I followed her suggestion. I just never thought about bidding less, I guess. Now I feel terrible, because I also paid the sellers extra to leave the washer, dryer, and refrigerator. Do you suppose I could have bargained for them?"

Not only could she have bargained; she could have cleaned up. You need to know the techniques of bargaining and use them to your advantage.

First, you should inspect the house from top to bottom several times. Look for faults and any major defects. Make sure the seller hasn't painted over the basement walls and floors to hide water leaks and that he likewise hasn't painted over upstairs walls or ceilings to hide roof leaks. Look behind pictures and furniture to make sure there are no holes or cracks in the walls. Your broker should arrange one time for you to go over the house thoroughly in the seller's absence.

When you go through the house in the seller's presence, ask him as many questions as you can about the condition of the house (refer to the "Inspection Checklist" in Chapter 6, p. 85). Remember the basic law is *caveat emptor:* Buyer beware. The seller is not required to disclose any damages or defects unless you specifically ask about them. Make a list of questions you intend to ask; then note all the faults and get bids on them. It's also advisable to have a professional inspector examine the house and give you a written report on its condition and ball-park estimates, if he will, for necessary repairs. Each item is a negotiating point for you.

Ask the seller about the energy efficiency of the house; whether it's insulated, and if so, how well. Also ask to *see* utility bills for the past year. If the house is a real energy sieve, you probably should bypass it. If you can improve the situation by insulating it, find out how much necessary energy improvements will cost you—that's a big bargaining point.

Make sure the seller and broker are quoting you the actual sales prices of recently sold similar houses in the neighborhood and not simply telling you the asking prices on those houses. If you're in doubt, have a certified appraiser give you a written estimate of the home's value. Neighbors can also be a valuable source of information about the house—they're usually willing to tell you about its chronic problems and what other homes on the block have sold for.

Now take your list of shortcomings to the owner, with the estimates of how much it will cost to bring the house up to standard, and make a low verbal offer. If the broker or seller accept that bid immediately, you probably haven't hit the seller's rock-bottom price yet. So say you need further time to consider your decision and then make your bid in the written offer even lower, or insist upon some concessions. You can ask the seller to include the washer and dryer or other appliances.

If the seller won't accept your low bid, then you'll have to compromise on the difference. But give in gradually—coming up at $100 increments until you hit the lowest price the seller will accept. As long as the negotiations are verbal, haggle all you want. Once your written offer is accepted, you can no longer reduce the price, unless it is specified that subsequent defects discovered in the house will reopen the negotiations. With a new house, you may not have much negotiating power with the builder, unless he's overbuilt and needs to get rid of his surplus.

If you really feel unsure of yourself in the negotiations, it may be wise to have your attorney handle this process for you to avoid personality conflicts and becoming overly emotional or overanxious and blowing it.

If the house has recently changed hands, you can check the last selling price at the county courthouse. The revenue or tax stamps on the deed will indicate how much the owner paid for the house, or the sales amount may be stated on the deed. If you think the owner has unreasonably jacked up the price, this information can be a negotiating card.

You should avoid buying a house when it first comes on the market and the asking price is the highest. You should also avoid buying in the spring when prices are highest. Remember—houses hit the lowest prices in mid-winter. Most buyers spend about three months shopping before purchasing a home.

Your negotiating ability will also be determined by market conditions. If it's a seller's market, buyers bid up the prices of houses, and you may not be able to get the seller to come down from his asking price. You should try though. Often, if you catch the seller at just the right moment, when he's fed up with showing the house, he'll accept your bid on the spot, even against his broker's advice. Then get it in writing *immediately!*

On the other hand, if it's mid-winter and there are a lot of houses on the market, you'll be in a good bargaining position. Also, if the seller is anxious to move into a new home or sell because he's being transferred, you'll have a strong negotiating advantage.

The Offer to Buy

Money first exchanges hands when the offer to buy (also called the binder, sales agreement, or purchase agreement) is made. When you make the offer, you deposit "earnest money," usually a sum between $250 and

$1,000, as your serious intent to purchase the home. This earnest money should be held in an escrow account by your broker or attorney and never turned over to the seller. The offer, a written, legal contract, describes the property and sales price and should include a number of protective clauses for you, as stipulated in Chapter 7.

In some states, the practice is for the buyer to sign a preliminary binder at the time he puts down his earnest money. Then a second agreement, the sales contract, is drafted to stipulate the details of the purchase. Where this is the procedure, the sales contract should contain all of the protective provisions that would otherwise be written into the offer to buy. And your attorney should review this document before you sign it.

In addition to those provisions noted in Chapter 7, make sure these protections are included in the offer to buy or sales contract:

- The seller keeps the property insured until closing in an *amount equal to the sales price.* The seller's existing insurance often only equals the amount of his mortgage, which is much lower than the present sales price. In case of fire, most standard contracts give the seller the option of turning insurance proceeds over to the buyer or of restoring the property. But restoration doesn't require the seller to replace anything new in a house that is not new. As the buyer, you should insist on your own protection with such a clause: "In the event of fire or casualty damages exceeding $4,000 (or some reasonable amount), the buyer can cancel this contract and receive his deposit back."
- If the seller defaults on the agreement, he must pay X amount of damages (this amount, to be determined by you and your attorney, should be as much as or double your deposit). Most standard contracts, weighted in favor of the seller, don't contain this provision.
- A possession clause, protecting you if the seller doesn't vacate the premises by closing day. This clause should include a penalty to the seller and provide for expenses incurred by you for accommodations and meals until you can occupy the home.
- In the case of a new house, the remaining work to be done and all other responsibilities of the builder should be spelled out in detail, with a provision for specific damages in the event that he does not fulfill all of his obligations.
- If you're getting a VA- or FHA-insured loan, make certain there's a clause stipulating that you may withdraw your offer and receive your deposit back if the house does not appraise for the amount offered. Under these financing methods, if the house or buyer fail to meet requirements set by the insuring agency, your deposit does not have to be returned in full. Therefore, make sure your contract specifies that it can be cancelled and all monies refunded if the house doesn't appraise for the amount offered.
- It's stipulated who will pay the property taxes. (Property taxes are due at different times of the year depending on where you live, and it should be stipulated who will pay for which portion of them. If you buy the house in June, you don't want to get stuck with the whole year's taxes.)
- You may also wish to put an arbitration clause in your contract, a new concept that may meet with resistance from the seller or the broker. Arbitration, however, is faster and less expensive than litigation. An arbitration clause should contain wording similar to this: "In the event of any dispute involving this contract or the sales transaction, the parties to this contract agree to

submit to binding arbitration under the rules of the American Arbitration Association."

You can revoke your offer at any time prior to notice of acceptance—it's the acceptance that constitutes formation of a contract. Also, you should know that if the seller rejects your offer, he can't later accept it and bind you, because the offer is killed forever by his rejection. Make sure that all parties involved sign the offer and that you get a written copy of it.

Once the offer to buy or sales contract is signed, you should immediately start shopping for financing. To assist you with this task, this section will explain the various methods of financing that should be considered. Financing is a highly individual matter, which should be tailored to your specific needs, economic situation, and income potential. Here you will learn the advantages and disadvantages of each method and how to select one appropriate for you.

Mortgage Loans

Most homes are financed by mortgage loans. Following is a rundown of the traditional mortgages with fixed rate, fixed payment, and fixed term that have been in use for years.

Conventional Loans

The most common form of mortgage, the conventional loan allows you to borrow a certain amount of money over a set period (usually between twenty-five and thirty-five years) at the prevailing market interest rate. The size of your payment remains the same for the term of the loan. The standard down payment is twenty to twenty-five percent of the home's appraised value, although this varies depending on whether money is tight and whether you live in a state with prohibitive usury ceilings.

A number of states have interest rate ceilings—also called usury ceilings or usury rates—set by state law. These usury ceilings limit the interest rates that can be charged, often below those rates prevailing in other states. The net effect is to force mortgage lenders in these states with ceilings to curtail lending or demand large down payments. (At the time of this writing, Congress was considering whether to make permanent a temporary preemption of state usury ceilings.)

Many lenders—particularly savings and loan associations—will write you a conventional loan on a *new* house for only 5 or 10 percent down with the purchase of private mortgage insurance (PMI). (Banking regulations, however, limit the number of these low-down-payment mortgages that an institution can make.) You pay an added fee for PMI, usually at the closing or as part of your monthly mortgage payment. Conventional loans can usually be processed quite rapidly, generally within a few weeks.

FHA-Insured Loans

The Federal Housing Administration (FHA) insures mortgages against default on both new and existing homes in an effort to encourage lenders to write loans for persons who can't qualify for conventional loans. Within the past few years, a large proportion of the FHA-insured borrowers have been single buyers, and single women in particular—a constituency lenders are now eager to reach.

The down payment on an FHA-backed loan is low—3 percent of the first $25,000 of the home's appraised value (or $750) and 5 percent of the remainder—up to $67,500 for a single-family dwelling or condo unit. For example, to buy a $55,000 house, you'll need a down payment of $2,250. Since the FHA guarantees loans for single-family dwellings only up to $67,500, anything over that amount will have to come out of your pocket, along with the required down payment. (FHA will insure two-to-four-family dwellings for larger amounts.)

Repayment periods are long—ranging from thirty to forty years—and interest rates are set by the FHA, usually about one percentage point below prevailing market rates. (The interest rates, down payment requirements, and maximum loan amounts are subject to periodic review and revision by the FHA. But once you take out an FHA-backed loan, the interest remains the same for the term of the loan.) The buyer is required to pay an additional .5 percent for mortgage insurance. You should realize that although the interest rate is lower and settlement costs usually minimal, because of the low down payment you will pay considerably more interest over the term of the loan than you would with a conventional loan. There is no prepayment penalty if you pay off the loan early.

Anyone is eligible for an FHA-insured loan. You apply for one at an FHA-approved lending institution, which sends your application to the local FHA office. The home is examined by an FHA inspector to assure that it meets the Minimum Property Standards (MPS) set by the FHA. If it does not, the seller must make the needed repairs before the deal can be closed. The house is also appraised by the FHA for market value and based on that appraisal, the agency decides the loan amount it will insure. If the FHA and lender agree that your income and assets qualify you for the loan, then it is approved.

There are a few drawbacks to the FHA-insured loan. First, many lenders refuse to make these loans because of the paperwork and red tape involved—often it takes up to three months to get the necessary approvals to close the loan. Second, many sellers refuse to take their homes off the market for the time required to process the loan or to comply with FHA property standards. Plus the seller is required to pay any points charged by the lender to make the loan.* Third, although the FHA is working to

*To compensate for the lower interest rates on government-backed loans, the lender often assesses charges called "points." One point is equal to one percent of the mortgage. So, one point on a $50,000 mortgage is $500; five points $2,500. The FHA and VA require the seller to pay the points, although the buyer may be assessed a one-point service charge. Most sellers required to pay points pass the price on to the buyer by asking more for the house. It's not unusual for lenders to charge up to six or seven points on government-backed loans, and in times of tight money, the lender may charge more.

straighten up its procedures, inadequate appraisals by the agency and improper loans by lenders have forced some borrowers to default on their loans.

Mortgage banking companies write the majority of FHA-insured loans, and investigations have revealed that some mortgage bankers have engaged in fraudulent and shoddy practices to profit from the government program at the home buyer's expense. For example, one mortgage banker has been accused of falsifying the income levels and credit records of home buyers. The home buyers were forced to default on their loans when they couldn't meet their payments, and the lender foreclosed the mortgages, recouping his investment from the FHA. *Never* accept an eager loan officer's assessment of your ability to pay for the house unless he can show you exactly how, based on your income and assets.

If you buy a new house with an FHA-insured loan and you discover defects the first several years after occupying the house, the FHA will either make the builder repair the defects or reimburse you for the cost of the repairs. You must notify your local FHA office of the defects or any problems as soon as you discover them.

VA-Guaranteed Loans

The Veterans Administration (VA) guarantees no-down-payment loans for the purchase of new and used homes, including condos and converted condos, for eligible veterans—those who have served at least 181 days in active service. The VA guarantees up to 60 percent or $25,000, whichever is less, for a loan to buy, build, or repair a house. Interest rates, set by the VA, are usually about one percentage point below prevailing market rates, but are subject to constant review and revisions, as are the other terms of these loans. The VA requires an appraisal of the property, which must meet certain VA-set structural standards.

Unlike the FHA, the VA sets no limit on the amount that can be borrowed. If the property appraises for the price you have offered, no down payment will be required. If the amount you offer exceeds the VA-appraised value, the lender will require you to come up with the difference.

The maximum repayment period is thirty years. There are no prepayment penalties should you decide to pay the loan off, and the loans are assumable. The interest remains fixed throughout the loan. Because of the lack of a down payment, you will pay substantially more over the term of the loan than you would with a conventional loan. Many lenders and sellers are reluctant to deal with VA-guaranteed loans because of the red tape and approvals needed, which often require three months before the loan can be closed. Mortgage banking companies make the majority of VA-backed loans.

New homes built with VA-backed financing require three inspections by VA personnel. Those new homes covered by a ten-year insured warranty cleared through the VA or with the Home Owners Warranty are subject to only one inspection. Like the FHA, the VA has a program to help buyers of new and used homes recoup expenses for corrections of defects, if necessary.

You apply for this loan with a VA-approved lender. Spouses of personnel who died in the service or from a disability incurred in the service are also eligible for these loans. Veterans who have previously taken out these loans and paid off the balance are eligible to apply for another VA-backed mortgage. In rural areas, small towns, or credit-short urban areas, the VA provides direct mortgage loans for qualified veterans. The VA has direct financial grants to help permanently disabled veterans acquire specially adapted housing. In addition, the VA has developed some special programs for home improvements with solar energy for new and existing homes. For further information, consult your local VA office or write the Veterans Administration, Washington, D.C. 20420.

If you apply for a VA-backed loan, ask the agency if the interest rate is under review. The VA can raise its interest rate to any level regardless of usury laws in your state, and the lender can still demand the same high processing fees. A little advance checking can save you the hassles and disappointment Joe suffered. He applied for a VA-backed loan to buy a bungalow while he was doing graduate work. His meager income as a graduate instructor just qualified him for the loan. Then after going through all the red tape and waiting, when he went to sign the final papers to close the loan, he discovered that the interest rate had been increased thirty minutes prior to his closing appointment. Under the new terms, he couldn't afford the house. If the lender had notified Joe's broker of the impending increase, she could have gotten the loan closed that morning at the lower rate. So, you see, it pays to do some research and *never* take any of these procedures for granted.

FmHA Loans

The Farmers Home Administration (FmHA), a division of the U.S. Department of Agriculture, makes loans and guarantees loans for persons living in rural areas. Specifically, the borrower must buy or build in a community with less than 20,000 people that is not a part of a standard metropolitan area.

FmHA has three loan programs for persons in three different income categories. With all three programs, however, the FmHA bases loans on *adjusted* income, which it calculates by subtracting 5 percent from the borrower's gross income and $300 per dependent child.

Under the *Subsidized Loan Program,* persons with adjusted incomes of $11,200 or less qualify for interest credits, which may reduce the interest to as low as one percent. To illustrate how this program works, consider Alicia's situation. Her teaching position pays $11,500, and she has two children, which gives her an adjusted income of $10,325. FmHA figures a borrower should commit 20 percent of his or her income to housing. Based on that figure, Alicia has $2,065 available annually for housing, or $172 per month for payments on principal, interest, taxes, and insurance. Depending on the price of the house she chooses, Alicia would probably qualify for a one percent loan from FmHA.

Under the *Moderate Income Credit Program,* persons with adjusted incomes of between $11,200 and $15,600 qualify for loans of 9 percent directly from FmHA. Interest charged by FmHA is subject to constant review and revision, and you should check with your local FmHA office regarding rates and details of the program.

With both of the above programs, the FmHA conducts its own appraisals and will loan 100 percent of the appraised value of the house, which means that a down payment is not required. If the house appraises for less than you have offered, however, you will be required to pay the difference. Existing houses must meet certain structural safety standards set by FmHA, and new houses financed under these programs are subject to several examinations by FmHA inspectors to assure that they are properly built and meet the agency's structural and energy standards. Most houses financed by FmHA are relatively modest, and the maximum loan period is thirty-three years. Closing costs for these two loan programs are low—usually about $200–$300.

The *Above Moderate Income Program* enables persons with adjusted incomes of between $15,600 and $20,000 to obtain loans *guaranteed* by the FmHA from participating lending institutions (with the other two programs, funds come directly from FmHA). This fairly new program was implemented because of the lack of mortgage money in rural areas where required down payments on conventional loans are frequently 40 percent.

Under this program, the borrower pays a down payment: 3 percent of the first $25,000 of the home's cost and 5 percent on anything over $25,000 (the same as FHA down-payment requirements). The lender conducts the appraisal and handles all processing of the loan, although an FmHA inspector will examine the house to make sure it meets the agency's property standards and was properly appraised. The lender can't charge any points, but may charge you an origination fee of one percent of the loan amount. The other closing costs would be comparable to those on a conventional loan.

This program benefits persons like Kelly, a teacher who supplements her income by giving piano lessons. The mother of two, Kelly qualifies for a loan that will enable her to build a modest three-bedroom home on an acre of land. Tired of renting and unable to qualify for a conventional loan, Kelly has found a builder specializing in moderate-priced FmHA housing.

In most rural areas, there are a number of builders whose business consists almost exclusively of FmHA housing. Your local FmHA office can advise you of these individuals and perhaps suggest the more reputable professionals with whom you should deal.

To find out whether you qualify for FmHA financing, contact your local Farmers Home Administration office or write the FmHA, Department of Agriculture, Washington, D.C. 20250.

Alternative Mortgage Instruments

Grossly inflated housing prices, high interest, and tight money situations have locked many single, first-time buyers out of the market. Alternative mortgage instruments (AMIs), most of which require lower monthly payments in the early years of the loan and often a lower down payment than a conventional loan, have been created to assist first-time buyers. Many of these AMIs allow you to tailor loan terms to your particular financial situation and give you credit for your income potential. Some financial experts herald AMIs as the wave of the future in home lending.

This section will describe the various AMIs that may adapt to your needs. These instruments are not available everywhere, however, so you will have to contact local lending institutions to find out what is offered where you live. A good broker should be aware of the financing tools in your community and be able to direct you where to apply for these various instruments. In states where escalating payments or negative amortization (the charging of interest on interest because the lower payments in the initial years don't reduce the principal amount of the loan) are prohibited, some of these AMIs will not be allowed. That situation is expected to change as more single, first-time buyers enter the market and require creative financing instruments to afford their homes. You can speed that change by voicing your concerns to your state and federal legislators.

The Variable-Rate Mortgage (VRM)

VRMs are fixed principal loans with an interest rate that goes up or down, according to some key economic indicator (usually the cost-of-money index). This instrument, designed to protect lenders hurt by high inflation and the higher rates they must pay savers, can also benefit borrowers. Lenders sometimes offer VRMs with a slight discount from the current interest rate on conventional loans. The down payment you pay with a VRM is the same as that for a conventional loan.

To entice buyers to use VRMs, lenders frequently exclude prepayment penalties, and if you buy a new house, they may extend you your new loan at the same rate as the VRM on the house you sold. Lenders also may allow the buyer of your home to assume your variable-rate mortgage. (Most lenders don't permit buyers to assume existing conventional loans which were taken out when interest rates were much lower than those prevailing today. Bear in mind that the money market is subject to numerous and unpredictable events, and the lender must always keep a certain amount of funds on reserve and take in enough money in the form of savings and investments so he will have funds to loan out for mortgages. VRMs help to keep his inflows up.)

If you take out a VRM, the lender may allow you to later borrow against built-up equity without further credit checks. You should ask any lender offering VRMs to explain all the conditions of the loan to you—both advantages and disadvantages.

Consumer groups have strongly opposed VRMs, noting that anytime the lender hikes the interest rate, the borrowers' monthly mortgage payments increase. In fact, the borrower can usually choose to stretch out the life of the loan to a maximum of forty years rather than increase the monthly payments. Banking regulations limit the frequency and amount by which lenders can increase the interest. Interest rates can also decrease with VRMs, although that's not often the case.

All federally chartered savings-and-loan associations (S&Ls) can write VRMs. However, only one-half of the mortgages they write in a given year can be VRMs. Many state-chartered lending institutions can also offer these loans under state banking regulations. Some states have tie-in provisions, which give state-chartered associations lending authority comparable to that granted the federally chartered S&Ls. VRMs authorized for federal associations may have somewhat different terms than those offered by state-chartered institutions. You should make certain that you understand all conditions of any VRM you are offered.

VRMs have been very popular in California, where state-chartered lending institutions have been writing them since 1975. Proponents claim that this instrument will eventually replace conventional fixed-interest loans as the standard mortgage.

Federally chartered S&Ls, authorized by the Federal Home Loan Bank Board as of July 1, 1979, to offer VRMs, must follow these regulations:

- They can only change the interest rate once a year, and then by a maximum of one-half of one percent.
- They can only raise the interest rate 2.5 percent over the life of the loan, but there is no limit on how far the rate can fall.
- They must give you thirty days notice of any rate change and tell you what the new interest rate will be.
- When an increase is enacted, you have the option of: 1) prepaying the loan within ninety days of notification without penalty, 2) making higher monthly payments, 3) making the same payments but extending the payment period up to one-third of the original life of the loan.
- They must allow you to choose between a conventional loan and a VRM after fully disclosing the differences in rates and terms between the two instruments. The lender must show you side-by-side tables detailing "worst case" inflation scenarios with VRMs and their effect on your payments.
- If their key interest rate decreases, they must lower your mortgage rate.
- They can't increase the rate during the first year of the loan.

So on a thirty-year VRM of $90,000 at 10¾ percent interest, your first year's monthly mortgage payments would be $840.60, the same as they would be with a fixed-rate mortgage. Assuming the interest rate increased by one-half percent after one year, your monthly payment would be $874.80, and the third year it could increase to $909. If the interest rate climbed the full 2½ percent allowable, by the sixth year your monthly mortgage payments would be $1,013.40, whereas with a fixed-rate mortgage they would remain at $840.60 for the life of the loan.

On the other hand, if the interest rate declined by one-half percent, your second-year monthly payments would decrease to $807.30, and could conceivably drop as low as $676.80 by the sixth year, although that's not likely.

VRMs benefit most persons who sell their homes within a few years and can pass on their mortgages to the buyers. This is a common practice in California, where real estate changes hands rapidly.

In fact, most of these AMIs are structured so they benefit the buyer who remains in the home for only a few years, builds up his equity, and then moves on to another home. Only if you remain in the house for the life of the loan do you pay out the extra interest created by these AMIs. For example, with the VRM cited above, if you stay in the house for the full thirty years and the interest rate jumps the allowable 2½ percent, you'll pay out $358,570.80 compared with $302,616.00 with the fixed-rate mortgage. So as you're weighing the advantages of any mortgage, consider how long you're apt to remain in the house. And have the lender show you how much you'll pay out over the life of any loan you consider.

The Renegotiable Rate Mortgage (RRM)

The renegotiable rate mortgage, also known as the rollover mortgage, is similar to the VRM. However, the interest for the RRM is set at a fixed rate and then renegotiated at regular intervals, usually every three to five years. Federally chartered savings and loan associations are authorized to write RRM in which the interest rate can increase by five percentage points over the life of a thirty-year mortgage. But the maximum amount the interest may increase or decrease in any one year is one half of 1 percent.

For example, if you take out a RRM at 15 percent today, and interest rates are at 12 percent five years later when you renegotiate, the lender *must* offer you the mortgage at 12½ percent. On the other hand, if interest rates increase to 18 percent, the lender can raise your rate to 17½ percent. And five more years down the road, if interest rates are at 20 percent, the lender can hike your rate to that level. Whenever interest rates decrease, the lender *must* offer you the lower rate; but when they increase, the lender has the option of increasing your rate.

The refinancing occurs automatically, and you do not have to go through any additional approvals or closings, or pay any fees. The lender *must* notify you ninety days in advance of the renegotiation what the new interest rate will be. That notification will allow you time to shop around for another mortgage if you are not satisfied with the new rate. You cannot be charged a prepayment penalty if you decide to pay off the mortgage.

Because of the high rate of inflation, lenders will be more apt to offer the RRM, which gives them more flexibility than the VRM.

The Graduated-Payment Mortgage (GPM)

With the GPM, payments start low in the early years of the loan and increase to higher levels later. GPMs were developed to help young, first-time buyers with rising incomes who can't afford the high payments of conventional loans. The interest rate and length of the graduated mortgage are fixed, only the payment amount in the early period of the loan varies.

It's estimated that GPMs will enable about 2.5 million more first-time buyers to afford homes. Persons in the $15,000-to-$25,000 income range can benefit most from this program. The great advantage of GPMs is enabling persons to buy more expensive houses than their incomes would qualify them for with a standard mortgage or even with one of the basic government-backed loans.

There are some drawbacks to the GPM, however. Your payments will increase gradually over the first five or ten years of the loan and then level off at a figure higher than fixed-rate payments would be. During those initial years, you're paying primarily interest and building little equity in the house, and you will pay out more over the full term of the mortgage than you would with a conventional loan.

The most widely used graduated-payment mortgages have been those authorized by HUD and insured by the Federal Housing Administration. There are five different schedules for the FHA-insured graduated-payment mortgages, which can be used to purchase new or existing homes or condominiums. These payment schedule variations allow you to tailor your payments to your projected increases in income. After the initial five- or ten-year period of increase, payments level off for the remaining term (see Chart D).

The reason FHA-insured GPMs have succeeded where other GPM plans have not is the federal government's preemption of state laws prohibiting payment of interest on interest. Often, the lower monthly mortgage payments in the early stages of the loan don't cover all of the interest obligations. The unpaid interest is added to the principal mortgage balance, and the interest is paid on the entire balance; thus you get interest paid on interest. Of course, the immediate advantage of this situation for you is that your total monthly mortgage payment is tax deductible.

Anyone is eligible to apply for an FHA-insured GPM, available through FHA-approved lenders (usually mortgage banking companies). Your local FHA office can advise you which lenders in your area are making these loans.

You should ask the lender to explain which of the five GPM schedules is best suited to your income and income potential. The greater the rate or the longer the period of increase, the lower the first-year mortgage payments will be. If you expect rapid income increases, you might select a 7½ percent, five-year GPM. On the other hand, if you anticipate slower income growth, you might be better off with a 2 percent, ten-year plan.

Down payments required with the FHA-insured GPM are quite reasonable. On a $60,000 home, for instance, the down payment would range from about $3,000 to $6,700, depending on the plan you choose (see Chart D on p. 152). Because the mortgage cannot exceed 97 percent of the home's value, GPM down payments are generally a bit higher than those under the straight FHA-insured mortgage, but still lower than those required with a conventional mortgage loan.*

You will also have to pay a mortgage insurance premium of one-half percent per year on the average outstanding mortgage balance. The loan term required by FHA is thirty years, but the loan is assumable should you decide to sell.

The application and qualification procedures for the GPM are the same as those for the regular FHA-insured loan. You are required to have a satisfactory credit record, available cash for the down payment, and a steady income with the expectation of increases. FHA must inspect and approve the dwelling. Often the closing costs and loan processing fee you pay will be figured into the total loanable amount. The seller pays the points, but you should ask each lender with whom you check what he'll charge you for the closing costs.

The Flexible-Payment Mortgage (FPM)

Under this plan, you pay interest only, no principal, for the first five years of the loan. In the sixth year, payments are increased to a fixed level to retire the balance of the loan. The FPM was the first graduated payment plan to be implemented when housing inflation and a credit crunch made it impossible for single working persons to afford homes. Like the GPM, this plan assumes that your income will increase.

The reduction of payments during the first five years is not nearly as great as it is with GPMs, however. Therefore, you'll need a substantially higher income to qualify for an FPM than a GPM. FPMs have been used by first-time buyers whose incomes fell just short of qualifying them for conventional, fixed-payment loans. The down payment requirements are the same as with conventionals. The advantage, of course, is that during the first five years, your payments are totally tax deductible. The disadvantage is that you won't start building equity in your home until the sixth year of the loan.

The Pledged-Account Mortgage

This plan, offered by federal savings-and-loan associations under authorization from the Federal Home Loan Bank Board, substitutes pledged accounts for down payments. In other words, instead of making a down payment, you can secure your loan by pledging your savings account or the savings account of your family or your employer. This plan has a tremendous

---

*All terms—minimum down payment required, interest rate, maximum amount insurable, and the rate by which the annual payments increase—are subject to FHA review and adjustment to keep pace with changes in the housing and money markets. To compensate for the lower interest rate on these FHA-insured loans and the costs for processing them, lenders will charge points.

CHART D

SCHEDULE OF MORTGAGE PAYMENTS UNDER THE FIVE FHA-INSURED GPM PLANS

(Figures rounded to nearest dollar.)

DESCRIPTION OF THE PLANS

Plan I   Monthly mortgage payments increase by 2½% each year for five years.
Plan II   Monthly mortgage payments increase by 5% each year for five years.
Plan III Monthly mortgage payments increase by 7½% each year for five years.
Plan IV Monthly mortgage payments increase by 2% each year for ten years.
Plan V   Monthly mortgage payments increase by 3% each year for ten years.

LOAN FACTORS

Cost of house + Closing costs = $60,000   Interest Rate = 13%*   Term = 30 years

REQUIRED DOWN PAYMENT**MONTHLY PAYMENTS PLUS MORTGAGE INSURANCE***

YEAR	PLAN I DOWN PAYMENT $3,000 LOAN AMOUNT $57,000	PLAN II DOWN PAYMENT $4,850 LOAN AMOUNT $55,150	PLAN III DOWN PAYMENT $6,600 LOAN AMOUNT $53,400	PLAN IV DOWN PAYMENT $4,550 LOAN AMOUNT $55,450	PLAN V DOWN PAYMENT $6,700 LOAN AMOUNT $53,300
1	579 + 24 = 603	514 + 23 = 537	457 + 23 = 480	552 + 23 = 575	503 + 22 = 525
2	583 + 24 = 617	540 + 24 = 564	491 + 23 = 514	563 + 23 = 586	518 + 23 = 541
3	608 + 24 = 632	567 + 24 = 591	528 + 24 = 552	575 + 24 = 599	534 + 23 = 557
4	623 + 24 = 647	595 + 24 = 619	568 + 24 = 592	586 + 24 = 610	550 + 23 = 573
5	639 + 24 = 663	625 + 24 = 649	611 + 24 = 635	598 + 24 = 622	566 + 24 = 590
6	655 + 24 = 679	656 + 24 = 680	656 + 24 = 680	610 + 24 = 634	583 + 24 = 607
7	655 + 24 = 679	656 + 24 = 680	656 + 24 = 680	622 + 24 = 646	601 + 24 = 625
8	655 + 24 = 679	656 + 24 = 680	656 + 24 = 680	634 + 24 = 658	619 + 24 = 643
9	655 + 24 = 679	656 + 24 = 680	656 + 24 = 680	647 + 24 = 671	637 + 24 = 661
10	655 + 23 = 678	656 + 23 = 679	656 + 23 = 679	660 + 24 = 684	657 + 24 = 681
11	655 + 23 = 678	656 + 23 = 679	656 + 23 = 679	673 + 24 = 697	676 + 24 = 700

*The interest rate is subject to periodic review and adjustment by the Federal Housing Administration.
**Because the mortgage cannot exceed 97% of the home's value plus closing costs, there is a minimum 3% down payment on that amount. The down payment and loan amount are rounded to the nearest hundred dollars to comply with regulations of the secondary mortgage market.
****

potential to help first-time buyers afford homes. Unfortunately, it has not been widely implemented, so you'll have to check in your community for its availability.

The Flexible-Loan Insurance Program (FLIP)

FLIP was the first loan instrument to incorporate a pledged savings account with a graduated mortgage plan. FLIP can reduce your monthly mortgage payments by as much as 25 percent during the first year of the loan, thus qualifying you for a home you could not afford with a conventional or government-backed loan.

FLIP also eliminates the high down-payment obstacle by allowing you to put down as little as 5 percent with the purchase of private mortgage insurance (PMI). In order to get the greatest reduction on their initial monthly mortgage payments, however, most buyers put a minimum of 8 percent down. (For any down payment less than 20 percent, PMI is required.)

This is the way FLIP works. You put part of your down payment into a pledged savings account, and some of that money is withdrawn each month to supplement monthly payments, which are reduced for the first five years. The pledged account, which is in your name and accrues interest at the same rate as a regular savings account, can only be used to satisfy your mortgage obligation. In other words, you can't withdraw money from the account.

The FLIP Mortgage Corporation, Newtown, Pennsylvania, which created this plan, provides lenders a computer program to analyze your qualifications for mortgage financing under FLIP. Your payment schedule is then tailored to your means based on your current salary, the cash you have available for a down payment, and your projected income.

You deposit your pledged account with the lender when you take out your mortgage. The lender draws supplemental monthly payments from this account during the five-year period of reduced payments, wiping out the account in the process. (The pledged account acts both as a source of supplemental mortgage payments *and* an additional collateral for the mortgage.)

Because of the initial reduced payments you will pay more in interest over the life of the loan, and the subsequent level payments (beginning in the sixth year) are higher than the fixed payments of a conventional or standard government-backed loan.

FLIP has been well received by many lenders and can be offered by all federally chartered S&Ls and nationally chartered banks. It can be offered by state-chartered lending institutions where state banking regulations permit it. The plan has been especially well received by builders and developers who cater to single, first-time buyers. Those builders have often introduced FLIP into their communities as a means to market their homes. FLIP is available in most major housing markets, especially those in the Sunbelt states. As you're shopping for a FLIP mortgage, check with builders and developers of town houses and condos catering to singles, as well as with local lending institutions.

To illustrate how FLIP can work for you, consider the case of Chris. A twenty-nine-year-old professional with a $20,000 annual income, Chris would qualify for only a $40,000 house with a conventional loan. With a FLIP mortgage, she would qualify for a $47,700 house with a $5,500 cash down payment, part of which would go into her pledged savings account. With an 11 percent interest rate, Chris' first-year monthly mortgage payments with a FLIP loan would be $312.87 on her $47,700 home, compared to $401.90 with a conventional loan.

The second year, her monthly mortgage payments would increase to $336.28 (the interest remains fixed at 11 percent throughout the thirty-year loan). Her third-year monthly payments would be $360.99, the fourth year they would be $387.09, and the fifth year they would be $414.67. In the sixth year, they would level off at $443.78 and remain at that amount for the life of the loan.

If you apply for a FLIP loan, the lender is required to provide you a comparative disclosure statement showing how the terms of the FLIP mortgage compare with those of a standard loan.

Home Ownership Made Easier (HOME)

This program also incorporates a pledged savings account with a graduated-payment mortgage. Marketed by HOME, Inc., of Honolulu, Hawaii, this plan uses the five FHA-graduated payment mortgages in conjunction with the pledged account, which the borrower deposits when he closes the loan. Depending on the interest rate and plan selected, the borrower can reduce his first-year monthly mortgage payments by 8 to 25 percent, HOME claims.

HOME, Inc. charges you a fee of one-tenth of one percent of the initial loan amount, minus the initial savings account balance. The company notes that the lender may charge a higher interest for the HOME loan and may also require a minimum 20 percent down payment. HOME may be offered with less than 20 percent down if the borrower buys private mortgage insurance. As with the FLIP mortgage, after the graduated payments level off (either after five or ten years—see Chart D for the schedule of the FHA-GPMs), the monthly payments are higher than those with a conventional loan. You pay more over the life of a loan with HOME than with a conventional loan.

HOME claims that the plan results in a savings to the borrower during the first half of the loan, as the savings account is generally not depleted until after fifteen years. Thus, if you sell your home within fifteen years, you will pay out less with a HOME loan than you would with a conventional loan, according to HOME. The HOME mortgage is assumable.

HOME has not gained the acceptance that FLIP has, and only a few lenders have written these loans, which are still in the experimental stage. HOME has been approved for use by all federally chartered S&Ls and national banks. Some states have approved its use by state-chartered lending institutions. For further information about this new AMI, contact HOME, Inc., 745 Fort Street, Suite 1501, Honolulu, Hawaii 96813.

The Deferred-Interest Mortgage

Similar to the GPM, this mortgage lowers the monthly payments in the early years of the loan by allowing you to pay a lower interest rate initially. You will repay this deferred interest either later in the term of the loan with an extra fee or when you sell the house. Like all other instruments with reduced initial payments, this one assumes that your income will increase and is a mechanism to provide ownership to persons whose assets and salary don't qualify them under the conventional means.

You will have to check with your broker and various lenders for the availability of this mortgage where you live.

Inflationary pressures have created a special impetus for these AMIs and other mortgage innovations. Lenders, real-estate brokers, builders, and consumers are all searching for vehicles to make ownership more available to the growing number of single people seeking homes. A recent nationwide survey revealed that the overwhelming percentage of home buyers like the idea of having a choice among AMIs. They consider them pro-consumer and want alternatives to the standard fixed-payment mortgage.

Consequently, local banking and savings institutions across the country are experimenting with their own variations of AMIs. It behooves you, therefore, to make a thorough check of those alternatives available in your area. Call all the major lenders within any given metropolitan area—it may be that one has a branch in the suburb where you're looking that offers an AMI that will enable you to afford your home. Watch for new financial plans by following the real-estate section of your newspaper and reading local real-estate magazines.

One proposal now being promoted to assist home-buyers would provide a tax incentive for savings accounts used to accumulate down payments. Another proposal being considered would authorize three more graduated mortgage plans to assist persons in the $15,000–$24,000 income range.

This proposal, under Congressional consideration, would allow buyers the option of keeping initial payments at the lowest level for two or five years before they start to increase (under all of the existing GPMs, the payments begin to increase after the first year). It would increase the payments over a ten-year period at a rate of either 4 or 6 percent before leveling off for the remainder of the loan.

Proponents claim this plan will qualify the buyer for more house with a smaller down payment than any of the other graduated payment mortgages. They say it would reduce the monthly mortgage payments on a $55,000 house from $459 to $333 during the initial years of the loan, thus qualifying a buyer with an $18,000 income and a $2,250 down payment.

As a consumer, the bottom-line question you should always ask is how much any program will benefit you. Remember, lenders will only adopt programs that make money for them, so it pays to examine all aspects of any AMI carefully and compare them with other alternatives.

Other Methods of Financing

In addition to the mortgages already discussed, there are other methods of financing a home. These methods often evolve on a local level in response to any number of circumstances—usury limits, tight money, inflated prices, and seller's desire to delay capital gains. More of these techniques will undoubtedly be developed to assist the increasing number of single buyers entering the market. Some of these methods will benefit the individual with no money for a down payment or a limited amount of capital for a minimum down payment. Before you consent to any of these methods, you should have your attorney go over the terms of the agreement and get everything into a written contract. An experienced real-estate agent should be familiar with all of these methods, and may suggest some variations used in your area.

Contract Sale

Also called land contract or installment sales contract, contract sale is often used when money is tight and lenders aren't making mortgages. This is a method whereby the buyer makes direct payments to the seller, who retains the title to the property until the contract is paid off. Often after the buyer has built up some equity in the house and proven his credit-worthiness, he can take out a mortgage on the property and pay off the seller. Developers have often used this method to sell unimproved lots, although before entering into such an agreement you should be sure of *exactly* what you're getting, as this can also be a con scheme to unload a bad piece of property. Sellers of existing condo units may also sell on contract if lenders won't write mortgages for the condo (the case in some cities).

The immediate advantages to you may be a small down payment and no closing costs—a boon if you don't have a lot of cash on hand. However, you may pay a higher interest rate and more for the property than if you were buying it outright. For the risk he undertakes and the servicing of the loan, the seller frequently jacks up the price. It is your prerogative, of course, to barter for the down payment, interest rate, and sales price. If the seller is particularly anxious to get rid of the house, you may be able to negotiate very favorable terms. At this point, it's a good idea to get an attorney involved in the transaction.

Get an attorney familiar with contract sales who can negotiate an agreement to your benefit. You must have a written contract with the seller to protect your rights, and you shouldn't sign any documents until your attorney has reviewed them.

Usually it's much easier for the seller to repossess the property if you miss a payment than it is for a lender to foreclose a mortgage, so make sure you have all terms of the purchase spelled out in the contract. Since you won't have title to the property, it's possible for the seller to attach liens to the property, or even sell it if he chooses. A shrewd attorney will protect you against these possibilities in the contract. Since you won't own the property, you may not be able to make any major improvements or physical changes without the seller's consent. These terms should be spelled out in the contract.

The contract should give you the right to pay any default on the mortgage by the seller; otherwise you'll have no protection against a possible foreclosure. You should also have the right to pay taxes, insurance, or other obligations neglected by the seller, and whatever payments you make should be credited to your account with the seller. The contract should stipulate whether you can prepay the seller without penalty. In the course of drafting the contract, your attorney should make a title search to ensure there are no encumbrances, liens, or judgments against the property. He should also make sure that all parties concerned sign the contract—all persons named on the title must sign the contract. Like an offer to buy, the contract should contain a full description of the property.

Finally, make sure you have adequate insurance coverage on the property. You will be responsible for damage to the home, but you probably won't be covered by the seller's policy. Therefore, it's advisable that you maintain your own insurance policy with the seller as a co-insurer. Check with your insurance agent and attorney about how to obtain adequate coverage, and have these specifications included in the contract.

Older persons anxious to defer capital gains are often good sources for contract sales. Ask your broker about prospective contract sellers, and also watch the real-estate section of your newspaper for homes for sale by owner.

Buy the House, Lease the Land

In order to make new homes affordable for young, single buyers with good incomes but little down payment money, some developers will sell the house and lease the land under it. Says one East Coast developer, who markets his houses this way to twenty-five-to-thirty-four-year-old first-time buyers: "It's good for builders, bankers, and buyers. A builder who takes his profit on the leasing of his land and isn't too greedy about making a big profit up front on the houses he builds can provide many more houses for much less money and, thus, sell more of them to buyers who can't afford large down payments."

The lender gets a secure investment, and you, the buyer, can use the value of the land under the house to lower your down payment. The lender, working in conjunction with the developer, provides mortgages based on both the value of the land and the house. The lender holds first lien on the land.

To illustrate how this method can work for you, consider if you had to get an 80 percent mortgage on a house and lot valued at $47,000. The down payment would be $9,400. For a $40,000 house on a $7,000 leased lot, however, you could get a loan of $37,600 with a down payment of only $2,400. In addition to your monthly mortgage payments, you would pay $50 a month or so for the land lease.

Watch for builders or developers offering these terms in the real-estate section of your newspaper. And, of course, have your attorney go over the agreement before signing anything.

Assume the Mortgage

Lenders may refuse to allow buyers to assume conventional loans written at rates considerably below today's interest rates. (A clause in the existing mortgage may prohibit its assumption.) Or they will require that an assumed mortgage be refinanced at the current interest rate, in which case you may be better off completely refinancing the house with your own mortgage. Variable-rate mortgages (VRMs) are usually assumable, and FHA- or VA-backed loans are always assumable.

The problem with assuming a loan is that you may be required to come up with a substantial down payment in order to pay the seller for his equity built up in the home. That obstacle can be overcome by finding a seller who will take back a second mortgage (discussed in the next section). Closing costs will be non-existent or minimal.

Clark, who decided to relocate from his native New York to Albuquerque, got an extraordinary deal by assuming a loan. When he arrived in his Sunbelt city, Clark discovered that the decent apartment complexes all had long waiting lists. By shopping around, he found a recently divorced man anxious to get rid of his three-bedroom ranch home, which held only bad memories for him. The seller allowed Clark, who had only $1,500 in his pocket, to make a minimal down payment and took back a second mortgage. He then arranged for Clark to assume the existing VA-backed mortgage of 5½ percent—a whopping 5½ percent below the going rate then.

Second Mortgages

Particularly helpful for first-time buyers with limited cash, second mortgages have gained wide acceptance where real-estate prices are highly inflated and money is tight. California, the source of so many innovations, has pioneered the development of various second mortgage arrangements.

Basically this is the way it works. You want to buy a $50,000 house, but you only have $5,000 for the down payment and the lender insists upon an 80 percent mortgage of $40,000. The seller is anxious to unload the house, since he's already bought a new one and doesn't want to get stuck making two monthly mortgage payments. You ask the seller to take back a second mortgage of 10 percent or $5,000, and he agrees. Then you make monthly mortgage payments to the lending institution where you have your first mortgage, as well as monthly payments to the seller for the second mortgage, which is in the form of a note with the terms agreed on between you and the seller.*

You can negotiate with the seller on the interest rate, the amount of the monthly payments, and the length of the second mortgage. If the seller is extremely anxious to get rid of the house, he may agree to an interest below prevailing rates. However, he may require the entire $5,000 be due and payable within five years—a so-called balloon payment. In California, usually the real-estate agent negotiates the terms of the second mortgage and writes them into the purchase agreement. You should have your attorney look over this document to ensure that your interests are fully protected. This example may also be referred to as an 80-10-10 because you take an 80 percent first mortgage, the seller takes back a 10 percent second mortgage, and you put 10 percent down.

The flexibility of second mortgages is further illustrated by the deal Laurel worked out. After looking for several weeks, Laurel found a $65,000 house she wanted to buy, and the seller, who was being transferred to another town, wanted to sell rapidly. Laurel's income, however, did not qualify her for a mortgage at the going rates nor did she have the cash for a down payment. The seller still owed $53,000 on his 8 percent FHA-backed mortgage, which he would allow Laurel to assume. He also offered to take back a $6,000 second mortgage if Laurel could come up with the other $6,000 for the down payment.

Laurel's parents were willing to provide her a gift letter stating they would give her $6,000 which would not be repayable. (The gift letter is a formality required by the lender who usually will not allow borrowed money to be used for a down payment. Privately, Laurel and her parents agreed she would repay them the money later when she could afford it.)

So now Laurel had the $12,000 necessary to assume the loan. The seller put up the additional $6,000 in exchange for a note stipulating that he would receive 10 percent on his loan, to be repaid at the rate of one percent or $60 per month over five years, at which time the balance would be due. Laurel was delighted because she assumed the low monthly payments on the existing 8 percent mortgage (FHA-backed loans at the time of this writing were at 13 percent) in addition to the $60 she pays the seller. The seller was pleased because he didn't have to wait around for a new FHA loan to be processed and he has the $6,000 note at 10 percent—an excellent investment of his money. When the balloon payment is due in five years, he'll collect $5,225.40 from Laurel.

There are endless variations that can be worked out to accommodate both buyer and seller. You should know, though, that most lenders will only allow a 10 percent second mortgage with 10 percent down on an 80 percent mortgage. If you find the seller or broker trying to talk you into a deal where

---

*Some lenders forbid their borrowers to have second mortgages, so check practices in your area regarding this method. Also, sellers often demand interest rates higher than the current mortgage interest rates. Usually, the second mortgage will have to be paid off within a few years.

you put less than 10 percent down, check immediately with the lender. Some unethical brokers and anxious sellers do attempt illegitimate manipulations of this formula.

You can also go to a mortgage broker to arrange for a second mortgage or get a private individual willing to invest money at prevailing mortgage interest rates to take back a second mortgage for you. A good and reputable real-estate agent should be able to help you with these details.

The Wrap-Around Mortgage

This method is often used when money is tight and lenders aren't investing their money in mortgages, or when the seller is unwilling to take back a second mortgage. Assume that you want to buy a $50,000 house on which the seller now has a $40,000 mortgage at 8 percent. You want to put down $6,000, all the cash you have, and you want the seller to take back a second mortgage of $4,000 so you can assume his existing loan. The seller does not want you to asssume his loan but he does agree to take back a note from you on his terms.

The seller requires you to put down $6,000 and then he will give you a note for $44,000, the balance of the home's price, at 10 percent to be amortized over twenty-five years. (Your monthly payments to the seller will be about $386). The seller continues to make payments on his 8 percent $40,000 mortgage while you are making payments to him on $44,000 at 10 percent. In effect, what he has done is wrapped your mortgage around his mortgage, and his yield is going to be about 12 percent on the deal. Meanwhile, you're satisfied because prevailing mortgage interest rates are about 11 percent and you've gotten your loan for only 10 percent. This technique can also benefit the seller who wants to defer capital gains on the sale of his home.

Wraparounds have frequently been used in the Sunbelt states, where real-estate markets are really hot. The sellers often don't need the capital on their houses so they're willing to reinvest it with the buyers at a better rate of return than they could get through other channels.

Rent with the Option to Buy

You may have to work through a broker, but first check the rental section of your newspaper to find an owner willing to go this route. Most owners listing their houses want to sell them outright. If you don't have cash for a down payment, what you want to do is locate an owner who will lease to you for several years, with all or part of your rent payments going toward the purchase. You should by all means have a legal contract stipulating the terms of your agreement.

The seller may want you to buy the house by a certain date—at which time you will have to qualify for a mortgage. If a date is not specified, the contract should stipulate that when the owner decides to sell you have the first option to buy. An owner who does not want the capital gains of a sale may sell you the house on contract after the initial rental period. The immediate advantage to the owner is getting a good tenant who will take care of the property. Any number of arrangements can be worked out with a willing owner. Just make sure you get everything into a legal contract and all terms approved by your attorney before signing anything.

Buy the House through an Urban Homesteading Program

The U.S. Department of Housing and Urban Development (HUD), as well as many cities, have programs whereby you purchase a house for $1 or are given title to the property with the agreement that you rehabilitate it and live in it for a certain number of years. If you don't have much cash, but enjoy carpentry and are handy, this is an excellent avenue to home ownership. See "Rehabilitation Housing," p. 57, for more information on homesteading programs. If there isn't one in your community, you may be able to initiate one.

Sources of Financing

Failing to shop around for financing is a major mistake single buyers often make. They allow their brokers, attorneys, friends, or the sellers to recommend a lender. Consequently, they end up paying much more than necessary, and they may even become the victims of unscrupulous lenders who qualify them for larger loans than they can afford. When this happens, the buyer may be forced to default because he can't keep up the payments.

As a single buyer, it's essential that you work with an open-minded professional who can create a financial package geared to your needs and means. Shopping around for the right lender can help you avoid the painful and costly pitfalls that Dorrie experienced.

The public relations director for a large, Denver-based firm, Dorrie was steered by her broker to a mortgage banking company in which his brokerage owned the controlling interest (a fact she discovered too late). Dorrie, a first-time buyer, took the referral on good faith. But she ended up paying exorbitant fees due to delays caused by the mortgage company's fumbling and failure to process her loan promptly. The loan officer lost her employment-verification report and withheld other documents she legally had a right to review. In addition, the lender delved illegally into some personal matters, which Dorrie's attorney nevertheless advised her to provide in order to expedite the process and get the loan closed.

"It was a very emotionally distressing and draining ordeal for me. I was asked if I had always been honest and paid my debts. It really hit me in the ego—it was a demeaning experience and I got the impression that the loan officer had very antiquated ideas about doing business with a single woman," Dorrie said. "If only I had shopped around for the financing I could have saved myself so many hassles and I know now I could have gotten a much better deal. Since it was my first house, I didn't bargain for the sales price or for any of the loan terms—it didn't even occur to me to do so."

This section will outline the various sources of financing—both the conventional and innovative resources you can shop in your search to get the best terms. In Chapter 9, you'll be advised of the questions you should ask a prospective lender and the steps of the standard loan procedure, as well as your legal rights in the process. Some of the sources listed here may not be available in your community, but there should be other alternatives and it's up to you to discover them. A good ethical broker, attorney, or your personal banker should be able to assist you in this effort.

Savings and Loan Associations (S&Ls)

These banks write the majority of mortgages on one- to four-unit residential dwellings. Whether federally chartered (regulated by the Federal Home Loan Bank Board) or state chartered (regulated by your state banking commission), S&Ls frequently offer generous terms and are apt to be the first lenders to experiment with alternative mortgage instruments and creative financing. Of course, the lender's willingness to try innovative financing will depend on the economic climate in your community. If it's extremely conservative or if money is really tight, then the lender will probably not want to take on new risks.

In any event, you should check with local S&Ls regarding terms. And if you have an account with a savings-and-loan association, start there, where you may get more favorable terms as an established client. Single women should shop at those S&Ls established by and catering especially to women. These institutions often offer educational courses in home buying and financing for their clients.

Commercial Banks

Commercial banks are the next major underwriters of mortgage loans. They usually require larger down payments and may stop writing mortgages altogether when money is tight. If you're a long-standing client of the bank, however, the institution may make a special exception for you—or if your parents or other relatives have large sums on deposit at the bank.

Also check the bank's trust department, which is a completely different division than the mortgage loan department. Often the trust department will have clients willing to invest their money in mortgages, and you can work out a deal with a trust officer. The trust department can also be an excellent source for second mortgages.

Women's banks provide some special educational services for female home buyers. Check the Yellow Pages for women's banks in your area, or write the National Association of Bank Women, Inc., 111 East Wacker Drive, Chicago, Illinois 60601, for a list of women's banks.

Both S&Ls and commercial banks often refuse to write government-backed mortgages because of the red tape and time involved, so you may have to shop other sources for those loans.

Mutual Savings Banks (MSBs)

Mutual savings banks, which were the nation's first savings banks, write both conventional and government-backed mortgages. MSBs concentrate on writing home mortgages, and many of them offer alternative mortgage instruments. Mutual Savings Banks are chartered to operate in seventeen states: Massachusetts, New York, Connecticut, Maine, New Hampshire, New Jersey, Washington, Pennsylvania, Rhode Island, Vermont, Indiana, Maryland, Wisconsin, Alaska, Delaware, Minnesota, and Oregon.

Most of the approximately 500 MSBs operate under state banking charters, although federally chartered MSBs have recently been authorized. If you live in one of the seventeen states where MSBs operate, be sure to check terms offered by these savings institutions.

Mortgage Banking Companies

Mortgage banking companies write the majority of FHA- and VA-backed mortgages, but operate entirely differently than the previously mentioned lenders. Mortgage banking companies (also called mortgage service companies, mortgage companies, or mortgage banks) do not accept deposits from customers. Their sole function is issuing and packaging mortgages into portfolios, which they sell to large investors or into the secondary mortgage market. For this reason, mortgage bankers maintain close contact with local real-estate agents and builders, who are urged to bring their buyers qualified for government-backed loans (a major source of financing for single buyers) to the mortgage banking firms. The mortgage banking companies earn their money from the buyer through fees charged for originating and servicing the loan.

Mortgage banking companies have come under fire for charging excessive fees. Congressional hearings into mortgage banking practices have found these lenders engaging in fraud and shoddy practices at the buyer's expense. Specifically, mortgage bankers have been accused of fraud in falsifying the income levels and credit of home buyers. Congressional reports also cite mortgage bankers for failing to screen buyers properly and to determine if the property is structurally sound and fairly valued. The result of these abuses is invariably that the home buyer defaults on his loan, loses his house, and the mortgage banker recoups his investment through the 100 percent FHA-insured program.

Mortgage banking companies are also under federal scrutiny for illegal charges to buyers and failure to comply with consumer legislation and antidiscrimination regulations. Unfortunately, *there in no one public agency that regulates the lending practices of mortgage bankers,* hence the widespread abuses. Mortgage bankers are exempt from the reporting requirements of other lending institutions. HUD is supposed to supervise mortgage bankers, but that relationship poses a serious conflict of interest, since it is also HUD's duty to encourage the issuance of government-backed loans, which in many areas only the mortgage banking companies will handle.

Chances are, if you apply for the popular FHA-graduated payment mortgage or any other government-backed loan, you will obtain it through a mortgage banker. So make sure you establish from the outset the nature of the animal with which you're dealing. Mortgage bankers vary in size and may be part-time businesses linked to real-estate firms, the central organization in major conglomerates, or subsidiaries of large banks. They may operate only locally or throughout a number of states.

If you feel yourself being steered to a mortgage banker by your broker or builder, start asking questions immediately: Demand a complete explanation of the mortgage banker's procedures in processing your application and loan. Ask how much you'll be expected to pay in fees—get it in writing if possible. Ask for a preliminary written estimate of closing costs, to which you are legally entitled (more on this in Chapter 9). And make sure the loan officer shows you precisely how your income and assets qualify you for your loan.

Mortgage banking companies have been accused by FTC officials of discriminating against minority persons and female heads of households. If you sense any irregular or illegal activity, contact the consumer protection division of the Federal Trade Commission, Washington, D.C., 20580, or a local FTC office. Unfortunately, the interlocking interests of the local real-estate industry often preclude your chances of getting another professional involved in the transaction to go to bat for you.

Beware that many real-estate agents will refuse to jeopardize their special relationships with local lenders to protect the interests of the buyer or seller, even when their legal rights are violated. Builders and attorneys who sit on the boards of the major lending institutions usually don't want to rock the boat. If you know the laws, you will be your own best advocate because you can threaten to present the illegal activity to the regulatory agency of the violator.

Credit Unions (CUs)

Credit unions, which are non-profit cooperatives of persons with a common bond of employment, association, or residence, are excellent sources of mortgage loans. State-chartered credit unions have been able to make long-term mortgages for years, and in 1977 Congress authorized federal credit unions to write thirty-year conventional and government-backed mortgages. If you belong to a credit union, that should be one of the first sources you shop. Not all CUs make mortgage loans, but many of the larger ones are establishing mortgage loan departments to service their members.

Because of their non-profit nature, credit unions can make loans at more favorable rates than other lenders. For example, under National Credit Union Administration (NCUA) regulations, the maximum loan origination fee that federal CUs can charge is one-half of one percent (except for government-backed mortgages, which require a one percent origination fee). Down payment requirements may be lower than those of other lenders, and interest rates may be slightly lower than prevailing market rates.

Also, the interest rates charged by federal CUs must include such items as the appraisal and the credit report fees, which other lenders generally tack on in addition to the base interest rate. There are no prepayment penalties, and interest must be paid on all of your money held in escrow accounts (for insurance and taxes). Most other lenders do not pay interest on escrow accounts, even though they are holding your money and using it. Closing costs are apt to be much lower at your credit union, which should process the loan rapidly. Credit union officials, who essentially work for you, should also be able to offer you sound financial counseling.

NCUA, which oversees the operations of all federal CUs, authorized these guidelines for one- to four-unit dwellings purchased as primary residences. Loans for vacation homes, investment property, raw land, and lots are usually available under a ten- or twelve-year mortgage program, depending on your credit union's practices. CUs may also be an excellent source for second mortgages and may allow you to borrow against share drafts for a down payment.

Small state-chartered CUs, which don't have the dollar volume of federal credit unions, may not be as extensively involved in the mortgage market. It's worth checking, however, to see what terms they offer. In any event, your credit union officer may have some valuable insights into the financial market in your area that will prove helpful to you.

To assure ample protection to members, NCUA regulations prohibit tie-in arrangements with real-estate brokers, insurance agents, attorneys, and other actors in the real-estate transaction. NCUA rules also forbid kickback or conflict-of-interest situations in which any CU official or employee would receive any compensation from another professional involved in the transaction. Fees charged the buyer are limited to the amount necessary to reimburse the credit union for its expenses—a big plus for you.

State Housing Finance Authorities (HFAs)

State housing finance authorities have been established in most states to make low-interest mortgages available to low- and moderate-income persons. These agencies raise money through the sales of tax-exempt bonds and then turn around and allocate funds to lending institutions throughout the state. The lenders make the loans, which range two to three percentage points below prevailing market rates, to qualifying borrowers on a first-come, first-served basis. To obtain these low-down-payment loans, many buyers have spent the night outside the bank waiting for the doors to open in the morning.

For Roger, a recent college graduate, his wait paid big dividends. Roger, who was on his first job and renting an apartment, hadn't planned to buy a house until he heard about the terms offered through his state's HFA. The prevailing interest of 10¾ percent completely locked Roger out of the market, but under the HFA program he got an 8 percent, thirty-year loan for

$40,000 and bought a two-bedroom suburban ranch house near his place of employment. His monthly payments are $293.52 (compared to $373.40, the monthly cost for a 10¾ percent loan). The total cost of Roger's loan over thirty years will be $79,246, as opposed to $134,424 with the market-rate loan.

Your real-estate agent or a local lender should be able to tell you whether your state has a HFA program and if you qualify for it. In Roger's state, persons with an adjusted gross income of $17,300 or less qualified for the loan (the adjustment is figured by deducting 10 percent from the buyer's gross annual income and $300 for each dependent).

Most HFAs set a limit on the maximum loan amount. And to hold down the buyers' costs, limits are also set on the amount lenders can charge for originating and servicing the loans.

FHA- and VA-backed loans are usually available under the HFA programs at the lower interest rate.* Conventional loans are offered with only 5 percent down and the purchase of private mortgage insurance. Every effort is made to keep the down payment and other costs low. Often, a certain percentage of the HFA loans must be made within the cities and another percentage must be made within small or rural communities where moderate-income persons have difficulty obtaining credit. These loans can be used to buy new or existing houses, to build new houses, or to rehabilitate older homes.

The guidelines for these programs vary from state to state, so you should check with a local lender about the terms and availability of these funds where you live. If you can't find a lender to answer your questions, contact your state legislator, who can tell you where to obtain the necessary information.

Local Mortgage Revenue Bond Programs**

Local mortgage revenue bond programs have been launched by a number of cities to assist low- and moderate-income persons (primarily those in the $14,000–$25,000 bracket) buy homes in town. Similar to the HFA programs, these local bonds are designed to generate money for loans to persons locked out of the conventional mortgage market, where down payments are often as much as 30 to 40 percent.

Basically, this is how these programs work. Local governments sell the bonds on which interest is exempt from federal income tax, and often state tax, too. Proceeds are turned over to local lenders who make low-interest mortgages to home buyers. Because the tax-free feature enables the cities to borrow at a relatively low rate, the mortgages carry rates two to three percentage points below prevailing market rates. In some cities, these programs give preference to first-time buyers.

---

*The FHA and VA set the maximum interest that can be charged on these government-backed loans, but the individual lender is free to charge a lower interest. When you're dealing with a conventional lender, he will probably charge the maximum allowable rate.

Chicago, which inaugurated this concept with the sale of $100 million in bonds, offered home buyers mortgages at 7.99 percent when the conventional rate was 10 percent. Down payment requirements were as low as 5 percent, a common feature of these programs (though you'll usually have to buy mortgage insurance whenever you put down less than 20 percent). Municipalities eager to retain young, middle-income home owners in order to stabilize or revitalize older city neighborhoods and to increase their tax bases are enthusiastic about these programs.

Most cities set maximum income standards for eligibility, and there may be a maximum loan amount. These programs are perfectly tailored to the needs of city-oriented singles who are apt to fall within the income specifications. Some cities stipulate the types of home and locations for which this financing can be used. It may not be used for investment property but usually can be used to buy condo or co-op apartments, new or existing detached houses, as well as duplexes.

Some states prohibit these local bond programs. And amidst charges that some cities have abused these loans by cutting interest payments for upper-income buyers, Congress is considering legislation that would limit these loans to low- and moderate-income persons. Their availability may well depend on how responsibly they're administered within the next few years. Presently, they are expected to provide a major source of financing for first-time buyers throughout the eighties.

You should find out if your city now offers or plans to offer such a program and if you qualify for it—check with a broker or lender. If such a program is being proposed where you live, it may be your avenue to ownership. These loans are usually processed quite rapidly and can save you thousands of dollars. Of course, they are in great demand, so you may have to wait in line to get in your application. That's why it pays to know in advance the eligibility requirements and when they will be offered. Then, if necessary, you can select a home in an area that will better qualify you for one of these bargain-basement mortgages.

Insurance Companies

Insurance companies often get involved in the mortgage market because these long-term loans are a secure investment of their funds. Many major insurance companies do not originate loans, but only buy mortgages in the secondary market. If an insurance company in your community writes mortgages, that can be an excellent source of financing for you. Frequently, insurance companies write the FHA- and VA-guaranteed loans. If you hold a policy with an insurance company, ask your agent whether the firm will write your mortgage loan. A good real-estate agent should be able to tell you which insurers offer loans, or you can call the insurance offices yourself—ask if they have a mortgage loan department. Large companies may make loans through their branch offices, which can be spread out over several states. Also, if you work for an insurance company, you may get preferred rates on a mortgage from your employer.

Your Company

Your company may have a program for helping employees finance their homes, particularly transferees. Many large companies make long-term mortgages, and others give short-term loans (often second mortgages) to supplement other mortgage sources. You will have to *inquire* about these services, since they're not apt to be offered you on a silver platter. There seems to exist a philosophy within established corporations that single persons do not require the perks provided family men, the traditional company executives. Fortunately, as more single men and women enter the executive ranks, these discriminatory practices are being broken down, albeit slowly.

More and more companies are subsidizing loans for transferred employees. For example, American Airlines, which moved its headquarters from New York to the Dallas-Fort Worth area, arranged for up to $60 million in mortgage loans at three Dallas banks for its employees. The interest rate was a low 8¾ percent, and American made up the difference to the banks (the prevailing interest rate was 10 percent) by keeping compensating balances on deposit. If you're a first-time buyer being transferred, this is an excellent time to tap company resources to get your home.

Also, many private universities are well endowed with funds for mortgages or will use their influence to secure mortgages for faculty members and administrators.

The Seller's Company

The seller's company is a possible source if the seller is being transferred. Most firms are eager to expedite an employee's transfer and may use their influence to secure a mortgage for the buyer, make a short-term loan to the buyer, or even endorse the buyer's note. Firms perform these services rather than buying the transferee's home outright and getting stuck with the cost of reselling it.

Your Brokerage Firm, Builder, or Developer

Brokerage firms, builders, or developers will often reserve funds at local lending institutions for mortgage loans to their clients. This is a common practice when money is tight. Major brokerage firms and developers reserve large sums on which they pay interest to ensure that their clients will be able to get financing. Incidentally, that's why the lending institutions want brokers, builders, and developers on their boards of directors.

The Seller

The seller may be willing to help you finance the home by taking back a note in lieu of cash or another method. For example, if the seller owns his home free and clear, a new first mortgage (short-term, typically ten years) can be drawn up between you and the seller. The seller carries back a note and a first mortgage on the property for an agreed-upon amount of money. Usually the monthly payments are not enough to amortize the mortgage during the ten-year period, so at the end of the ten years you make a balloon payment to the seller. By that time you will have built up enough equity in the house that you can refinance it with a mortgage from a local lender, and part of your funds you'll give to the seller for the balloon payment.

Here's how Lynda arranged the financing on her $50,000 home with the seller. The seller had a $40,000 loan which he would allow Lynda to assume. She only had $6,000 for the down payment, however. But she was starting a new job and her employment contract stipulated that she would get a $2,000 Christmas bonus. So the seller, who was anxious to get rid of the house, agreed to take back a second mortgage of $2,000 amortized over five years at four percent, and a third mortgage of $2,000 at no interest due on January 1.

If the seller is not in a position to take back loans, you should have him check with his lender. Often the seller's lender will write you a mortgage because he can increase the interest from the existing loan, hence his income.

Pensions Funds, Unions, Fraternal Organizations

These organizations can also be sources of financing or second mortgages. If you belong to a union, see if it has a loan program. Check whether your company's or union's pension funds are invested in mortgages. Your immediate family or close relatives may also help you with these sources. Ask around. Mortgages represent a secure, long-term investment and many different organizations are now putting their funds into them because of the high rate of return.

Private Investors or Relatives

Certain individuals may be willing to write you a mortgage. Often wealthy individuals eager to put their money in high-yielding investments will make their desires known to lenders, real-estate brokers, or they may even advertise in the newspaper or financial journals. Also, if you have wealthy relatives with the capital to invest, approach them about a loan.

9

Negotiating the Loan Terms and Settlement Costs

Since lenders sometimes apply stricter standards to single persons, it's crucial that you understand the steps of the loan process and shop for the best terms. This will put you in a position to bargain for the financial package and deal with discriminatory practices you encounter. These illegal, often institutionalized procedures, are usually subtly disguised maneuvers that you must watch for or they'll cost you more or prevent you from getting a loan.

Lenders, the conservative bastion of the financial community, often hold strong opinions on just which types of persons should be granted mortgage loans and the kinds of homes on which they will lend. For example, lenders have a number of ways of discouraging loans to two single, unrelated persons. Fundamentally, that's an illegal practice, but they have methods of getting around the law. Some lenders only like to loan on houses in certain price ranges of certain ages and sizes in particular neighborhoods. Other lenders prefer making loans only to persons who have owned homes before.

Furthermore, many lenders affect superior and dictatorial roles to intimidate the single buyer, who is expected to assume a hat-in-hand posture. Brokers usually contribute to this charade by telling you that getting the house depends on meeting all of the lender's demands. Or they will only show you "safe" houses, on which they know you can get a mortgage.

Privately, brokers have quite another opinion. As one broker, who spends much time wooing lenders, bluntly admits, "Bankers are pompous asses and intimidators. The borrowers carry the entire freight, and the origination fees they pay are pure profit to the lenders."

So what can he do about it? Nothing, he claims. "The lenders hold the cards, and they can get by with anything they want. If you fight them—even if what they're doing is illegal—you just don't get the money. I must cultivate my contacts with lenders—they have got to be your buddies, and we are at their mercy."

Fortunately, many of the blatant, as well as subtle, discriminatory practices are being broken down by citizens' activist groups. The groups are demanding to see loan records as authorized by the Community Reinvestment Act and Home Mortgage Disclosure Act. Both of these federal laws (see Chapter 10, which discusses the antidiscrimination statutes) require lenders to disclose their lending patterns, and provide sanctions against the lenders for selective and discriminatory practices. Of course, the financial institutions are fighting desperately to get these "unnecessary" laws repealed.

Now, against that backdrop, realize that you *do* have certain rights in the financial transaction. You are going to pay a substantial amount of interest and other fees for the money you borrow, and therefore, you deserve equal and dignified treatment.

Prepare yourself for the financial transaction by asking your real-estate agent to explain the loan process to you. Most brokers just gloss over the particulars, since this isn't their field, but their money does depend on your getting the loan and they're paid to understand the entire transaction. So grill your broker as much as you want about the process. Likewise, before applying for a loan, ask the loan officer to explain the process to you. If there's something you don't understand, stop him and ask for further amplification on that point. If you become confused, ask him to explain everything again.

Among lenders there often exists a resolute determination to preserve the mortgage transaction in language incomprehensible to the layperson. This leaves ample margin for abuse and can have dire consequences for the single buyer, as Janis will attest.

A thirty-three-year-old medical technologist, Janis was buying her first home by herself (having previously purchased a home with her former husband). She thought all the details had been taken care of and was feeling quite satisfied with how smoothly the transaction was proceeding. Then just three days before the loan closing date, she discovered that she would be required to pay $1,200 in closing costs at the closing.

Nobody—neither her loan officer nor her broker—had clearly informed her that the closing costs were due at the time of closing. And, in fact, the lender had violated federal law by failing to give her a copy of a special settlement costs information booklet that would have explained the procedure.

Janis panicked, since she had used all of her savings for the down payment. Fortunately, her parents were able to give her an emergency loan for the needed amount. But had they not, the whole deal would have been off, and the seller could have sued Janis for not making good on her legal commitment in the offer to buy.

Janis' broker adamantly insisted that she had received a copy of the settlement costs booklet and had been "made aware" of when her closing costs were due. He also maintained that the loan officer had explained the process, including the closing costs. Janis said the lender did briefly describe the process, which she had asked him to repeat.

"He seemed really annoyed with my stupidity and made me feel extremely foolish," recalled Janis, who, as a result, didn't ask any more questions and didn't have further contact with the loan officer.

Questions You Should Ask the Lender

When you're shopping for mortgage money, you should make a list of questions that you ask each lender with whom you visit, and keep separate records of their responses. Then when you've completed your shopping, you can compare their terms and decide where you will get the best deal. Here are some of the questions that should be on your inquiry list:

- What is your interest rate?
- What is the minimal down payment? If I put more down, can I get a lower interest rate? Do you require less down on a new house?
- Will private mortgage insurance be required? How much will that cost? Can I shop for my own private mortgage insurer?
- Do you allow second mortgages?
- Do you make government-backed mortgages?
- Do you make variable-rate mortgages or offer any of the other alternative mortgage instruments? If so, find out which ones, and the terms under which they're offered.
- Will you consider my income potential in qualifying me for a loan?
- How much can I expect to pay in closing costs? Can you give me a rundown of the various closing costs? If I pay a higher interest rate, is it possible to reduce the closing costs? (This is important if you're dealing with a limited amount of cash for the up-front costs.)
- What items will I be required to escrow? Often the lender will require you to place money in a reserve account (also called an escrow) for your property taxes, home insurance, and private mortgage insurance. If he requires escrows, ask whether he pays interest on these accounts.
- Can I use my own attorney to examine the title and handle other closing procedures?
- Is title insurance required? If so, can I choose the title insurance company?
- Can I select the providers of the settlement services?
- What is the maximum repayment period you allow?
- Approximately how long will the loan approval take?
- Will there be a prepayment penalty if I pay off the loan in advance of maturity? If so, how much and how long will it apply? Many lenders stick a steep prepayment penalty into the loan if you pay if off within three to five years. This is a common practice in California, where real estate turns over fast. Often the seller will require the buyer to use his mortgage lender (who then waives the prepayment penalty), or he will charge the buyer for the prepayment penalty.
- Will there be an escalation clause in the mortgage? Getting this information now can help you avoid nasty surprises later. Andy, for instance, was so excited about purchasing his first home and so trusting of the male loan officer that he didn't quiz him at all about the terms. Andy simply signed the documents without reading through them. Then one month after buying his $45,000 home, Andy discovered that the mortgage agreement stipulated that the bank could raise the interest rate to any level after three years.

- Will you require or permit a cosigner? If the lender requires a cosigner, you should find out why. This may be illegal. If you plan to buy with another single person, inquire whether the lender will consider both of your incomes for loan qualification.
- Will you include a home improvement loan as part of the financial package? This can be important if you're buying an older home or one that needs energy upgrades. Ask what terms he'll offer on the improvement loan.
- Will the loan be assumable? If you sell and the buyer assumes the loan, ask the lender whether he will charge you an assumption fee, raise the interest rate, or require other terms.
- What is the late payment charge? How late can my payment be before I'm charged? (Late payments can affect your credit rating, so you should avoid them, or go explain your circumstances to the lender if you get in a financial bind.)
- Will I be able to borrow additional money against the mortgage after I have paid off part of the original loan?

It's advisable to visit with several lenders when you're shopping for a home as the lender may offer you some good tips and perhaps even leads on prospects. If you already have a specific house in mind, you should ask the lender the terms he will offer on the house based on its price, your income, and assets. It will be helpful if you have filled out Chart B from Chapter 3 (page 12) and can show the lender the monthly breakdown of your budget and the funds you have available for housing.

Most lenders will only quote you their current mortgage rates and terms over the telephone. To get specific answers, you'll need to make an appointment to visit with each lender in person. Federal laws prohibit lenders from "pre-screening," that is, telling a person over the phone that he doesn't qualify for a loan based on his income or the institution doesn't make loans in a certain area. To avoid violating these laws, most lenders will require a face-to-face meeting to discuss the particulars of a mortgage loan.

After you get the suggested information from several lenders, you should go over your lists carefully, evaluating the terms to determine which institution will give you the most favorable financial package.

The Down Payment

Before applying for a loan, you should consider carefully how much you will put down. A 20 percent down payment on an average-priced home of $70,000 is $14,000. If you have that much to put down, you may be able to get a lower interest rate on the loan, your monthly payment will be smaller, you'll pay less over the life of the loan, and you'll build equity in your home more rapidly.

If you're a first-time buyer with limited cash reserves, however, a $14,000 down payment may be impossible. Plus, you'll need an additional $1,000 or so for closing costs and some cash for other expenses—moving, appliances, etc.

Some financial counselors advise putting the minimum amount down, noting that because of inflation you'll pay off your loan with cheaper dollars. If you have a large income but little savings, obviously you'll make a low down payment. But if your income is in the low to moderate range, you should put down as much as you can and keep your monthly payments low. Likewise, if your income fluctuates, you're better off keeping your monthly payments as small as possible.

Here are some alternatives to consider if you have a limited amount to put down:

- Apply for a FHA-backed loan or a VA-guaranteed loan, if you're eligible.
- Apply for one of the low-down-payment FHA-graduated payment mortgages or other alternative mortgage instruments with a low-down-payment requirement.
- Apply for a 5 to 10 percent down conventional loan covered by private mortgage insurance (PMI). With PMI, you could get a $50,000 home with as little as $2,500 or $5,000 down. Of course, you will pay extra for the private mortgage insurance. On a 5 percent down payment, the PMI premium is one percent of the mortgage amount, payable at closing. On a down payment of 10 percent or more, the premium is often one-half of one percent. After that first fee, you pay one quarter of one percent per year on the declining balance, and the premiums are included in your monthly mortgage payments. Premiums continue until you have paid off 20 to 25 percent of the mortgage, which takes about eleven years on a thirty-year loan. PMI is available through banks, S&Ls, and mortgage banking companies. About a dozen companies nationwide offer this insurance, with rates about the same everywhere.
- Obtain a second mortgage to cover part of the down payment, if the lender allows it. If you take out a second mortgage, you will get title to your home, but the lender of the second mortgage will get a second claim to your property. Also, because of the increased risk to the lender, the rate for the second mortgage may be higher than that on your first mortgage loan. Usually there's a balloon payment with a second mortgage. If you're buying a new home, look for a builder who will give you a low-cost second mortgage.
- Simply shop for a low-priced house. As one broker in the inflationary California market advises: "I tell my clients to buy an igloo if necessary. At the rate real estate appreciates here, I suggest they stay in the house for one year, by which time the property will have appreciated enough that I can get them into something more to their liking." Leslie, who works with many single, first-time buyers, says she then sells their original homes for no commission as a client service. She realizes that she'll get a commission on the house they buy, as well as many referrals from satisfied buyers and sellers.
- Shop for a house being sold on contract. Older persons often will defer part of the down payment, give you a generous second mortgage, or agree to terms to help you buy the home. Many older persons are very sympathetic to the plight of young, first-time buyers today. If they think you'll take good care of their home, which they have lived in for twenty or thirty years, they may bend over backward to work out a deal to help you. A good broker should be able to assist you, but you should also follow the real-estate ads for homes for sale by owner. Often contract sellers don't want to pay brokers' commissions.
- Buy with another person if the lender will consider both of your incomes on the loan application.

If after exploring these alternatives, you find you still need additional money to cover the down payment and closing costs, here are some methods of coming up with the extra cash. You'll have to make sure, though, that the lender will accept these methods. Many lenders, for example, refuse to allow you to borrow any part of the down payment.

- Get a gift letter from your parents or a friend. The gift letter has to state that the individual is giving you the money outright, with no expectation of repayment. Privately, however, you may arrange to repay the funds.
- Sell mutual funds, shares of common stock, or other assets.
- Ask your stockbroker for a loan. Brokers often lend money at rates up to 40 percent cheaper than what a bank would charge. In order to do this, you will have to have an account with your broker, as well as some stocks, bonds, or other securities to use as collateral.
- Borrow against the current value of stocks, bonds, treasury bills, or other securities. Generally, you can borrow up to 50 percent of the current value of your listed stocks, 70 percent of listed bonds, and as much as 90 percent of the value of T-bills and other types of government securities. If the current value of your securities falls, though, the value of your collateral falls and your broker will issue a margin call for more money to bring your collateral up to the required limit.
- Borrow against an interest-bearing savings account or certificates of deposit (CDs). Savings banks and S&Ls will usually lend you an amount equal to between 90 and 100 percent of any money in your account. If you borrow from a savings bank, you'll have to repay it on a fixed schedule. S&Ls don't always require a fixed repayment schedule, but you do have to pay the interest quarterly. Check with your lending institution to see how much you'll be charged in interest. When you borrow against CDs, you're not required to make monthly payments and can pay off the loan as you're able. Keep in mind that you may have a better chance of getting your mortgage from the thrift institution where you have your savings or CDs.
- Get a loan from your credit union. After you've been with your employer for a while, your credit union may loan you the needed amount on signature. For example, at one large company, employees can borrow $3,000 on a signature loan after five years of employment. If they have collateral to put up, they can borrow up to $25,000 at the preferred CU rates—usually lower than those of commercial banks or thrift institutions. Most credit unions will take repayment through deductions from your paychecks—a further convenience.
- Borrow against the cash value of your whole life insurance policy. This is often the cheapest source of money—you pay an interest rate of only 5 to 8 percent, depending on when and where you bought your policy. If you don't have a whole life insurance policy, check into borrowing against the cash value of your family's policy. These loans don't come due at a set date; they remain in effect as long as you wish. But, the benefits payable to a beneficiary under a life policy will be reduced by the amount of any loan outstanding, plus any interest due. Contact your insurance agent or write directly to the insurance company to get the specifics on your policy. Usually these loans can be made in a matter of days. Term insurance policies, including those group policies supplied workers by employers, build up no cash value.

- If you own your car outright, borrow against it or the cash value of any other valuable asset.
- If your folks are willing to help out but don't have the cash to loan you, ask them to consider borrowing against the equity in their home. Then they can give you the money with a gift letter.
- Check whether your State Housing Finance Authority makes loans for down payments. Some states will do this for first-time buyers with certain maximum income requirements.

Now, if you still don't have the necessary money for the down payment and other up-front costs, here are a few additional measures that may help, although they'll require a bit more time:

- Take a second job or do some free-lance work.
- Undertake a "forced" savings plan, where money is automatically deducted from your paycheck or bank deposit and put into savings. If you belong to a company credit union, have the CU deduct so much from your paycheck. You'll earn a higher rate of interest at most credit unions than at other thrift institutions. If you don't belong to a credit union, have your bank automatically transfer 5 to 10 percent of each deposit into your savings account.
- Sacrifice all vacations and unnecessary expenditures, until you have the needed capital.
- Invest in short-term certificates of deposit, or shop around to see what would be the best short-term investment of your money to produce the funds you'll need.

The Loan Process

Knowing your rights is every bit as important as understanding the steps of the loan process. Lenders are supposed to stick to factual data in collecting information from you and in evaluating your ability to carry a loan. Although most professionals will treat you respectfully and fairly, there are also those who will wax judgmental and wander beyond the legal border.

You need to be on your toes at every stage of this process, particularly if you're buying with another single person—whether a same-sex friend or a friend of the opposite sex. Pay close attention to the questions the lender asks you, make notes if you question the necessity or legality of the questions, and by all means, ask for an explanation if there is something you don't thoroughly understand. Also, make certain that you understand those documents you sign and the commitments they entail. Do not sign anything you have not read fully and do not comprehend completely.

Assuming you have done your shopping and found a lender offering terms acceptable to you, here are the basic steps you'll go through to obtain a conventional mortgage loan, although practices do vary from area to area.

- You make formal application for the loan, providing essential information such as your income and assets, place and length of employment, outstanding debts, and the amount needed. A form called the Residential Loan Application must be used by lenders selling their mortgages into the secondary market, either through the Federal Home Loan Mortgage Corporation or the

Federal National Mortgage Association. This standardized form is used by many other lenders as well.

If you're buying a new home, the builder may have you fill out the application and forward it to the lending institution. If you have any questions regarding the application, you should go directly to the lender.

When applying, you will be required to state the source of your down payment and closing costs and whether any part of the down payment has been borrowed. The lender can also inquire about your legal and financial position, as well as your insurance coverage. The application form stipulates: "This Statement and any applicable supporting schedules may be completed jointly by both married and *unmarried co-borrowers* if their assets and liabilities are sufficiently joined so that the Statement can be meaningfully and fairly presented on a combined basis. . . ."

In other words, if you are buying with another single person, the lender should consider both of your incomes. He will ask you how you plan to take title to the property and if you are buying with another person or persons. This is a matter that you should determine with your attorney, as it can have extreme legal ramifications (more on this in Chapter 11, "Special Tips for Single Persons Buying Together.")

The lender can ask you only the questions on this application form and cannot legally delve into your personal relationships. It's illegal for him to ask whether you intend to marry. If you're buying with another person, it's illegal for him to ask how long you've known that person or how long you've lived together. His business is not to pass moral judgments or solicit confidential information, but to collect the facts in order for the loan committee to determine whether your purchase represents a good investment of the institution's funds.

When you apply for your loan, make note of any questions you want to ask the lender regarding the form. And be sure to find out how much you will pay out over the life of the loan.

At the time you apply, the lender will probably charge you a fee of $75 to $100 for processing your application. This is also to discourage you from applying at several institutions, in case you're denied at the first one. This fee is usually non-refundable, regardless of whether the loan is made. At this point, you should also inquire whether it's the institution's practice to give out your name to mortgage insurers or others of their ilk. It's advisable to inform the lender emphatically you do not want your name provided to anyone except the parties principal to the transaction. This action can save you a lot of harrassing calls and offers of various services.

When you apply, the lender *must* give you a good-faith estimate of the closing costs you are apt to incur and a special informational booklet explaining the settlement costs and procedure. If he does not give these items to you in person, he has three business days in which to mail them to you. This good-faith estimate may not cover all items you will actually pay in cash at settlement, and the final charges may be higher. So you should ask the lender all the possible fees you could be charged at the settlement and the maximum you should set aside. If there's anything about the closing costs you don't understand, question the lender then or anytime prior to the closing.

Finally, ask the lender approximately how long it will take to process your application and when you can expect an answer. It should be within a few weeks.

STATEMENT OF CREDIT DENIAL, TERMINATION OR CHANGE

DATE _____ 19 ____

No. _____

> The Federal Equal Credit Opportunity Act pr:
> hibits creditors from discriminating against cred:
> applicants on the basis of race, color, religion, nationa
> origin, sex, marital status, age (provided that th:
> applicant has the capacity to enter into a bindin:
> contract); because all or part of the applicant's incom:
> derives from any public assistance program; or becau:
> the applicant has in good faith exercised any rig!
> under the Consumer Credit Protection Act. Th:
> Federal Agency that administers compliance with th:
> law concerning this creditor is:
>
> **COMPTROLLER OF THE CURRENCY**
> Consumer Affairs Division
> Washington, DC 20219

Dear _____

Your Application for (Description of account, transaction or requested credit): _____

has been acted upon (Description of adverse action taken): _____

PRINCIPAL REASON(S) FOR ADVERSE ACTION CONCERNING CREDIT:

- ☐ Credit application incomplete.
- ☐ Insufficient credit references.
- ☐ Unable to verify credit references.
- ☐ Temporary or irregular employment.
- ☐ Unable to verify employment.
- ☐ Length of employment.
- ☐ Insufficient income.
- ☐ Excessive obligations.
- ☐ Unable to verify income.
- ☐ Inadequate collateral.
- ☐ We do not grant credit to any applicant on the terms and conditions you request.
- ☐ Other, specify: _____

- ☐ Too short a period of residence.
- ☐ Temporary residence.
- ☐ Unable to verify residence.
- ☐ No credit file.
- ☐ Insufficient credit file.
- ☐ Delinquent credit obligations.
- ☐ Garnishment, attachment, foreclosure, repossession, or suit.
- ☐ Bankruptcy.

DISCLOSURE OF USE OF INFORMATION OBTAINED FROM AN OUTSIDE SOURCE

- ☐ Disclosure inapplicable.
- ☐ Information obtained in a report from a consumer reporting agency.

Name: _____THE XYZ CITY CREDIT BUREAU_____

Street Address: _____1004 ARTHUR STREET_____
_____ANYWHERE, USA._____

Phone: _____515 244 0000_____

- ☐ Information obtained from an outside source other than a consumer reporting agency. Under the Fair Credit Reporting Act, you have the right to make a written request, within 60 days of receipt of this notice, for disclosure of the nature of the adverse information.

By _____

Telephone No. _____

- After taking your application, the lender will conduct a credit check to make sure you are a good risk. At the same time, the lender will send out an appraiser to appraise the property and make sure it is adequate security for the loan. (See "The Appraisal," page 118, for a full explanation.)

  The credit check is often made through the local credit bureau, and you should ask the lender if he uses a credit scoring plan or point scoring plan to determine your credit-worthiness. Many major banks use these systems, which are frequently computerized, to attempt to discriminate statistically between good and poor credit risks by assigning points to personal situations. For example, living in one part of town may be worth 20 points, in another 6; owning a home 25 points, renting 7; having a home phone 15 points, no phone 3 points. Other variables considered include age of your car, time at your job, time at address, occupation, and maintenance of checking and savings accounts, as well as your income bracket.

  The lender totals the score for all these factors, which you have supplied on your application, and a total above the target can help you earn the necessary credit for your loan approval. Opponents to this credit scoring system charge that a score less than the target often results in denial of credit, regardless of credit performance.

  If your lender uses a credit scoring system, you should ask him to explain it to you, and find out which factors will be evaluated. You should also ask which agencies he will contact to determine your credit-worthiness. You want to make certain that he gets an overall picture of your credit history, including your past performance, which indicates you have promptly made all payments and are current on all installment debts.

A further word on point scoring systems: They may be illegal! The personal data used may be intimately related to personal characteristics that are illegal to look into under the Equal Credit Opportunity Act. Zip code and owning or renting information may involve racial discrimination; owning and renting information may involve marital status discrimination; time at employment may discriminate against women. These systems are also biased, since contrary to law, their users don't utilize random samples of applicants or acceptable alternatives to develop systems. In addition, the systems do not meet the law's criteria of objectivity. Users of these systems sometimes override their own systems by awarding credit to rejected applicants who complain, which discriminates against those who timidly accept credit denial.

Under the Federal Fair Housing Act, each applicant's credit-worthiness is to be evaluated on an *individual basis* without reference to presumed characteristics of a group.

The lending institution may also require a deposit verification to confirm that you have savings and checking accounts at the financial institutions you have stated. If this verification is required, you will probably be asked to fill out part of the form, stating the balances in your accounts and the account numbers, and be asked to sign a request for verification of deposit. If you don't see this form, ask if the lender uses it. Usually this form also asks the banker to whom it is sent if you have any outstanding loans, and if so, what type of loans, and whether your payment experience is favorable or not. The request may also ask how long you've had your accounts with the financial institution.

Your lender, in addition, may require a job verification. If so, this request for verification of employment will be sent to your employer. You should see the form and sign it prior to its being sent. Note the questions your employer is asked. Usually, he will be asked the length of your employment, position, base pay, earnings over the past twelve months, and probability of continued employment. Your employer is often also given the opportunity to make any remarks that he thinks might affect your eligibility as a loan applicant.

Once you sign any requests for verification, that is the last you'll see them. Then they'll be sent off to the respective parties. Keep in mind all the questions posed on those forms, in case you are denied credit and then decide to contest it.

• After your credit check is completed, your loan application with the credit report and required verifications goes to the lending institution's loan committee for consideration. This committee will analyze the appraisal, all the data on you, and any long-term debts you have. If that committee determines that you and the property you intend to buy are a good risk, then it will approve the loan. The committee can also disapprove the loan or simply defer it until a later date.

If the loan is approved, the lending institution then makes a loan commitment, a formal statement of exactly how much it will lend you and on what terms—interest rate, down payment, and repayment period.

If your loan is denied, the lender must give you a statement of credit denial informing you of the reason for the rejection. On this form, the lender must notify you of the source of any information obtained on you, such as the XYZ Credit Bureau. You then have the right under the Fair Credit Reporting

Act to make a written request within sixty days of receiving the lender's notice for disclosure of the nature of the information leading to the denial.

If you are turned down, you should obtain this information immediately. Check your credit bureau file for any misinformation or misunderstandings. Often, questionable items in your file can be clarified, clearing the way for loan approval. Time is of the essence, so don't get depressed about being denied. Proceed in a businesslike manner, and collect all the facts that can help you build a case as to why you should get the loan.

• Assuming your loan is accepted and you approve the terms, then a title search will be performed. This title search will be handled by your attorney, the lender's attorney, or a title company, depending on the practices in your area. In any event, you usually pay for the title search and title opinion. In most cases, the lender will require you to buy a title insurance policy protecting his investment, should a defect in the title be uncovered later. You may also want to purchase your own title insurance policy (for more information, see "Title Insurance," page 132).

When the title search is conducted, the *abstract*, the legal document outlining the history of ownership of your property, will be brought up to date. The abstract shows whether the title is free and clear or whether it has encumbrances or liens that must be taken care of before the property can be passed on to you. The abstract, which protects your claim of ownership, is often held by the lender or your attorney after closing, but it's up to you to make certain where this document is filed. Often the lender or attorney will give you the abstract for safekeeping or you may ask for a copy of it.

• The final step in the process is the settlement, or closing, a procedure which is conducted in a number of different ways across the country. The closing, or final settlement between the buyer and seller, usually involves a meeting of the various principals—the lender, the brokers, the buyer and seller, their respective attorneys, and a representative of the title company. At the closing, which is held at the office of the lender, title company, or other settlement agent, you will sign a *promissory note* (also called *consumer mortgage note*). This is the written agreement in which you guarantee repayment of the mortgage loan. This note specifies the interest, principal, and repayment terms and should also state whether you can prepay the loan without penalty. You should receive a copy of this note.

You will also sign the *mortgage document* in which you pledge your property as security for the loan, thus creating a legal claim on the property until the debt is paid in full. This document is recorded at the county courthouse in some states and then held by the lender. Most lenders will also give you a copy of this document.

In some states, notably California, the buyer receives a *deed of trust* (also called *trust deed*), which is similar to the mortgages used in other states.

At the closing, the seller gets the down payment from you, plus a check for the balance of the selling price from the lender. You pay the closing costs—all those expenses involved in transferring ownership of the property to you and in processing the loan. The settlement agent will give you a uniform settlement statement to sign, itemizing each of the closing costs, and you will receive a copy of this form. You will also receive a federal truth-in-lending statement, disclosing the annual percentage rate on your loan and some other particulars (more on this later).

After all of these matters have been taken care of, you will receive the *deed* to your property—the legal document representing your ownership of the house and property. There are three main types of deeds—warranty deed (also called deed with full covenant), bargain-and-sale deed, and quitclaim deed. Usually, the buyer receives a *warranty deed*, stating that the sellers are conveying the premises free and clear of all liens and encumbrances. This is the most desirable type of deed, since it gives you certain assurances backed by the seller. (Your attorney should see that you get the proper deed; discuss any questions you have with him.) The deed is notarized and a copy of it is filed with the county recorder. *Make certain this is done*, since it is your legal proof of ownership. It does occasionally happen that a negligent settlement agent doesn't see to this final step, which puts the new owner in a very precarious position.

If all the details of the sale have been worked out in the offer to buy or sales contract, the closing shouldn't take much time and should be a smooth transaction. Just make certain you understand those documents you're signing—that's why it's a good idea to have your attorney present. Most real-estate and mortgage contracts are still in the time-honored legalese incomprehensible to most buyers, but there is a strong move afoot to require plain-talk contracts in non-technical language, presented in a clear and coherent manner for consumers.

You will usually come to closing within thirty to forty-five days of the date you applied for your loan, though this time period can vary considerably, depending on the circumstances involved and the market conditions.

The Escrow Closing

In some parts of the country, predominantly the western United States, the settlement is conducted by an escrow company or escrow agent and is called an escrow closing. The escrow agent may be a lender, a real-estate agent, or a title company representative. Or the escrow company may be a wholly owned subsidiary of a real-estate company. In an escrow closing, the parties—the buyer, seller, brokers, attorneys, lender—do not meet face to face around a table to sign and exchange documents and funds.

Instead, the buyer and seller sign an escrow agreement that requires them to deposit specified documents and funds with the escrow agent. Usually an attorney is not involved in the closing. The escrow agent requests the title report and policy, drafts the deed and other documents, pays off existing loans, and adjusts the taxes and insurance between the buyer and the seller. The escrow agent also computes the interest on the loans and the settlement costs, and he may acquire the hazard (home-owner's) insurance. He obtains all the necessary signatures from buyer and seller, and if all the papers and funds are deposited with the agent within the agreed time, the escrow is closed. The escrow agent then records the appropriate documents and gives each party the money and documents to which he is entitled, including a copy of the uniform settlement statement.

Escrow closings usually cost consumers more because the rates of escrow companies are *not* regulated, and so they are able to gouge the already fee-ridden single buyer. Moreover, a number of escrow companies have been found guilty of embezzling funds, price-fixing, and illegal kickbacks.

The major disadvantage to this type of closing is that you don't have the opportunity to ask questions of the other principals at the settlement meeting. Usually, the real-estate agent refers the buyer to an escrow company, which may be a subsidiary of his brokerage firm. If you are involved in an escrow closing, it is *imperative* that you shop for your own escrow agent and do not allow yourself to be steered to one by your broker, the seller, or any other party to the transaction.

There can be substantial differences in the fees of various escrow agents within one area, and you should call around and get quotes. Usually, the fee is computed on a sliding scale based on the home's price. For example, one Los Angeles-based escrow company charges a base fee of $90 plus $1.25 for every $1,000 of the sales price. The fee may be split between buyer and seller, but this arrangement should be negotiated prior to your signing the offer to buy and should be stipulated in that document.

It's a good idea to ask the escrow agent to account for each item on your final uniform settlement statement and to ask to see receipts for disbursements if you question any item.

For instance, when Cal received his uniform settlement statement from the escrow company following his purchase of a $69,500 house, he realized there were many items he didn't understand. His closing costs totaled $1,747.35—$205 of which he paid to the escrow company. In addition, the escrow company charged the seller $155 for a closing fee and another $10 for document preparation. That a hefty $370 escrow fee.

Cal paid $884 for a loan origination fee, $12 for a credit report, $50 for document preparation, $16.50 for tax service, $10 for a sub-escrow to the title company, and a $50 loan tie-in fee, to mention just a few items. He was baffled by those last two charges. So he went to the escrow company (a small, three-person operation) following the closing and asked for a line-by-line explanation of the charges.

"They reacted very defensively, really in a very paranoid way," Cal said. "They thought I was attempting to hang them from the yardarm. However, when they realized my intent was to find out what the various items meant they were quite willing to answer the questions.

"I noticed they worded their answers very carefully, although they were very accommodating. People don't generally question them, and they were surprised that I would come in and dig into it in detail. They questioned my motives, and rather than replying that I was checking their accuracy and honesty, I told them it was because I might be moving again and wanted to know as much as possible about the process."

Cal discovered that he had paid through the nose for the escrow company's services and could have saved a good bit of money had he shopped for his own escrow agent.

You should ask your attorney or a disinterested, but knowledgeable, third party to recommend a few reputable escrow agents you can contact for bids. Ask each agent you contact to explain the various fees he will charge you.

The Settlement Costs

The settlement costs (also called closing costs) comprise a significant portion of the overall purchase price. You may pay $4,000 or more in settlement costs—all due when your loan is closed. Since this is money you must have on hand in addition to the down payment, $1,000 can make the difference between being able to afford a home now or continuing to rent. Therefore, it's vital that you find out about settlement practices in your locale and shop for the best terms.

Closing customs and costs do vary significantly from area to area, and the time to inquire about these matters is when you first start shopping for a home. For example, Lila, a newcomer to the Washington, D.C. area, discovered by shopping around that the settlement costs for a house in Maryland were more than $1,000, while the closing costs for a similarly priced home in Virginia were less than $450. No Maryland real-estate broker or lender would provide Lila this information, which she ferreted out herself by questioning various lenders, brokers, and home owners. She found that in Maryland, the buyer traditionally pays for *all* the closing costs.

If you have a fixed amount to spend, shopping for settlement services can be as important as shopping for economical houses. So after you've decided the type of house you want and have a location in mind, go to various lenders and ask how much they'll charge in closing costs for the type and price house in the specific neighborhood. Also ask them to explain the settlement procedure they follow. (Closing-cost terminology varies in different parts of the country, so have the lender explain each item you'll pay.) Lenders may not give out this information over the phone, or if they do, they're apt to just give ball-park figures. It's advisable to visit in person with loan officers.

Before you start your settlement shopping, there are a few facts you should understand and warnings you should heed in order to save yourself time, grief, and money. First, settlement costs often are figured as a fixed percentage of the home's sales price or the mortgage amount and not based on the actual cost of providing the settlement services. This is particularly true in highly inflated markets, where a lot of settlement providers get involved in the transaction. Mortgage servicing fees will escalate as lenders attempt to keep pace with inflation.

Thus you should ask each lender what his loan origination fees are, how those fees are set, how much he charges for processing of documents, and if he will charge you points.* Try to get precise quotes on the specific

---

*One point is equal to one percent of the loan amount. Who pays the points is a matter of agreement. On a conventional loan the points may be split between buyer and seller. On an FHA-backed loan, the buyer can pay only one point. Points, which are one-time fees paid at closing, usually are listed as the loan discount on the uniform settlement statement. Lenders charge points to compensate them for making a loan at less than the going market interest rate. In states where the usury limits are set by law, lenders may charge as much as ten points or more to make a loan.

settlement costs you'll be charged. The lender is not obligated to provide you this information until the day of closing, unfortunately. But if you present yourself as a knowledgeable consumer, lenders might be amenable to giving you pretty accurate estimates. If they won't, you should just keep shopping.

Second, you should know about escrows or reserve accounts, also called impounds. At the closing, lenders often require buyers to place funds in a reserve account to cover the property taxes, hazard (home-owner's) insurance, mortgage insurance, and other annual assessments. Escrows are usually required for these items if you put less than 20 percent down. As you shop, ask each lender how much money he'll require you to escrow—this can make a substantial difference in your total closing costs. There is a legal limit on the amount the lender can require you to escrow (more on this in the next section).

Many lenders hold your escrow funds without compensation to you, or they pay only a nominal rate of interest. Ask each lender if his institution pays interest on escrows, and if so, how much. Federal credit unions pay the same dividend on escrow accounts as they do on regular share accounts. New federal laws may soon require other lenders to pay a nominal interest rate on escrows.

Third, you should beware of the so-called dry settlement, a problem encountered by some single buyers. In a dry settlement, the attorney or escrow agent handling the closing fails to disburse funds promptly, thus profiting from interest on your money. To avoid this problem, shop carefully for a reputable attorney or escrow agent. Following the closing, you can also ask to see receipts verifying that funds were disbursed.

Fourth, find out from each lender whether he will require you to use certain settlement providers. It is legal for the lender to do this, but if he does, he has no excuse for not being able to give you precise quotes on all the closing costs you'll be charged. You should also ask the lender what his business relationship is with the required providers. Often you'll find it's become customary over the years for the lender to refer his borrowers to a certain broker, attorney, title company, and escrow company. Conversely, those individuals or companies will refer their clients to that specific lender. In the process, the clients end up paying higher prices.

If you feel yourself being steered to specific providers of settlement services, or if the lender requires certain providers, check their fees against those of other providers in your area. If you have to pay substantially more at the lending institution requiring specific providers, then go to another lender.

Fifth, you should know that some lenders may be willing to absorb the closing costs in a higher interest rate. In other words, if you can't afford the up-front closing costs, they will agree to drop these expenses and charge you a higher interest—one quarter or one half percent more. True, that will increase your monthly mortgage payments, but if you only have so much cash and can afford the higher payments, you'll have to go that route to obtain your home. Check also with your hometown or personal banker.

Sometimes he won't charge you any closing costs, especially if he's been your family's banker over the years.

Although local practice generally dictates which settlement services you'll be required to pay, how much they'll cost, and how the settlement will be conducted, the sharpest warning that can be sounded is SHOP AROUND! Single buyers are too often led to believe that involved professionals—brokers, lenders, attorneys—represent their best interests in arranging for settlement services, so they don't vigorously shop. Invariably, they end up paying excessive fees.

For instance, Marie and Ron bought the same town-house units in a Virginia suburb of Washington, D.C., within a few months of each other. Marie shopped around for a lender offering low closing costs and bargained with the seller (the builder) over the closing costs. Consequently, she paid only $757.81 in closing costs and points for her $66,700 town house. On the other hand, Ron, who did not shop around and got his financial package through the builder, paid about $1,000 more than Marie in closing costs.

It's important to note that you can bargain with the seller over who pays which closing costs. If the lender charges points, you can negotiate with the seller who pays them—you may decide to split them. Other negotiable items include the title search fee, inspection fees, and who pays which portion of the taxes.* Since there are no legally fixed rules about who pays which fees, any item is theoretically up for negotiation. You may find yourself bound by local convention, however, if the lender insists upon one party paying certain charges. Stipulate your agreement on who pays which costs in the offer to buy or sales contract. And remember, the broker who is the seller's agent is not apt to stick up for you in your effort to get the seller to pay more costs.

Your ability to get the seller to assume some settlement costs will depend on such factors as his eagerness to sell, the length of time the house has been on the market, the interest of other buyers, and your eagerness to buy. Don't become so anxious to get the house off the market that you fail to bargain over these expensive fees.

The items you can expect to pay are all listed under section L, Settlement Charges, on the uniform settlement statement, the form you will receive at closing. Each item on this statement will be explained in a settlement costs book you will receive from your lender.

What you'll ultimately pay will depend on market conditions, house

---

*At some point, you probably will encounter the term "prorations." Prorations are a division of the continuing costs of owning a piece of real estate between the buyer and seller so that each pays a fair share. When you're bargaining for closing costs with the seller, you should also discuss the prorations. Prorations are necessary because taxes, insurance, and some other costs are not paid daily, but in one or two installments a year. Depending on when the sale occurs, the seller may owe the buyer for funds due but not yet paid or the buyer may end up owing the seller for money already paid but not yet due. Normally, prorations are made on the day of closing and when the deed is transferred into your name. It's advisable to consult your attorney about how the prorations should be figured and make sure all appropriate items are included. In addition to taxes and insurance, other items that may be prorated are water, gas, and electric bills; coal, oil, or propane gas on hand; garbage removal; home-owners' association fees; and any other continuing item related to the property.

prices, and the part of the country in which you live, as well as the other factors previously mentioned. For instance, Cal paid $1,747 in closing costs for his $69,500 home in southern California. The escrow company handling his closing was recommended by the broker who also arranged for the financing. Marie, who bought about the same time Cal did, paid only $757 in closing costs for her $66,700 Washington town house, but she shopped after her attorney had gone over all of her documents. She paid no points or loan origination fees, which she negotiated for the seller to pay. Cal, on the other hand, paid $884 in loan origination fees and another $66.50 in loan processing fees to the mortgage banking company, in addition to the escrow company's $205 charge.

Barbara, who moved to Iowa from Atlanta, and financed her $55,000 home through a commercial bank, paid only $307 in closing costs. She paid no loan origination fees or points and was assessed by the lender only for the appraisal, credit report, title search, attorney's fee, survey, recording fees, and state tax stamps.

Duke, who bought a $39,900 condo in a medium-sized midwestern city, didn't fare as well. He paid closing costs of $2,070 to the mortgage banking company, which charged a 5 percent loan fee, one-half percent of the purchase price for a reinsurance premium (private mortgage insurance), plus fees for the appraisal and credit report. Duke did not shop for settlement costs and, in fact, went to the mortgage banking company recommended by the broker and builder of the condo complex.

Tamara, who bought a $48,000 detached house in the same town as Duke, paid only $983 in closing costs. She got her financing through a local bank after inquiring around about rates. She wasn't charged a loan origination fee or points, but she did pay a $720 loan closing fee, as well as for the title search, attorney, recording fees, and state tax stamps.

These examples demonstrate the importance of shopping for settlement providers and services. Another important step that can save you money and aggravation in the closing is to know your consumer rights under the Real Estate Settlement Procedures Act.

The Real Estate Settlement Procedures Act

Over the years, there have been repeated complaints that the providers of settlement services—title companies, attorneys, escrow companies, mortgage lenders—are interrelated and steer the buyer from one to another without the opportunity to shop. As a result, in 1974 Congress passed the Real Estate Settlement Procedures Act (RESPA), requiring the mortgage lender to give the buyer and the seller advance disclosure of actual closing costs they would incur at settlement. Both parties were to be notified a minimum of twelve days prior to closing.

In 1975, the savings-and-loan industry and other mortgage lenders, charging that they were subjected to undue burdens in preparing this information, succeeded in weakening RESPA.

The important message for you in this little history is to shop independently for all financial services. If the principals in the real-estate transaction can't find a legal way of getting around the law, they often resort to very subtle tactics of questionable legality. RESPA does still provide you some protections, which you should know about and exercise. Lenders often gloss over these requirements or minimize them at best.

- RESPA requires the lender to give you a special HUD-prepared booklet on settlement costs within three days of the time you apply for a mortgage loan. Most lenders will not advise you to read this booklet, and some, in fact, may even fail to give it to you. Make sure you receive this booklet, and read it. It outlines the rights and obligation of the various parties under RESPA and advises you how to file complaints and seek damages if your rights are violated. In addition, it describes in detail all of the settlement-cost items you might possibly face.
- Also within three days of your mortgage application, the lender is required to give you a good-faith estimate of the settlement costs you'll pay at closing. Note, however, this is only an estimate, and the lender is not required to give estimates of how much you'll pay for the hazard insurance premium or how much you'll be required to escrow. Often, costs increase by the time you get to settlement, especially the number of points the lender charges. The lender must give you dollar amounts for each estimate and not simply an estimate as a percentage of the total purchase price. You should quiz the lender about *all* the possible closing costs you can expect to pay.
- RESPA does allow the lender to require you to use specific settlement service providers as part of his agreement to make your loan. If the lender does require specific providers, though, he must give you the names, addresses, and phone numbers of those providers and advise you of the services they will render. In addition, if the designated provider has a business relationship with the lender, this fact must be disclosed. This requirement is intended to alert buyers to potential conflicts of interest. If you question the lender's estimate, you can call the specified providers yourself. If estimates seem too high, go to another lender.
- RESPA requires that the uniform settlement statement be used by the settlement agent to disclose all charges paid at or before the closing. Those charges paid before the settlement (for example, if the lender requires you to pay for your credit report when you apply for your loan) must be itemized on this statement and designated POC—paid outside closing. The person conducting the closing must fill out this statement and give you a copy. In the case of escrow closings or where you don't attend the closing, the settlement agent must mail this statement to you as soon as the transaction is completed. You should ask that individual approximately when you can expect to receive this form.

This form is required to protect you from imprecise or obscure settlement-costs statements, which shield unnecessary or inflated charges. Go over this statement carefully when you receive it. If you do not pay any closing costs or if you are informed when you apply for a loan that you will only pay a fixed dollar amount for all settlement charges, then the uniform settlement statement does not have to be used.

One further word: A lender is prohibited from charging you for preparing or distributing this statement. Any other individual conducting a settlement *can* charge you for handling this form.

- One business day prior to closing, you have the right to inspect the uniform settlement statement to get an idea of exactly how much cash you'll need at the closing. The settlement agent may not have all the costs available at this time, but is obligated to show you, *upon your request*, what is available. This right is explained in the RESPA booklet, but you can be sure you won't hear about it from the lender or anyone else. The settlement agent usually doesn't want to be bothered with this request, so it is never emphasized. If you want to exercise the right, it's advisable to make a written request for inspection a few days prior to the closing. This requirement does not apply in the case of escrow closings or when you don't attend the closing.
- RESPA prohibits any party in the real-estate transaction from giving or taking a fee or thing of value for the referral of business. It also prohibits charging a fee or accepting a fee when no service has been provided.

  Prior to the passage of RESPA, lenders, attorneys, brokers, and settlement service providers frequently paid each other fees for referrals of business. Generally, these payments were made in return for a phone call. Therefore, if any party wanted to increase his business, he did so by paying higher referral fees rather than offering better services at lower prices to consumers. Ultimately, the buyer always paid for these activities. *Recent reports to HUD reveal that RESPA has not effectively done away with these activities, but has merely driven them underground.*

  If you are the victim of such a scheme, RESPA provides redress for damages and penalties to the offender—you will find an explanation of your legal rights in the RESPA booklet. You should avoid these situations by effectively shopping for services. You don't want to be tied up in a legal hassle right after buying your home—that can take all the joy out of ownership.

  Incidentally, if you're dealing with a large brokerage firm with a subsidiary title insurance company and mortgage banking company, you may not receive quality service at a competitive price from those subsidiaries.
- The seller cannot require you, as a condition of the sale, to buy your title insurance from a particular title company.
- RESPA limits the amount that the lender can require you to place in an escrow or reserve account. Previously, lenders often required unnecessarily large escrows from buyers and got the free use of their money. The formula for figuring the maximum amount that can be escrowed is explained in the RESPA information booklet.

Finally, you should know that RESPA covers all transactions where a federally related mortgage loan is used to buy a one- to four-family dwelling. Any lender that is federally regulated or insured or is a creditor under the Consumer Credit Protection Act is federally related. This designation also pertains to all loans that are governmentally insured, guaranteed, supplemented, or assisted. If you find the RESPA requirements are not being observed, you should ask your lender and attorney about the practices in question.

RESPA does not apply to mortgage loan assumptions, contract sales, cash sales, or lease-purchase agreements. RESPA supercedes any state disclosure laws covering your home purchase, unless those laws make more stringent requirements than RESPA. For further information on RESPA, consult the information booklet you receive from your lender.

Truth-In-Lending

The Truth-In-Lending Act (TIL) requires the lender to disclose to you the effective interest rate you will pay on your mortgage loan. This rate is generally higher than the rate the lender initially quotes you or the contract rate stated in the mortgage note, because it includes many of the charges you pay at closing.

The lender is required to give you a federal truth-in-lending statement as part of the uniform settlement statement. TIL requires that all credit terms and fees associated with closing be disclosed on this form, so you know exactly how much you are paying. All these costs will be added to the contract interest rate to reveal the total finance charges as an *annual percentage rate* (APR).

Since the lender is not required to give you the TIL statement until closing, when you file your loan application you should ask the lender to provide a TIL disclosure covering all of the loan terms. The TIL statement should indicate the loan amount, contract interest rate, number and amount of payments, total amount financed, the total finance charge, and the APR. This statement should also stipulate whether there are any provisions for variations in the interest rate or prepayment penalties.

Charges that will be used to figure the APR include the total mortgage amount, the total interest paid, the loan origination fee, any points, prepaid interest (a fee that covers the interest between the date of settlement and the date of your first loan payment), any lender's inspection fees, mortgage life and disability insurance premiums, as well as mortgage insurance premiums, if that coverage is required by the lender.

The FTC is currently investigating whether creditors, specifically mortgage bankers and other mortgage lenders, are correctly charging consumers for the cost of credit and are complying with the TIL requirements. The FTC wants to determine whether credit information is being disclosed in such a way that consumers can easily compare the terms available from different sources. If you believe you have been overcharged under provisions of TIL or not adequately informed of the terms of your transaction, you can contact the FTC, Division of Credit Practices, Washington, D.C. 20580.

This law provides criminal penalties for violators, as well as civil remedies. You may sue if the lender fails to make the required disclosures. You can sue for twice the amount of the finance charge—for a minimum of $100, up to a maximum of $1,000—plus court costs and attorney's fees.

Also, you should know that if you take out a loan using your house as security, this law gives you a three-business-day cooling-off period in which to cancel the transaction. The creditor must give you written notice of your right to cancel, and if you decide to cancel the transaction, you have to notify the creditor in writing of your decision.

This law pertains to all credit transactions and not just mortgage loans. For further information on the law or any questions regarding your credit transaction, you should contact a Federal Reserve Bank.

10

Avoid Discrimination: Know Your Rights as a Single Buyer

Kathryn, a forty-year-old divorced woman with two children, owns her own business and two income properties. Recently, she sold her home and went to the bank for a mortgage to buy a new house. Even though she has an excellent credit record and properties on which to borrow, she had to show the lender her income tax return several times to substantiate her income. She shudders as she recalls the numerous delays purportedly for credit checks and the additional references the lender required.

"I don't think those things would have happened to a man," Kathryn concluded.

Steven, a twenty-five-year-old commercial artist, had the cash down payment and qualifying income for the $36,000 home he wanted to buy, but was unable to get a loan. He was told by several loan officers that for "a person by himself" they would require a minimum of 20 percent down, although a married couple could get a loan with only 10 percent down. They cited the fact that there would be no income to fall back on if something happened to Steven.

Steven had been at his job three years and had a top-notch credit history. His only outstanding debt was a car loan of about $2,000.

"Finally, one lender admitted that as a single man I was unstable and too much of a risk," Steven said. "I appreciated his frankness, because all the other lenders had sidestepped the fact of my being single by saying that my income just didn't qualify me, when married friends with the same income as mine were getting loans. They were just trying to get me to back down so they didn't have to bother with me."

Reports Steven, who is now renting a house with the option to buy, "I think it's much easier for a single female to buy a house—even if she has a couple kids and is divorced. Lenders consider males much more mobile and, hence, unstable."

Both Kathryn and Steven were the victims of illegal, sexist discrimination. And there are a host of prejudicial practices that lenders and other participants in the real-estate transaction perpetrate on single buyers. The problem is most buyers don't know their legal rights and the remedies available to them.

Had Kathryn and Steven known their rights under the Equal Credit Opportunity Act, they could have warned those lenders they were courting lawsuits and reported them to the federal agencies regulating their institutions. Under those circumstances, the lenders probably would have changed their tunes and written the loans with a minimum of hassles. Unfortunately, neither Kathryn nor Steven consulted attorneys about their difficulties or learned the laws affecting them.

Off the record, one loan officer at a major bank admits, "There are many subtle ways of turning down mortgage loans. The lender can apply more rigid standards for the single individual—require a longer minimum time on the job, be much more selective on credit requirements, or pick out different points on the application and impose stricter qualifications.

"The lender can appraise the property lower than the market value so the person has to come up with a larger down payment," she adds. "Lenders always fear more liability with a single person. In turning down a loan application, we might even tell the individual that he or she hasn't banked with us for one year."

Furthermore, lenders sometimes discourage single persons from even applying for loans, either verbally or by charging a large fee for the application. Since federal banking regulations require lenders to keep records of the applications as well as the race and sex of the applicants for compliance monitoring of the laws, many lenders don't want data in their files showing the loans were denied. So they avoid taking the applications.

The owner of a large Midwest-based, real-estate brokerage firm, notes, "With the passage of all the consumer laws, the buyer expects the broker to look after his rights and interests, but that's not the broker's job."

Reports one of his agents: "If I ran into a violation of the buyer's rights, I would not tell the lender and force the situation, because it would jeopardize my relationship with the lender, who I rely on for loans."

Of course, that presumes the agent knows the laws; many agents don't. In any event, no agent is going to willingly rock the boat. Remember, the real-estate establishment is a powerful industry, relying on certain tacit alliances.

The job of knowing your rights and making certain they are observed so that you get your loan at the going rates without any extra penalties, conditions, or fees rests squarely on you. As more singles enter the housing market and gain the acceptance and confidence of lenders, incidences of discrimination are apt to decrease. And, in fact, there are many seasoned and professional loan officers who now write mortgages based on the facts and avoid prejudicial and personal judgments. You should seek out these individuals.

Presuming you have the qualifying income for the loan you seek and an adequate credit record, these are some of the practices for which you should watch:

- The lender applies stricter terms to you than to a married couple. He may ask for a higher interest, shorter maturity, larger down payment, or additional fees.
- You are denied a loan or stricter terms are applied to you based on the racial or ethnic composition of the neighborhood where your prospective home is located.
- You are refused a loan or offered less favorable terms because of the age of the neighborhood's homes, the income level of its residents, or the size or price of its homes.
- The home is appraised for less than its actual value on the basis of any of the above-mentioned factors.
- The lender refuses to count steady part-time or overtime earnings in your overall qualifying income.
- The lender refuses to consider steady income from alimony, public assistance programs, disability insurance, Social Security, or unemployment payments.
- The lender requires stricter standards or denies you a loan because you have not previously owned a home.
- The lender makes loans only to "preferred customers" or others with whom he has business or personal relationships.
- The lender gives undue weight to credit difficulties in the distant past.
- The lender tells you he provides no loan service at branch facilities in lower income or minority neighborhoods or in inner-city residential areas.
- You are discouraged from filing a written application.
- The lender refuses to discuss loan terms or answer any questions unless you pay a substantial fee and file an application.
- A lender tells you over the phone that he doesn't loan in a specific area or your income doesn't qualify you for a loan. Such tactics, known as "pre-screening," have typically been used to avoid making a record of denying loans to women and minority persons.
- The lender requires you to have a cosigner.
- You encounter unexplained delays in the processing of your loan.
- The lender asks you personal questions beyond the scope of those on the loan application.
- The real-estate agent consistently steers you to specific neighborhoods. Naturally, the agent will show you houses in neighborhoods within your means. However, if he steers you away from certain neighborhoods where you specifically ask to look, that may be illegal. Racial minorities have traditionally been the victims of this type of steering—the agents would only show them houses in integrated neighborhoods. Some single buyers, particularly divorced women with children, have felt the cut of this type of discrimination where brokers steered them away from family residential areas. The broker, who regularly served those areas, did not want to jeopardize future clients by injecting into their neighborhoods a single individual who they would regard as disruptive because of a different or alternative life-style.*
- You are buying with another credit-worthy individual, and the lender refuses to make a mortgage loan in both of your names or discourages you in any way. For example, a single man and a single woman applied for a mortgage loan at

*Some communities, to eliminate communes from their neighborhoods, enacted zoning ordinances preventing unrelated persons, or more than a certain number of unrelated persons, from living together. Such ordinances are illegal, according to the federal fair housing laws, and you should contact an attorney if you encounter them.

their local bank, where they both had established accounts. The banker told them he would only count the man's income in processing the loan, and on that basis the couple could not afford the house.

The Laws You Need to Know

Within recent years, a number of laws that specifically protect the rights of single persons have been passed. Here is a rundown of the legislation you will need to know to assure full and equal treatment as a single buyer.

The Equal Credit Opportunity Act (ECOA)

This landmark legislation, implemented in 1975, really opened the mortgage market to single persons. Prior to passage of ECOA, it was often impossible for singles, who were routinely looked upon as bad risks, to obtain home loans. For single women—now the fastest growing segment of the home-buying market—this law has been a real boon, particularly for the divorced, separated, and widowed, who have always faced difficulty establishing their credit-worthiness.

ECOA prohibits discrimination in any aspect of the credit transaction because of your marital status, sex, age, race, national origin, or religion. All institutions which regularly extend credit are covered by the act.

Under the provisions of ECOA, the lender may not:

- Discourage you in any way from applying for a loan.
- Refuse to make you a loan if you qualify for the type of mortgage loan and terms you're seeking.
- Lend you money at terms different from those granted to a married couple or person (or persons) with similar income, expenses, credit history, and collateral.
- Stall your loan application or delay it without a viable explanation.
- Rely on a property appraisal that considers the racial makeup of the neighborhood.
- Ask you about birth control practices or child-bearing plans. A lender may not assume that you will have children or discount your income for that reason.
- If you are separated or divorced, ask you for information about your spouse or former spouse, unless you rely on that individual's income or on alimony or child support from that individual. Then, the lender may ask you for a statement that those payments are regularly made on time.
- Ask you whether you receive alimony, child support, or separate maintenance payments unless he first tells you that you don't have to disclose such income unless you want to use it to get the mortgage. However, a lender *may* ask whether you have to *pay* alimony, child support, or separate maintenance.
- Refuse to consider your income from alimony, child support, separate maintenance payments, public assistance programs, disability insurance, Social Security, an annuity, unemployment payments, or a part-time job, if these are steady items. (Most lenders won't count tips as part of your income and aren't required to do so. In special markets, underwriting rules permit adding these gratuities to your base salary in figuring your qualifying home-buying income.

In Las Vegas, where many single buyers' incomes include a high percentage of tips, the FHA considers this income, called "tokes." Usually, though, the buyer has to give the lender a "toke statement" of how much income is based on gratuities.)

- If you're credit-worthy and have the qualifying income for the loan you seek, require a cosigner on the loan.
- By the same token, the lender can't refuse to allow you to have a cosigner, if necessary.
- Assign any value to sex or marital status in credit scoring plans.

ECOA requires the lender to notify you whether your loan has been approved within thirty days after you apply and any necessary appraisals, credit checks, or government approvals have been completed. If your loan is denied, the lender must immediately either notify you or advise you in writing of the specific reasons for the rejection or advise you that you can request the specific reasons within sixty days. Examples of *specific* reasons are: Your income was too low; you haven't been at your job long enough. Indefinite and vague reasons, such as "You didn't meet our minimum standards" or "You didn't receive enough points on your credit scoring system" *do not comply* with the law. You can challenge the reasons for the refusal and try to buttress your case as to why you should get the loan. A good real-estate agent should help you in this effort.

The Equal Credit Opportunity Act was expanded in 1977, adding special provisions to assist separated, divorced, and widowed women. Traditionally, the credit of a couple was reported in the husband's name only, so many women who married and changed their names had no credit records. Effective June 1, 1977, this law required creditors (such as Master Charge, VISA, or any department store) to report information on shared accounts to credit bureaus in both spouses' names. This gave married women the ability to establish credit easily in their own names. If you are separated, divorced, or widowed, you should visit your credit bureau to make sure all relevant information is in a credit file under your name.

ECOA also went a bit further in assisting separated, divorced, and widowed persons. It forbids a lender to use against them any unfavorable information about an account they shared with a spouse or former spouse, if they can show that the bad credit rating does not accurately reflect their willingness or ability to repay their loans.*

The most recent regulation promulgated under ECOA binds builders to observe all of its provisions. Builders, as you will recall, are often party to the financial arrangements in the sale and involved in drafting the offer to buy. The law bars builders from "steering" buyers or in other ways denying them equal credit rights.

---

*If you've had major credit problems in the past, you should tell the lender about them from the outset, as they will probably be found during the credit check. If there were mitigating or unavoidable circumstances behind previous credit problems, explain them to the lender. Such problems shouldn't prevent you from getting a mortgage if you've since reestablished your credit.

To further illustrate what constitutes illegal activity under this law, consider these incidents.

Thirty-one-year-old Bess had held her well-paying job for several years when she applied for a home loan. The lender asked her if she was married, and she told him no. He then asked how she planned to make her mortgage payments after her child was born.

Replied Bess, "I don't think I'll have to worry about that—I believe you have just taken care of it for me."

Indeed, he had. The court ruled that Bess' rights under ECOA had been violated by that inquiry into her personal affairs. The settlement she received will cover her house payments and expenses for a long while.

Even though Marlene's income and assets qualified her for the 10 percent down payment and mortgage payments on the $40,000 house she was buying, the lender required her father to cosign her loan.

Says Sally Gold, of the FTC's Bureau of Consumer Protection: "It's clearly illegal to ask for a cosigner if the person qualifies for credit. The applicant can sue the lender, and the law provides for substantial penalties."

If you do need a cosigner because you fall short of the necessary income, down payment, or credit record the lender requires, you have the right to choose your own cosigner. You could choose a friend, a parent, or other relative. As long as that individual is credit-worthy, the lender must accept him or her as the cosigner. You may encounter pressure from the lender for that cosigner also to live in the house. Without that condition, the lender often reasons, he has no assurance the cosigner would make the payments if you couldn't. If you run into that situation, consult your attorney.

So what do you do if you are discriminated against or think your rights have been violated?

First, you should describe the facts to your attorney and let him advise you how to handle the situation. If you don't have an attorney, you can consult a local legal aid society or housing advocacy group. Often attorneys affiliated with these type organizations are familiar with discriminatory patterns and practices and can best advise you what to do. In any case, the lender or other party should be informed and given the opportunity to rectify the situation.

ECOA authorizes persons whose rights have been violated to sue in Federal District Court for recovery of actual damages and punitive damages of up to $10,000. You can also recover attorney's fees and court costs. If, for example, you were required as a single buyer to put 20 percent down, instead of the going rate of 10 percent, you could sue later for that extra 10 percent and up to $10,000 in punitive damages for each violation. If you win, the lender has to pay for your attorney fees and court costs.

You can also join other people (for example, a number of single buyers against whom a lender discriminates in higher terms or other conditions) and file a class action suit. You can recover punitive damages for the class of up to $500,000 or one percent of the lender's net worth, whichever is less.

You should report violations to the appropriate government enforce-ment agency. Ask the lender the name and address of the federal agency regulating his institution and send your complaint to that agency. Inciden-tally, just taking that action may persuade the lender to write your loan if he realizes his actions are definitely unjustified and prejudicial.

The Department of Justice has recently established a special unit within its Civil Rights Division to investigate complaints and take legal action against ECOA violators. Contact the Housing and Credit Section, Civil Rights Division, U.S. Department of Justice, Washington, D.C. 20530.

For more information about ECOA or advice regarding a complaint, you can contact any Federal Reserve Bank in your area or write the Division of Consumer Affairs, Board of Governors of the Federal Reserve System, Washington, D.C. 20511.* Information pamphlets on ECOA are available from the Federal Trade Commission, Legal and Public Records, Room 130, Washington, D.C. 20580.

The Federal Fair Housing Act

Enacted as part of the omnibus Civil Rights Act of 1968, this law has been amended to prohibit discrimination on the basis of sex, race, color, religion, or national origin. This legislation, directed at real-estate agents and sellers, along with other providers of real-estate services, was initially passed to give minority persons equal access to the housing market. When expanded to ban sex discrimination, it was intended to help single women, particularly the separated, divorced, and widowed, who were experiencing difficulty obtaining suitable housing.

This act makes it unlawful, on the basis of those factors mentioned, for anyone to:

- Refuse to sell or rent housing to a person.
- Discriminate in the terms, conditions, or privileges of the transaction.
- Discriminate in the availability of brokerage services.
- Indicate any preference in advertising.**

Regulations implemented under this law by the Federal Home Loan Bank Board (FHLBB) make it illegal for savings-and-loan associations to:

- Engage in practices that discriminate on the basis of marital status or age.
- Refuse to lend to a woman because of her sex.
- Subject a woman to higher standards of credit-worthiness.
- Impose different loan eligibility criteria on women than on men.
- Require as a condition for granting a mortgage loan information on birth-control practices or child-bearing capability.

*Federal Reserve Banks are located in Boston, New York, Philadelphia, Cleveland, St. Louis, Minneapolis, Kansas City, Dallas, and San Francisco.

**For example, a major Chicago newspaper excluded the real-estate section of its Sunday paper distributed to black and Chicano neighborhoods. The Justice Department is investigating this case, where the advertising department allegedly succumbed to pressure from builders and developers who wanted to keep minority persons out of their projects.

- Consider only the non-overtime income of the primary wage-earner.*
- Apply rigid or arbitrary rules relating to the borrower's prior history. For example, rules which disfavor applicants who have frequently changed jobs or residences may be considered rigid and arbitrary.

Regarding underwriting standards which have a possible discriminatory effect on women, the FHLBB regulations stipulate: "Each loan applicant's credit-worthiness should be evaluated on an individual basis, without reference to presumed characteristics of a group. The use of lending standards which have no economic basis and which are discriminatory in effect is a violation of law even in the absence of an actual intent to discriminate."

To ensure compliance with this provision, single women should request and examine the credit scoring system or plan the lender uses to process the loan application. Plans that assign a value to marital status, job title, the applicant's neighborhood, having a phone in one's own name, or other basic criteria which adversely affect women *violate* the Federal Fair Housing Act.

You will notice that some provisions of this law overlap those of ECOA; but enforcement procedures vary. HUD, which has responsibility for ensuring compliance with the Fair Housing Act, will collect information it needs to secure the shelter or get damages when a person's rights are violated. HUD has a toll-free number (800-424-8590) that you can call day or night to complain if you believe you've been treated unfairly. HUD will refer your complaint to one of its regional offices for follow-up. You should also inform your attorney of the matter or consult a local housing advocacy group or legal-aid organization.

You can go to court for any violation, and the offender, if found guilty, must pay damages as well as court costs and attorney fees. HUD may also refer the case to the Justice Department for action by the U.S. Attorney General, especially where it appears there is a pattern of discrimination.

Despite the enactment of legislation and antidiscrimination efforts by brokers' and lenders' groups, the nation's leading fair housing official recently announced that fair housing problems persist across the country. Incidents surface regularly of brokers steering minority persons either to or away from certain areas.

As a single person, you could also be a target of this type of steering. If you suspect it, report the offending real-estate agent or other party to HUD as well as to the local Board of Realtors and your attorney. Where widespread evidence of this kind of steering exists, the Justice Department will investigate.

State and Local Fair Housing Law

A number of states and cities have enacted their own fair housing statutes, which cover both discrimination in the search for a home and in the credit transaction. In some cases, these laws are more stringent than the federal statutes. Find out about the laws where you live, either by contacting

*This practice could adversely affect two or more single persons buying together, where only one individual holds a full-time job or where one individual has a higher income.

the consumer protection division of your state attorney general's office or local consumer housing groups. If you live in a state that has ratified an Equal Rights Law, you will have added protection.

Anti-Red-lining Legislation

Red-lining is the practice by mortgage lenders of refusing to make loans on houses in areas that they consider undersirable. When red-lining occurs, it usually prohibits borrowers from getting loans on older homes in inner-city or ethnic neighborhoods. Some state and local governments have enacted laws declaring red-lining illegal. And with the strong federal emphasis on inner-city revitalization, many lenders are more readily making loans in older sections of cities.

To encourage inner-city rehabilitation, Congress passed the Community Reinvestment Act (CRA) in 1977. This legislation requires that financial institutions applying for changes in status—branches, mergers, deposit insurance, charters, etc.—show they have made "continuing and affirmative" efforts to meet the credit needs of the local communities in which they are chartered. Frequently, lenders divert all their funds away from the inner city and into the wealthier suburbs.

This act directs the four federal agencies that regulate banking to encourage institutions to meet community credit needs and to assess each institution's record in meeting those needs.

CRA, as well as the Home Mortgage Disclosure Act, can affect you substantially if you're interested in inner-city rehabbing and have difficulty getting financing. The Disclosure Act, which has a 1980 sunset provision, requires lenders to disclose where they make mortgage loans by zip codes, so neighborhood and consumer groups can tell where red-lining occurs.* You can ask to see this information at any time at your bank, savings-and-loan association, or credit union. If there is an active consumer housing organization in your community, seek its help if you have trouble getting a loan for a home in an older neighborhood.

You can also send complaints to any Federal Reserve Bank or the regulatory agency of the lending institution. On the surface, it would appear that the Federal Fair Housing Act prohibits red-lining, but the practice persists. (For additional assistance you can seek in cases of red-lining, see "Rehabilitation Housing," page 57.)

The Fair Credit Reporting Act

This law requires any lender denying you a loan to immediately inform you that you can request in writing, within sixty days, the nature of the information on which the rejection was based. You also have the right to be told the name and address of the consumer reporting agency responsible for

---

*A fierce battle over extending this important legislation is anticipated. The major financial institutions strongly oppose extension, while consumer activists and neighborhood groups maintain it is essential to continue the process of inner-city redevelopment.

preparing the consumer report used to deny you credit. Within thirty days of the denial, you can obtain, free of charge, the nature, substance, and sources of information collected about you by the consumer reporting agency. You can request to see this information anytime, but the agency is allowed to charge a fee for the disclosure if it doesn't follow a denial.

This act also gives you the right to have incomplete or incorrect information reinvestigated, and if the information is found to be inaccurate or cannot be verified, you can have the information removed from your credit file. When your version of a transaction differs from that of the credit reporting agency, you can have your version placed in your file and included in subsequent consumer reports. You can also request the agency to send your version to certain businesses without charge. You can sue a company for willful or negligent violations of this law, and if you win, you can collect attorney's fees and court costs.

Says Sally Gold, of the FTC's Bureau of Consumer Protection, "The FTC urges citizens who are rejected credit to challenge the rejection. Many credit scoring systems are clearly discriminatory, and those who challenge the rejection and ask the lender to examine their past credit records usually get credit."

This legislation provides additional protective measures in the advent of adverse action. You should know that it covers all credit transactions, not just mortgage loans. The FTC is charged with investigating violations, and for more detailed information on this law or to report a violation, contact the nearest regional office of the FTC, or you can write the Fair Credit Reporting Act, Federal Trade Commission, Washington, D.C. 20580.

Enforcement of Consumer Protection Laws

"Housing-related disputes touch the lives of millions of Americans every year. The scope of the problem—the disputes that are ignored, shunted aside, or left to fester over time, due to inadequate dispute resolution capability, is an added dimension of a tremendous social and economic dilemma," says Randall Scott, director of the National Housing and Justice Field Assistance Program.

The antidiscrimination and fair housing laws have *not* been rigorously enforced since their passage. The tide is changing, however, as consumer groups with heightened awareness of the pervasive discrimination in obtaining housing and financing begin to exercise their collective clout and as more single women and men buy homes.

Leading the vanguard in the enforcement effort was a coalition of civil rights and fair housing organizations, which in 1976 sued the four federal regulatory agencies to make them use their enforcement powers to end the routine discriminatory policies of lenders. As a result of that suit, the agencies agreed to implement new enforcement programs to search out and prevent illegal lending practices.

The regulatory agencies have since begun beefing up their civil rights staffs, which have uncovered evidence substantiating the charges of discrimination that the coalition alleged in its suit. One of the leading members of that coalition, the Center for National Policy Review, has compiled an excellent handbook on fair mortgage lending. The booklet discusses loan seekers' rights and advises how to recognize discrimination and to file a complaint. It explains the new enforcement programs, and lists consumer-oriented groups throughout the country with expertise in various areas of housing.

This booklet also contains a directory of federal regulatory agencies. You can obtain a copy of this handbook by writing the Center for National Policy Review, Catholic University Law School, Washington, D.C. 20064.

To handle the increasing number of discrimination and other housing-related cases, housing courts and fair housing offices are being established in a number of cities. If you have a grievance or complaint regarding any housing matter, contact a local consumer housing organization and/or your attorney for advice on how to proceed. Any local housing advocacy group or neighborhood justice center should be able to assist you. If you believe your personal rights have been violated, you can also contact the American Civil Liberties Union.

Finally, you should know that amendments to the existing statutes and new laws to expand the scope of the present legislation are constantly being proposed. Some of these proposals are legitimate efforts to achieve equal opportunity in housing; others are bureaucratic boondoggles. Government, by no means, has played an even hand in the effort to obtain equality in the housing market. It, too, is fraught with special interests and industry tie-ins. The moral is: You are your own best advocate if you proceed in an informed, methodical manner.

11

Special Tips for Single Persons Buying Together

"Marcus, the man with whom I lived for five years, died, and a great uncle whom he never met is going to get the house and all the property even though Marc and I bought it together," laments Nancy.

Many persons of the same sex and opposite sex are doubling up, even tripling up, to buy homes. Cohabitation for members of the opposite sex has become socially acceptable, and career persons, unwilling to be penalized as married couples by either the tax or Social Security systems, often choose to live together.

Unfortunately, these individuals frequently fail to specify their arrangements and agreements in legal contracts. Hence, they encounter a situation similar to Nancy's. Or worse, they end up in court battling over the property. Since the precedent-setting *Marvin* v. *Marvin* case, the number of palimony suits has multiplied across the country. And the courts generally hold that what happens after a breakup depends largely on how the cohabitants handled their finances while together. Thus, without a legal document you leave yourself wide open for trouble.

Says Polly Blanton, an Atlanta attorney who handles closings for many same-sex and opposite-sex friends buying together, "The main thing singles have to look out for is how they choose to hold the property, and many of them are oblivious to the fact or simply refuse to deal with it. This can lead to some disastrous situations.

"To protect themselves, unmarried couples must have a legal instrument declaring how they will hold the property and what each person's rights and obligations are."

The worst mistake you can make is to base your purchase on an informal, friendship understanding. In such an instance, if your friend later decides to move out or quit paying his or her share, you will be responsible for the entire mortgage if you have both signed the mortgage note. The lender will go after whoever is living in the house or capable of paying, even if that requires going to court and suing. If you eventually want to sell the house and your friend resists, you would have to sue to force a sale of the property. Necessary repairs and routine maintenance can become a hassle without a proper legal agreement. Suppose the roof needs reshingling and your friend can't afford or won't agree to pay for part of the repair. How do you resolve the dispute?

Unless you get the arrangement contractually set up from the outset, there can be endless difficulties, which consistently leave you at the mercy of the other person and any unforeseen events. Step one in buying with another individual is to find an open-minded attorney competent in real-estate transactions. Younger attorneys frequently are more sympathetic and knowledgeable about the arrangements for people living together.

Legal Advice and Arrangements

If you consult an attorney prior to applying for a loan, he can advise you of your legally protected rights and guide you through the loan process. For individuals buying together, lenders often turn the transaction into a Grand Inquisition. They illegally demand proof of how long you have lived together or quiz you about the particulars of your relationship or when you intend to marry.

Notes Blanton, "Where they have no assurance of a marriage license holding two people together, lenders make value judgments which I think are totally invalid. I say you don't know how long a marriage is going to last so what's the point of trying to pin down two single people on the future of their relationship?"

Unfortunately, she adds, most couples don't come to her until after they've gone through the lender's grilling. By that time, they feel humiliated from having someone critically probe into the inner recesses of their lives. Consequently, they are even more reluctant to discuss their relationship, which handicaps Blanton's ability to help them.

For example, she was shocked to learn *after the fact* that a lender, as a condition for granting the mortgage loan, required two single males to sign an agreement stating they had lived together for two years and purchased all of their property jointly during that period.

Taking Title to Your Property

In addition to helping you with the loan process, your attorney should advise you how to take ownership of your property. The two main ways for persons buying together to take title are as "joint tenants" or "tenants in common." However, you should carefully check out the laws regarding property in your state as they vary greatly.

Joint Tenancy

Joint tenants share equally in the property. Both have a right to the use of the whole property, and if one dies the survivor inherits the house, the land, and the mortgage. Also called joint tenancy with the right of survivorship, this form of ownership supercedes any will in passing the property to the surviving partner, who automatically becomes the sole owner upon the death of the other. A joint tenant can sell his share of the property, although this may involve court action.

Tenants in Common

Tenants in common own the property in equal parts. If one tenant dies, the other tenant does not get the decedent's part. It becomes part of his or her estate and is distributed according to his or her will or, in the absence of a will, according to the laws of intestacy.*

As you see, how you take title determines who will inherit your share of the property. The property's worth should also be considered in deciding how to hold it. Because of the variables involved and the differences in state laws, it's impossible to lay down general rules. You should consult both your attorney and tax accountant about the best method for you to take title.

Drafting the Contract

After you've determined how to take title, the next step is to draft a contract (also called a non-nuptial agreement), spelling out the rights and responsibilities of each person, as well as what happens in the event of the departure or demise of one or both persons. *This contract should be signed prior to the closing.*

The majority of single buyers fail to sign this agreement, thereby making it a valid contract, prior to the closing. Typically, they just let the matter slide, which results in some unholy cat fights later.

Sign the document, and make its existence and whereabouts known to your heirs, parents, or any persons who might contest the disposition of the property following your death. You should store this contract in an appropriate place for safekeeping. Normally, your attorney will retain a copy, and a copy may also be attached to the abstract.

Although your specific circumstances will dictate the stipulations in your contract, here are some of the provisions it should include:

- A description of the property and how it is to be held.
- The portion of each person's monetary contribution toward the purchase, including the down payment and closing costs.
- The amount of the mortgage and whether it is jointly financed.
- Each person's monthly contribution to the mortgage payment.
- Each person's contribution to the insurance, taxes, and maintenance expenses.
- How and where records are to be kept of each person's contribution.
- What happens if one person fails to make his/her payment.
- How the property will be divided in the event of a sale.
- What happens if only one person decides to sell. The other person should be given the first option to buy the seller's share, and the property's value should be computed by an independent appraiser. Method of payment should also be designated—whether in cash at the point of the seller's departure or over a period of time.

*These laws, which vary from state to state, designate how property or an estate will be divided when there is no will.

- How property is to be disposed of if one person dies. (This provision is usually unnecessary if you take title as joint tenants. If you take title as tenants in common, the surviving party often is given the first option to buy from the decedent's heirs.)
- What happens if both persons cease wanting to live together but both want to remain in the house. Who stays may be determined by the flip of a coin, with the winner having the option to buy out the loser's share, according to a specified formula and based on an independent appraisal. (Since most persons don't have immediate access to the cash necessary to buy the other person's share, repayment is usually set up over a period of time, such as five years. Or, the property may be refinanced.)
- What happens in the event of the disappearance or mental disability of one person. Usually the co-owners agree to give each other power of attorney over the house. So if one person should disappear, say for ninety days, or be declared mentally incompetent, the other owner is free to sell the house or encounter any encumbrance on the property.
- An appendix listing all furnishings purchased jointly.
- Also ask your attorney about including a provision that in the event of a breakup, the remaining party (buyer) can obtain a release from the bank releasing the departing party (seller) from the mortgage debt. As long as both names are on the mortgage note, each person is fully liable for the entire loan amount and the entire taxes. The buyer should transfer everything into his/her name so the seller can't make later claim to the property. (However, if the lender doesn't think the buyer's income will support the monthly payments, he may not remove the seller's name from the mortgage note. These details should be worked out contractually in advance.)

Without a protective contract, the parents or children of the deceased or disabled partner could claim half of the house.* In fact, that's exactly what happened in Jack's case. He and Darlene jointly bought a house, although he made the major monetary contribution to the purchase. When Darlene was killed in a car accident, her family fought for her share of the house. Consequently, Jack had to sell the house and give half of the profits to Darlene's family, even though he had made most of the payments.

Look over the agreement (page 205) drafted by two women who built a duplex together. Because Esther had children who she wanted to inherit her half, the women decided to hold the property as tenants in common and each drafted a will.

Personal Property Agreements

To avoid legal snarls over the division of material goods in the event of a breakup, it's advisable to have property agreements regarding household possessions. Couples often agree that each person retains complete ownership of all possessions owned prior to their cohabitation. It's best to make and sign a list of the more valuable items you each own for future reference. If

*This presumes that all co-owners are single or legally divorced. If one of the parties is legally separated, but not divorced, the surviving spouse could claim a share of the property.

one person gives the other a major item, it's a good idea to prepare a statement setting forth the facts.

You can draft your own written agreements, similar to the following, for major purchases and ownership understandings. Signed copies of these agreements outlining your intentions should be kept by each of you, and one should be filed with your attorney. In the agreement, stipulate who will own the item, who will pay for it, what will happen if you break up or one of you dies.

If you decide to purchase major items jointly, you should also protect yourself with an agreement outlining each person's obligations and how the property will be divided if you break up. When you have questions about property or purchases, consult your attorney. You should conscientiously maintain precise records of all your financial contributions and transactions.

Couples with track records advise against joint bank or credit accounts as well as joint purchases. Do not cosign loans or credit agreements unless you are willing to assume all payments if your friend cannot or will not pay.

Although such formal agreements may seem to go against the grain of an affectionate, trusting relationship, they may be the very elements that later preserve your friendship. Or at least enable you to part ways as civil adults.

Always remember that if you get into a legal dispute, a court settlement will probably be based on how you handled your finances together. If you held property or bank accounts jointly, without the benefit of protective contracts, that would make recovery easier for a partner seeking greater equity.

Kingsford, who bought his first house—a country home on several acres—with a male friend, explains the guidelines they followed. Since both men were divorced and making substantial child-support payments, they needed to pool incomes for the down payment and closing costs. They took title as joint tenants, but with the formal stipulation that if their arrangement proved unsatisfactory, each would have the option of buying the other out.

AGREEMENT

Bonnie Wolslegel and Esther I. Maier hereby agree to the following:

1. We, the undersigned, have purchased, as tenants in common, Lot 46 of East Side Annex Assessor's Plat No. 19, City of Wisconsin Rapids, Wood County, Wisconsin. We built a duplex on said property.
2. We have contributed equally toward the purchase of said property and have jointly financed a mortgage with the Wisconsin Rapids Savings & Loan of Wisconsin Rapids, Wisconsin, in the amount of $38,200.00 to purchase said property.
3. Each party shall pay one-half of the monthly payments due and owing Wisconsin Rapids Savings & Loan.
4. Each party shall pay one-half the taxes on said property and one-half the insurance premiums on said property by the date on which said payments are due.
5. Should either party fail to make a payment as described in paragraphs 3 and 4, the other party shall have the right to make said payment, and said amount shall be added to the share of the party who makes the payment.
6. Upon the sale of said real property, each party shall be entitled to one-half the net proceeds realized from said sale unless payments have been made under

paragraph 5, in which case each party shall be entitled to that percentage of the net proceeds from the sale of the house that corresponds to the percentage of the payments she has made of the total payments made.

7. Each party shall keep a record of all payments made. All payments shall be made by check or money order.

8. If either party should want to sell her share, the parties shall attempt to agree as to the value of the share. If the parties are unable to agree, the value of the share shall be computed in the following manner:

A. An independent qualified real-estate appraiser shall appraise the value of the property.

B. All encumbrances (mortgages, deeds of trust, etc.) on the property and the cost of selling said property shall be subtracted from the appraised value to determine the equity in the house.

C. The selling person's share in the equity shall be that percentage of the equity that corresponds to the percentage of the payments she has made of the total payments made pursuant to paragraphs 3 and 4. The other party shall then have the right to purchase the selling party's interest. The purchase of either party's respective share shall be a cash purchase. If the other party does not purchase the selling party's share, the selling party may sell her share on the open market.

9. Upon the death of either party and within three months of said death, the other party shall have the right to purchase the deceased party's interest in said real property from the heirs of said deceased party. If the surviving party and the heirs of the deceased party cannot agree as to the value of the property at the time of purchase from the heirs, the value shall be computed as specified in paragraph 8.

10. Each party shall sign all documents necessary to accomplish the provisions of this agreement.

11. The provisions of this agreement may not be altered except by a written document executed by both parties before a notary public.

12. This agreement is binding upon the heirs and assigns of each party.

13. Each party enters into the above agreement and makes the above promises in consideration for the other party entering into the agreement and making said promises.

Dated this _____ day of _____, 1978.

_____
Bonnie Wolslegel

_____
Esther I. Maier

STATE OF WISCONSIN
COUNTY OF WOOD   SS

Personally came before me, this _____ day of _____, 1978, the above named Bonnie Wolslegel and Esther I. Maier, to me known to be the persons who executed the foregoing instrument and acknowledged the same.

_____
Kenneth M. Hill, Notary Public
Wood County, Wisconsin
My Commission is permanent

AGREEMENT

John Anderson and Mary Miller agree as follows:

1. That the Amana microwave oven and Kitchen Aid dishwasher* purchased in January, 1980, belong exclusively to John Anderson.

2. That the power lawn mower and Maytag washer and dryer purchased in June, 1979, belong exclusively to Mary Miller.

Dated_____   _____
John Anderson

Dated_____   _____
Mary Miller

*It's advisable to also include the serial number of each item for absolute identification.

AGREEMENT

John Anderson and Mary Miller agree as follows:

1. That all the furniture in the living room and bedroom at 701 Marble Street, Houston, Texas, belongs to Mary Miller and that Mary Miller is solely liable to pay any and all obligations due and owing on this furniture. The furniture includes:
   A.
   B.
   C.
   D.

2. That all the furniture in the study and kitchen at 701 Marble Street, Houston, Texas, belongs to John Anderson and that John Anderson is solely liable to pay any and all obligations due and owing on this furniture. The furniture includes:
   A.
   B.
   C.
   D.

Dated_____   _____
John Anderson

Dated_____   _____
Mary Miller

"Both Paul and I consulted our individual attorneys and worked out a contract," King said. "I think that was essential; otherwise the friendship would have broken down, because it's very easy to have misunderstandings about what verbal agreements were made. I would never advise anyone to just make a verbal agreement regarding a property purchase."

Since both men held demanding jobs with heavy time commitments, they had a formal agreement regarding each one's responsibilities for household tasks and maintenance. Their contract stipulated they would make equal contributions to the down payment and monthly mortgage payments.

They opened up a joint bank account as a household account to which they both made equal monthly contributions from their personal accounts. From the joint account, they paid the monthly mortgage payment, the utilities and other household bills, as well as the groceries and maintenance expenses.

After about one year, Paul changed jobs and sold out his interest in the house to King. Because they had the contract as a point of reference, there were no disagreements. They simply figured up Paul's contribution to the house and the property's current value. Then King bought Paul out, based on his outlay and the current value of his share.

King transferred the title and mortgage note into his name alone. Since he had the qualifying income to keep up the mortgage payments, the changeover was a simple process to which the lender readily agreed.

Wills

If you or your friend have sizable holdings outside of your shared property or if you own the property as tenants in common, you both should have wills. Having a legal will is the only way to assure that your estate will be distributed according to your wishes. If one or both of you have children or parents still living, you should definitely consult your attorney about drafting a will. When a large amount of assets is involved, you should also visit with a tax accountant for advice on estate planning.

Taxes

If you're at all familiar with the tax system, you know that married working couples pay more in annual income taxes than two single persons with the same incomes. And the difference can be substantial if husband and wife earn anything like the same amounts of pay.

Take, for example, a working couple where the wife earns $10,000 and the husband $15,000. If they file a joint return claiming the standard deduction, their income tax will be $4,057, or $535 more than the tax on two singles with those same incomes. At higher levels of income, this marriage penalty is even stiffer. A husband and wife, each of whom earns $30,000, must pay $3,654—about 24 percent more—than two single people with the same incomes.

Since the U. S. Supreme Court recently refused to review a challenge to this marriage tax, it's apt to remain in force for a long time, thus making cohabitation more desirable. There are about two dozen additional tax rules that benefit singles and penalize married couples. For instance, married couples can write off only half as much of a capital loss against ordinary income in one year as can two singles. The same general rule applies in the treatment of moving expenses, investment credits, and depreciation. Keep these factors in mind as you contemplate or enter a purchase with another single individual.

You should consult a knowledgeable tax accountant, who can point out all the rules that will affect you and can prepare your tax returns. Also make sure you set up your bank accounts so that you can both claim deductions for interest and depreciation, if applicable.

Insurance

One study conducted a few years ago found that unmarried couples definitely face discrimination from the insurance industry, and shopping around is difficult since many companies not only charge such couples higher rates, but may refuse to insure them altogether. That study revealed that unmarried couples often had difficulty obtaining property insurance, and the individuals frequently paid higher rates for car insurance. Obtaining life insurance was not as difficult.

Some of those barriers undoubtedly have been broken down over the past couple years, as the number of persons buying property and living together has increased. Before buying any insurance, you should compare the policies offered by different companies on the basis of cost and benefits. You will, of course, need property insurance and should visit with several agents about the best way to hold this policy.

If you have children or one of you is financially dependent on the other, life insurance is probably a good idea.

Even though they both have well-paying jobs, Doug and Lisa, who combined incomes to buy a home, took out $50,000 life insurance policies on each other. If one dies, the other will receive the cash necessary to buy out the decedent's share of the house from his or her heirs.

Other single buyers take out mortgage life policies so that in the event of the death of one, the other will receive the cash to pay off the mortgage.

Discrimination

"We will not make loans to gays or two unrelated single people. We worry about what would happen if the relationship would change, and we don't like dealing with the liabilities that could result from a split-up. Where there is no marriage or legal binding relationship, it's much more difficult to collect the money." This statement comes from a loan officer in an expanding Midwest city known for its liberal and tolerant attitudes.

Rather than refusing the loan outright, she said, the lending institution resorts to more subtle tactics. The loan officer will be instructed to accept only one person's income on the loan application or to impose more rigid credit standards on the couple.

These practices violate the Equal Credit Opportunity Act (ECOA), which prohibits discrimination on the basis of sex or marital status in the terms of credit or financing. ECOA also forbids the lender to consider only the income of the primary wage earner.* (For more information on ECOA, see "The Laws You Need to Know," page 193.)

Unfortunately, notes Blanton, most single buyers don't know enough about the consumer laws to catch lenders in these violations.

Nevertheless, she detects considerable headway in unrelated couples' ability to get loans. Prior to passage of ECOA, she said, two single women could not get a loan together, while two single men could. Now, she reports, the barrier has been significantly lifted for both female buyers and opposite-sex couples, since lenders can't demand a marriage certificate before granting a loan.

It's illegal for the lender to inquire how long applicants have lived together or to require proof of, or consider, the length of time persons have cohabitated. ECOA also prohibits lenders from asking when a couple intends to marry or considering, as a condition for granting the loan, the stability of the relationship, which is at best a subjective judgment.

Nonetheless, lenders do consider all of these factors, although they would never state them as a reason for denying a loan nor would they ask any of those questions in the presence of the applicants' attorney. Lenders are much more discriminating about lending to two unrelated people and often pressure couples to get married.

"Before closing a transaction I have been told by lenders to get statements from buyers of when they were married or if they were planning to get married, even though they just said that to assure they would get the loan," Blanton says.

Noting that lenders can use any information volunteered by the applicants, Blanton advises singles buying together not to provide any information about the nature of their relationship or their intentions.

"If the lender asks whether you are using someone else's income to qualify for the loan, say 'yes,' and give that person's name, but don't volunteer any other information," recommends Blanton.

Unrelated couples who have difficulty getting conventional financing should apply for an FHA-backed loan. With these loans, the lender—usually a mortgage banker—only takes the application and forwards it to the local FHA office, where the decision to make the loan is based strictly on factual data.

Dorothy Johnson, a loan officer with Banco Mortgage Company, says, "We have an awful lot of singles buying together. As long as they are both employed and FHA and our underwriter in the secondary market go along

---

*In other words, if one of you earns more or one of you works only part-time, the lender must count both of your incomes according to ECOA.

with it, we're happy to make the loans. We never ask how long they've been living together, because that's a violation of the law."

Despite the law, lending institutions differ greatly on their policies of loaning to unrelated couples, so you may really have to shop around to obtain mortgage financing. On the other hand, if you both have qualifying incomes and present yourselves confidently and knowledgeably to the loan officer, your application may sail through. Above all, avoid the puritans, who attempt to subject you to a demoralizing battery of personal questions.

Elinor, who carefully researched her rights before deciding to buy a house with her male roommate of three years, reports, "Unmarried couples do not have the benefit of law and custom regarding marriage and property behind them. Therefore, they need special and sympathetic counsel from a competent attorney."

Elinor, whose joint purchase was made in a major city where such arrangements are increasingly common, concluded that most real-estate agents and lenders are more interested in profits than preaching.

"The changing mores make life more complicated for those who must determine which loans are bad risks. We found the indication of stability lenders most frequently use with unmarried persons is the length of time they have lived together," she said.

Elinor and her partner, both established professionals in their city, were up front with the lender about their relationship and their intentions and found that approach worked best for them. However, they were also cognizant of the laws and their rights.

As an example of what can happen if you don't know the laws and don't deal with a straightforward lender who gives you firm commitments, consider Renee's and Sam's experience.

Because of their unusual circumstances—building a dome in a rural community as an unmarried couple—Renee and Sam went to a savings-and-loan association in a nearby town recommended by the broker who had sold them the land. In fact, the broker personally introduced them to the head loan officer, who, he assured them, was "a pretty free-thinking fellow."

Renee, who handled most of the financial details, did not shop around for a loan and now realizes she should have.

"But at the time, I considered myself so lucky to have gotten the loan without any difficulty," she said. "I was really green at the beginning, and there were so many things I didn't know about."

Although the lender did not inquire whether they intended to marry or ask other personal questions, he refused to count as income $2,500 which Renee receives annually as a property settlement from her former husband. The loan officer quoted Renee and Sam an interest rate of 9¼ percent on their $46,000 loan, but failed to give them the required estimate of closing costs or any other information concerning the closing.

Several weeks later when Renee phoned the lender with some questions, he informed her that the closing costs would be about 2 percent of the loan amount. (The law requires a dollar estimate of closing costs be given within three days of the loan application, along with the informational booklet describing the Real Estate Settlement Procedures Act.) Renee, however, proceeded in good faith, anticipating a maximum $920 in closing costs. When she went in for the closing, she was handed a bill for $1,200 in closing costs and told the interest rate would be 9¾ percent—which figures out to a 10½ annual percentage rate.

"I told the lender that the 9¼ percent was originally stated to me as the interest rate and 2 percent as the closing costs. He told me, 'Oh, you must have misunderstood,' " Renee recalled.

So, although Renee and Sam were congenially received by the lender and not subjected to embarrassing questions, they were the victims of a more subtle and devious form of discrimination. The lender deliberately withheld certain required disclosures and then penalized them with higher charges at the closing.

Since the passage of ECOA, Blanton said she has handled closings for a variety of singles—two, often three or more persons—buying together. Sometimes children are involved, and divorced parents join other like-minded individuals to buy a duplex, triplex, or quadruplex. Depending on your relationship to the person or persons with whom you're buying and the type property involved, there are certain details that warrant your attention.

Opposite-Sex Buyers

Persons of the opposite sex with qualifying incomes, if they are honest about their relationship, provide the required information on the loan application, and give no indication of an intent to marry, often encounter little or no resistance at major metropolitan lending institutions. In small towns or rural areas where these arrangements are uncommon, such couples may have difficulty obtaining a loan. If you run into problems with a lender, you should diplomatically call the laws protecting you to his attention. If you gain no ground with that approach, point out that you can report violations to the lending institution's regulatory agency.

Says the president of one small-town savings-and-loan association, "Some single guys buy together here, but there is a raising of eyebrows with singles of the opposite sex buying together—it goes against the social grain."

Although he knows the laws, the S&L president admits that an application from an unmarried couple, "because it is something different socially, may well be looked at more closely."

It is important to make your intentions known as two singles cohabiting. To avoid involving yourself in a common law marriage, you should at all times use your own names and not open any unnecessary joint accounts. Although only a handful of states (13) still recognize common law marriages, states that do not provide for common law marriages within their own borders may recognize such marriages which were properly formed in other states that do recognize them. A legal contract should provide adequate protection, but you should also discuss this matter with your attorney.

Same-Sex Friends

Today, loan applications from two single females are more readily approved than those from two single males. Because there are more women remaining single and moving into high-paying career positions who know the laws, lenders are eager to write them loans. The women's movement has helped significantly to raise the consciousness of most lenders. Now it is the single males buying together who are more suspect.

"Two women buying together do not present the threat to the masculinity of the male loan officer or real-estate agent that two men do," believes Blanton. "Lenders automatically assume two males buying together are gay. Before ECOA, lenders routinely disapproved loans to gays because they thought the relationships were unstable. The law now encourages them to go along, but they would probably find a way to deny them the loan if they could."

In fact, there is no federal law prohibiting discrimination on the basis of sexual preference. Only in those communities that have passed ordinances establishing equal rights for homosexuals do these individuals have legal recourse. And then, it's a decision of whether one wants to press the matter, risking the possibility of publicity, on the heels of an initially embarrassing encounter.

To avoid these confrontations, there are several alternatives to explore. One is to deal with an open-minded broker and lender. In Atlanta, a number of gays who experienced the sting and humiliation of discrimination in their search for homes formed their own real-estate company. They then cultivated contacts with unbiased lenders.

One Atlanta mortgage banker who routinely writes loans for gay couples, says, "All I want to know is whether they have the money to make the payments, a good credit record, and whether they plan to continue living together. That's a legitimate concern when I'm making a loan based on both of their incomes."

Another course to pursue if you have difficulty getting a loan is to apply for an FHA-backed mortgage. The loan officer simply collects the facts and forwards them to the FHA, which makes the final decision on the basis of your qualifications. The officials who must approve the loan never meet the applicants, and their main concern is whether you and your friend represent a good investment.

A third alternative for same-sex friends is to have one partner with a qualifying income take out the mortgage in his or her name alone. You can combine your funds for the down payment and closing costs and have the person with the higher income take out the loan.

For your own protection, you can then have each of your contributions and your agreement defined in a formal contract. Blanton advises gay couples who have difficulty obtaining loans to follow this course. Usually, she says, a satisfactory agreement can be worked out with the attorney to protect both parties. For example, following the closing, an agreement of common tenancy can be inserted in the deed records to reflect the co-ownership.

However, since banking practices and laws vary in different states, you should consult an attorney practicing in real estate about the best method for you.

Cosigners

Although the law allows you to have a qualified cosigner of your choice, lenders sometimes balk at this request or impose impossible conditions. For instance, if your credit record necessitates a cosigner (this is your first home and you're really extending yourself to buy it; you've just been divorced and don't have substantial credit in your name), the lender may quiz you in detail about your cosigner.

The key, again, is: Don't answer the unasked question and don't volunteer unnecessary information. You will undoubtedly be asked your cosigner's name and income. If you present the facts in a businesslike manner and your cosigner's credit checks out satisfactorily, the loan should go through.

Blanton, who has handled a number of closings involving cosigners, states, "The matter of cosigners is a very fuzzy area in the law and the handling of mortgages."

That's partially because the law mandating lenders to accept qualified cosigners is unknown to many single persons and, therefore, has not been widely used. Also, lenders unfamiliar with this practice are reluctant to branch into a new area that presents potential underwriting risks for them.

Non-Resident Co-Buyers

If you're short of the cash for your purchase but have a friend or relative who will put up the necessary capital, you can buy as co-owners with the help of a willing lender.

Ilene, a thirty-eight-year-old career woman in Houston, decided she wanted to buy a home and start building equity, but she didn't have the cash for a down payment. Her brother, a contractor in Nevada, agreed to provide her the money as a co-buyer.

The lender warned Ilene that his institution did "not prefer" such co-buying situations, particularly when one buyer resided out of the state. But Ilene persisted, and the lender asked for a gift letter, which her brother provided, stating that he had given her $10,000.

Following the closing, Ilene's attorney drafted an agreement, which states that her brother is a shareholder in the property relative to the percentage of his investment. Ilene, however, is the prime owner, holds the mortgage in her name alone, and makes all of the payments. If she sells, her brother gets a portion of the profits based on the percentage of his investment. If Ilene dies, her brother inherits the house.

"This was an arrangement of mutual convenience for us," Ilene said. "I needed the money, and Elliot wanted an equity investment in real estate."

Provided you have a cooperative lender, there are any number of arrangements you can work out to the benefit of both parties. For example, Claudia, who lives in Philadelphia, wanted a home of her own, but needed some financial help. So her friend Brenda, who lives in a Los Angeles apartment and travels extensively on her job, agreed to help with the financing. That way, Brenda gained the equity accrual and tax advantages of ownership without the day-to-day responsibilities.

Duplexes and Tandem Houses

Many single persons who want their own living space, but can't afford detached homes of their own, pool funds to buy duplexes. This concept has become so popular that many builders are constructing tandem houses with two bedroom suites and common living spaces to accommodate two single persons who join resources to buy. Some tandem homes are designed so that one of the owners will have an upstairs bedroom and bath plus a sitting-room loft overlooking the downstairs living area. The other person will have a bedroom and bath of his or her own downstairs.

Purchasing a duplex or tandem home can be a very satisfactory arrangement, provided both parties methodically follow the steps of the real-estate transaction and take the proper legal measures. Jill and Anita, two nurses working on graduate degrees, demonstrate the ease of purchasing a duplex with a mutual strategy.

Both women were paying astronomical rents for their Santa Barbara apartments, but neither could afford to buy a house by herself. They figured if they could get the money for the down payment, buying a duplex would substantially decrease their monthly housing expenses and enable them to build equity. Moreover, buying a duplex would give them enough flexibility so that if one decided to move, she could either rent out her half or sell it to the person remaining.

"It was really an ideal situation, offering all the benefits of home ownership without the constraints," Jill said.

Each woman made a list of requirements for her half of the duplex and areas on which she could compromise. The two then contacted a female real-estate agent they knew and trusted and explained what they wanted.

Each wanted two bedrooms and an enclosed garage. Jill wanted space for gardening, southern window exposures, and a laundry room; Anita wanted a large kitchen, a fireplace, and minimum yard space for which to care.

The agent took them to see four duplexes, and they made an $82,000 offer on the one which met their requirements. The owners, a young couple who had been transferred to San Diego, were asking $84,000 for the property. The husband had already been commuting several weeks, and his wife, tired of showing the place and left with the power of attorney, accepted the $82,000 offer.

Jill and Anita got their loan at the seller's bank—the practice in California so the seller doesn't have to pay a stiff prepayment penalty. The women took title as joint tenants.

On the advice of Jill's brother-in-law, an attorney, the women drafted their own contract stipulating what each person's responsibilities were, both financially and for maintenance of the property. The contract also stipulated that if one of them wanted to sell, the duplex would be appraised at fair market value and the other owner would have the first option to buy the entire property. If she did not want to buy the other half, it would be sold on the open market. If they both decided to sell, they contractually agreed to split the proceeds.

The women sent signed copies of the contract to their parents and kept their own copies in places known to each other.

"We talked about having an attorney draft a contract for us, but we decided we had known each other nine years and we trusted each other so we didn't think we would get into any hassles," Jill said. "The only area about which we felt uncomfortable was if something would happen to either of us whether our family members would carry out our wishes. That's why we wrote out a contract and sent signed copies to our parents. I would not recommend someone else handling it that way without consulting an attorney, though."

One year later, Jill took a job in the Midwest and Anita married. When they had the duplex appraised, it had appreciated to a value of $110,000. So for $55,000, Jill sold out her interest to Anita and her husband, who refinanced the property and put the deed in their names as husband and wife.

"Since we didn't go through a broker, and all the legal details had been taken care of just one year ago, we didn't need to repeat anything, so there were no fees entailed in refinancing the property," Jill said.

If you decide to buy a duplex with a like-minded friend, you should consult an attorney about how to set up the financing and the contract. You should also seek the advice of an experienced insurance salesperson on the best method to arrange your home-owner's coverage.

Jill said the trickiest part of their transaction was setting up the property insurance. The insurance companies they contacted had no mechanism for insuring the property and personal affects of two unrelated people co-owning a duplex as separate residents. The insurer would cover the contents for one-half of the duplex under an owner's policy, but the other half had to be insured under a separate tenant's policy.

"Even though the property insurance was taken out in both of our names, the company would insure only one-half for contents. So we called Anita's side the owner's half and my side the tenant's half, and we took out a tenant's policy as a rider to the main insurance policy," Jill said.

12

Advice for the Single-Again

Over the past decade, the divorce rate in America has doubled, and in this time the number of widows has increased to more than twelve million. The U.S. Census Bureau predicts that one in three persons between the ages of twenty-five and thirty-five will get a divorce. More than one-fifth of all U.S. households now consist of live-alone persons, and the fastest-growing family type is that of the female-headed household. By the end of the seventies, there were more than eighteen million families maintained by women.

Death or divorce generally dictate major readjustments in one's housing arrangements and life-style. Such drastic events often strike women the hardest, because, traditionally, they have fewer economic resources than men and often depend upon their husbands for support.

This chapter will address the needs of divorced and widowed individuals, pinpointing the problems they encounter and suggesting solutions to ease the transition to a single household. Special attention will be given to the needs of the single-again woman. Because the problems of the divorced and widowed often overlap, a person in either situation would benefit from a thorough reading of all the material presented here. You should, however, pay particular attention to the section discussing your situation.

Divorce and Property Settlements

Usually the first impact of a separation is a drastically reduced income for both parties. If you own a home with your spouse, often that home has to be sold because it would be too costly for one person to maintain. In some cases, one spouse remains in the family home and the other spouse has to find alternative, affordable shelter. As a result of the inflated prices of real estate, it has become quite common to divide the equity in a jointly owned home, enabling both parties to purchase other homes.

Naturally, circumstances and needs vary. Where there are children, considerable property, and assets to divide, a settlement can be a complicated matter. On the other hand, where both partners agree to part and divide property equally, the dissolution can be relatively simple. If there was a prenuptial contract specifying how property and assets would be divided in the event of divorce, you'll know exactly what you will receive and will have a good idea of your financial status. Because of the high incidence of remarriages, contracts have become popular in recent years. In any case, you must be extremely careful to tailor your housing adjustments to your circumstances.

For example, when thirty-two-year-old Jennifer's seven-year marriage ended, she had a full-time job and was working part-time on a graduate degree. She and her spouse had no children and had never owned a home, so all they had to divide were furnishings and some savings. After a period of apartment dwelling with rambunctious neighbors who disrupted her studies and sleep, Jennifer decided to invest in a place of her own. Because she didn't have enough money by herself for a down payment, she used her assets from the settlement to invest in a duplex with another divorced woman, who had received a substantial cash settlement as her share of equity in a jointly owned home with her spouse. By pooling their resources, both women were able to afford modest homes of their own.

Not all settlements, unfortunately, are as easy and amicable as Jennifer's. Often the situation is tense and emotionally strained. There are strong disagreements over the terms and conditions of the divorce. It's a time of frustration, stress, and insecurity for everyone. Then the best thing you can do is *sit tight*. After undergoing a traumatic divorce, you should give yourself a cooling-off period of at least one year before plunging into a purchase. Most persons recovering from the ordeal of a divorce aren't prepared to confidently and competently make the major decisions required in the hydra-headed operation of buying a home. You need time to take stock of your situation, get some sound advice, and get your affairs in order before you take any action.

During and immediately following a divorce, you're a target for unethical opportunists, such as the real-estate agents who read the published divorce notices and then contact the spouse awarded the property with an offer to sell it and help the person buy another home. Agents who resort to these tactics, preying on the vulnerability and desperation of the just-divorced and rushing them into a sale, are to be avoided, as Angie can attest.

Divorced only two weeks and worried about the expense of maintaining her large house, Angie started looking around for a smaller, more modest place for her two daughters and herself. The broker who so swiftly stepped in to handle the sale of her $85,000 home tired quickly of trying to find something suited to Angie's reduced income and referred a new, young agent to help her. After three weeks, unable to locate any decent prospects in her price range, Angie grew panicky as the date she had to vacate her present home neared.

Then the young agent, eager to make his first sale, showed Angie a sixty-six-year-old house for which the owner was asking $34,900. Overlooking the fact that the house had no For Sale sign posted, Angie was immensely relieved to find something that met her budget and needs—it was close to her work and a school for the kids, although it was not in the best neighborhood. The agent warned Angie she couldn't get the house for any less than $32,500, and Angie's offer of $33,500 was immediately accepted. She then took a friend with her to inspect the house for defects.

Although the water pressure seemed low, the owner assured Angie the plumbing was good, and she accepted the owner's reason for water in the basement. The woman said she had just washed her dog. When Angie asked about the roof, the owner reported it was in good condition and had been checked the previous summer when the house had been painted.

Angie signed the purchase contract in January, but due to foot-dragging by the agent and the owner, she was unable to get occupancy until March. During that period, she learned the agent and owner were close friends, and he had purposely delayed the closing until the woman returned from a two-week vacation. Meanwhile, Angie had to put her furniture in storage and move in with her mother, because the new owners were taking possession of her former home.

Finally, Angie got into her new house. One week later, she lost all water pressure and discovered that the water line to the street was heavily corroded and had to be replaced. The plumber told her that the previous owner had the pipes flushed to make the pressure appear adequate and disguise the problems. Next, the kitchen and bathroom pipes had to be replaced. The plumber warned her that the hot-water heater was dangerous and should also be replaced. Before she had lived in the house one month, Angie had paid $2,500 for plumbing repairs.

As the March snow melted, Angie discovered there were big holes in the south side of the roof, which had to be reshingled. Part of the upstairs ceiling collapsed and had to be replastered. As spring rains came, water poured into the basement. All of these defects should have been pointed out by the agent or noted on the lender's appraisal, which would have red-flagged the home's poor condition.

"Why weren't these people looking out for my best interests? All of these things have happened to me alone," Angie despaired. "It's been just like having the weight of the world on my shoulders.

"I've never had to handle these things before—my husband always took care of them, and he would have known what to do. I didn't know what to look for, and it's been so frustrating because the house looked cute and right and I thought I could call the roofer or the plumber if I had problems. I had no idea it would cost so much. I guess because I was going through the divorce, I just overlooked a lot of things."

Angie, a credit union loan officer, said she felt stupid for allowing herself to get into such a predicament, because she would have handled a car purchase much more cautiously. She finally realized that she had overreacted when her husband left and stopped making child-support payments. She subsequently learned that she could have stayed in the family home and gotten the court to order her ex-husband to make the payments. That would have given her time to begin the reorganization of her life and allowed her to look at a number of homes, methodically evaluating their merits, before jumping headlong into a purchase.

Moreover, she wouldn't have been so financially strapped had she bided her time. The agent rushed her into a 20 percent down payment, conventional loan by telling her no FHA loans were available. With a little shopping around, Angie could have gotten an FHA loan with less down and a lower interest rate and had more to spend on necessary repairs and redecorating.

Sadly, Angie's confidence in her ability to act independently was completely undermined by the sequence of crises.

"You have to be stupid to be taken as I was," Angie concluded. "The main thing I learned is not to trust anyone ever again. I trusted my attorney to watch out for my best interests in this deal and he didn't help one bit. And the broker betrayed me."

When You're Separated

If you and your spouse are separated pending a divorce, it's often wise to postpone the purchase of another home until the divorce is final. Not only from an emotional standpoint is it advisable, but from a legal one as well. If you buy property while still married, your spouse probably will be required to sign the mortgage note and deed and will automatically acquire an interest in the property. Later, to get the property transferred into your name alone, you'll have to get a quitclaim deed from your former spouse. If there are major disputes or ill feelings between you, you definitely should not enter into a transaction until the divorce is final.

Marjorie learned this lesson the hard way. Eager to get rid of a large home that held bad memories, she signed an offer to purchase on another home midway through her divorce. Then when she went to close, her husband refused to sign the documents necessary to complete the sale of their jointly owned home, leaving Marjorie without the funds for the down payment on the house she was buying.

Veteran divorce attorney Ray Conley counsels his clients to contemplate "the hassle factor" if they're considering buying property prior to the divorce. If they suspect their spouses will give them trouble, he suggests waiting until the proceedings are final. Although it's possible to ask the court to order an uncooperative spouse to sign a quitclaim deed, waiving rights to the property, the purchaser can still encounter difficulties with the lender. And frequently, Conley notes, the courts are reluctant to take long-term actions, such as ordering a quitclaim deed, until the final settlement is decided.

"Lenders call the shots on what security they want to loan money," he said. "They can require a spouse or an ex-spouse as a cosigner, if the purchaser is dependent on child support and alimony."

As divorce and property laws vary from state to state, you should consult your own attorney. However, it is almost always inadvisable to purchase property with another person until your divorce is final because your spouse will automatically inherit a portion of your holdings if anything happens to you.

If you will be dependent on child support and alimony for income, you should also wait to buy a home. First, you want to know how much money you'll be receiving; and second, you want to make sure that the payments are being made regularly before committing yourself to a down payment and monthly payments. You will also want to know whether your decree contains an inflation clause that will increase your payments in relation to the escalating cost of living. Many women who were divorced several years ago, before such clauses were routinely included in settlements, are now struggling to keep up house payments and maintenance, as well as to clothe and feed growing children.

Says one midwestern mortgage lender who has handled many loans for divorced persons, "If an applicant is in the middle of a divorce, it's a sticky situation. One-third of the women we see never receive their payments. So we often tell them to wait until the divorce is final and we can find out whether they'll actually collect the money awarded them. Then we can check with the court to make sure the payments are being made on time."

If the equity in a jointly owned home is going to be divided in the settlement, you should also wait to find out exactly how much money you will receive. Conley reports that there are three common methods of handling the disposition of a home in a divorce: 1) The house is sold and the proceeds are split according to a formula agreed on by the two spouses or ordered by the court; 2) the house is awarded to one spouse, who retains ownership, and the other spouse signs a quitclaim deed relinquishing all interest; or 3) the equity in the house is frozen and one spouse continues to live in the house.

In this latter case, which is used in an increasing number of divorces, a formula is worked out so that if the inhabiting spouse decides to sell the house, the other person at the point of sale is awarded a sum in proportion to his or her equity at the time of the divorce. (As a practical matter, the departing spouse usually quitclaims the property to the remaining spouse and a lien is placed on the house declaring that the departing spouse's share must be paid before a sale can be concluded.)

Here's how the frozen equity method works: Assume that you and your spouse jointly own a home valued at $60,000. You still owe $40,000 on the mortgage, which puts your equity at $20,000. One half of $20,000 is $10,000, which is one-sixth of $60,000. So the ratio of equity to market value for your spouse is one-sixth, and that is the proportion of the proceeds that person will receive when you sell the house.

Closing costs and real-estate commissions can also be figured into the formula for the division of profits. Another aspect to keep in mind if you sell your house is capital gains taxes and how they will be paid if neither one of you purchases a more expensive house within the required time frame to defer these taxes. Consult an attorney knowledgeable in tax law or a tax accountant for advice. You should also realize that support payments are taxable income and anticipate the taxes you will have to pay on them.

Naturally, there are always exceptions to these general guidelines about postponing a purchase pending a court decree, as Louise's circumstances and experience prove. Married for twenty-five years to a very prominent man who had become an alcoholic, Louise finally decided she could no longer endure his illness and abuse, since he refused any effort at rehabilitation. She had been looking at houses for several years—ever since their four children had left home and their large prestigious house had become too much to maintain for two people. In the course of looking, she had developed a feel for the real-estate market, and when she spotted a thirty-year-old, two-story frame house, she knew that was where she wanted to live.

On a Saturday night, Louise looked over the house, which was being sold by the owners, and the next day she deposited a $1,000 earnest money check with the couple. She convinced her husband that if they stayed together, the $36,500 house would be a good investment, and so he willingly cosigned the papers necessary for the mortgage and closing.

Louise, who had always been a homemaker, lived in the house, receiving support from her husband, for one-and-a-half years before she filed for divorce. In the divorce decree, she was awarded the house (which had appreciated to a value of $60,000), as well as other property the couple jointly owned, and half of the family home where her ex-husband still lives. The court awarded her $1,000 per month in alimony, which she doesn't always receive in the full amount from her ex-husband. Since there was no inflation clauses in the decree, Louise often has trouble making ends meet and reports that she "lived on a shoestring" when she unexpectedly had to insulate the upstairs and pay for other major repairs.

She believes, however, that purchasing the house when she did was her only ticket to sanity.

"Buying this house was like getting an ace in the hole for me, because I knew he would never leave again—he had left once. And I felt very trapped in our home. I needed a place where I could go in a hurry," Louise said. "So I acted very impulsively and just lucked out on this house.

"My husband was sick and really out of it at the time. I don't think he ever truly believed I would divorce him. He had another woman. It was the first occasion that he had ever been unfaithful, and I just couldn't take that. So there was a lot of emotion involved, and I was frantically trying to get out of the situation."

Fortunately for Louise, the couple had considerable assets and well-established credit. Louise didn't check with a loan officer prior to depositing the earnest money or quiz the owners in depth about the house. The only checking she did was to call a real-estate agent she knew who assured her over the phone that the house would be a good buy.

"I really didn't know much about the financial arrangements, so I just went to the bank on Monday and took their word for what they were going to give me," Louise said. "I just assumed that the banker, my attorney, and the insurance man were looking after my best interests and I would be protected in the purchase.

"I guess I was very cavalier about all the financial details, but I think a woman whose husband left and didn't have enough money, as I knew we did, would have to be much more attentive to these details."

Financing Tips and a Few Precautions

If you will be transferring a home into your name alone following a divorce, the lender will want to see a copy of the quitclaim deed signed by your ex-spouse. The lender may also request to see a copy of your divorce decree. If you have questions about the lender's procedures, contact your attorney.

If you are buying a home and are dependent upon child support and alimony as a primary or partial income, the lender may require your ex-spouse to cosign the mortgage note. This is not a universal rule or practice; it depends on the customs of the lender and how much security the lender demands. The lender may allow another financially secure individual as your cosigner. If you do not have an established credit record in your name, the lender may be well within his rights in requesting an ex-spouse or other person of your choice as a cosigner.

If you *do* have your own credit record, however, the lender may be straying beyond the legal boundaries of the Equal Credit Opportunity Act in requiring a cosigner. You should consult your attorney or a local civil rights agency, which may be able to tell you whether that lender has a history of discriminating against divorced women.

If you are using support payments as part of your qualifying income for the loan, the lender can require proof that support payments are regularly made on time. Likewise, if you make support payments, the lender may want verification that you're current on these payments. Many lenders are in the habit of checking with the appropriate court authorities.

Although some of these conditions may seem demeaning to you, you unfortunately have no choice but to tolerate them as best you can, unless the lender violates your rights. Many lenders' requests often rely on subjective judgments of the conditions they believe must be met to ensure a secure loan. If you suspect the lender has made illegal demands, consult your attorney at once. If your attorney merely tries to pacify you and advises you to go along with the lender's requirement in order to get the loan, then you will have to decide whether to pursue the matter. Attorneys who handle real-estate closings frequently don't want to rock the local lending establishment with a public challenge of their procedures.

Divorced women applying for loans have routinely been subjected to illegal and prejudicial practices, which continue because they do not challenge these actions. If you believe that you have a good case, it may be necessary to consult a civil rights attorney, the local chapter of the American Civil Liberties Union, or a government civil rights agency. By exposing these illegal activities, you can stop the pattern of discrimination and gain redress for the violation of your rights. (See Chapter 10 for more information on the remedies to which you are entitled.)

If you can assume a loan, you can avoid the hassles involved in taking out a new mortgage.

Marion, for instance, had to sell her new two-thousand-square-foot ranch home after her divorce because she couldn't afford the payments and maintenance. Through a friend, she located a thousand-square-foot tract house where the owners allowed her to assume their 5¼ percent loan. She gave them a down payment of $18,000 and assumed payments of only $155 per month, including taxes.

"It was a real find," says Marion. "The house was easily worth $33,000, and I got it for $27,000. Because of increased taxes, the monthly payments are now $171, but the house was recently appraised at $52,000."

Many lenders do not allow buyers to assume the previous owner's low-interest mortgage, but that rule may be modified as the result of one woman's challenge of such restrictions in California.

In July 1975, Cynthia Wellenkamp bought a home whose previous owner had a $19,000, 8 percent mortgage from the Bank of America. Wellenkamp paid the seller the amount of the equity in the property and then tried to pick up the balance of the loan at the same 8 percent rate. But the bank, noting there was a restrictive clause in the original mortgage agreement prohibiting assumption of the loan, insisted on a new interest rate of 9¼ percent.

When Wellenkamp refused to accept the higher interest rate, the bank started foreclosure proceedings. She, in turn, filed suit to stop the foreclosure. The case ultimately went to the state supreme court, which, in a precedent-setting ruling, determined that she could assume the mortgage at the old interest rate and didn't have to comply with the bank's demands. As a result, lenders in California must allow assumptions. And there may be challenges of assumption restrictions in other states as buyers refuse to accept loans at today's higher interests when they could assume loans at half those rates. Fear of such a challenge may also cause lenders to ease their restrictions.

Solutions for the Suddenly Single Woman

Suddenly single women, whether widowed or divorced, face similar problems. The major one is economic, and the next is psychological—adjusting to the shattering changes that have turned their lives inside out. Yet, the two problems are inextricably intertwined, because one's ability to adjust depends on options, which are severely limited without a substantial economic base.

One-third of the female-headed households have incomes below the poverty line, and one-half of the approximate five million widows over age sixty-five live below the official poverty line, according to government statistics. Only 14 percent of divorced women are awarded alimony, and of these, less than half get their payments regularly. Widows, hard hit by estate taxes, often have to sell jointly owned property to meet these obligations. If widowed when they are young, they discover their husbands' insurance and other benefits only last for a short period.

Thus, women who do not hold well-paying jobs or who have not worked outside the home for a number of years find themselves in precarious situations following a divorce or death. Even if they have a job, often their salaries were simply considered "add-on" income to that of the major wage earner, the husband. Because of the salary disparities between men and women, the wife with a career frequently makes substantially less than her spouse. These women whose financial resources are cut drastically or cut off entirely usually are forced to sell family homes and seek more modest shelter.

Compounding the problem, however, is the fact that many women have not independently managed their finances or shared equally in the management of family finances and investments—they left the major monetary decisions up to their husbands. Financial analysts report that many women know a little about bits and pieces—like a savings account, house payments, or life insurance—but they don't look at the big picture. Consequently, they are left high and dry because of bad planning or no planning and a total lack of cooperation on the part of their husbands.

Abandoned abruptly and alone for the first time, many bright and capable women become desperate.

"These women don't know their rights and they're not prepared to make the necessary financial decisions. They're just ricocheting around in a state of shock," observes one female bank officer, who often finds herself counseling divorced and widowed women who don't know where to turn for help.

Moreover, because they don't know their rights, these women are totally unequipped to deal with the discrimination and prejudice they're apt to encounter.

Underscoring the magnitude of the problem, a recently released HUD study revealed that female-headed households are less well housed than the general population. The study found that they live in older housing and their homes suffer more from deficient plumbing and maintenance. In fact, 12 percent of the more than eighteen million female-headed households live in dwellings with major structural flaws. The study reported that to afford *adequate* housing, nearly half of all female household heads must spend one-fourth or more of their incomes on house payments.

To combat the obstacles these females confront, HUD undertook the Women and Mortgage Credit Project in 1979. Announcing the need for the project, former HUD Secretary Patricia Harris, said, "Women are faced with assumptions that prejudice against them has ended. We know that there is continuing discrimination against women because of the false assumption about women as credit risks. Old and false impressions die hard."

Despite passage of the Equal Credit Opportunity Act and the Federal Fair Housing Act (see Chapter 10 for a complete rundown on these laws), women face discrimination on several fronts. The HUD project directors claim that many lenders and real-estate agents have failed to grasp "the full scope of equal credit and fair housing laws" and have refused to recognize that women are credit-worthy.

A previous HUD study, "Women and Housing," found that divorced and widowed women often received condescending treatment from brokers, who perceived them as inferior in conducting business transactions. As a result, brokers used discriminatory credit criteria in qualifying female prospects. They steered divorced women away from certain neighborhoods and houses, equating the entry of "divorcees" into the area with declining property values. They also advised sellers to accept the bids of married couples over those of the women buyers, because the brokers felt they would have less trouble qualifying the couples for loans.

Lenders, in turn, were found to exercise subjective judgments and personal bias in deciding whether to extend credit to these women. Holding to the myth that a divorced woman or widow is inherently unstable and incapable of conducting her own affairs, lenders often required male cosigners and mortgage insurance. Or, the loan officer demanded to see a copy of the divorce decree, required the woman to pay off all outstanding debts, and requested extensive documentation of her work history and her equity in a previous home. In some cases, lenders even insisted on a clause in the closing papers stipulating that the monthly mortgage payment would be taken out of the woman's paycheck.

As a result of women's lack of awareness about these practices and their rights, and in the absence of complaints by them, little was done to end these harassing tactics, the "Women and Housing" report concluded. And now that laws forbid such blatant discrimination, many lenders and brokers merely use more subtle methods.

To break down these barriers, the Women and Mortgage Credit Project has launched a national campaign concentrating on the grass-roots education of women about basic credit and housing finance concepts, as well as their credit rights. "Women and Mortgage Credit" seminars will be held in twenty to twenty-five cities in the course of the two-year project to inform women of housing options, how to obtain credit, and the step-by-step procedures of acquiring a mortgage. Simultaneously, a massive informational program is being directed at lenders to advise them of their legal obligations and the credit-worthiness of women. And the project has commissioned research into the ongoing incidence of prejudice and discrimination against female buyers.

HUD Assistant Secretary Donna Shalala, whose office oversees the project, said it will focus on the special needs of displaced homemakers, minority, elderly, and low-income women—constituencies which include many divorced and widowed women.

For more information on this project, you can write to Women and Mortgage Credit, Assistant Secretary for Policy Development and Research, Room 8204, U.S. Department of Housing and Urban Development, Washington, D.C. 20410.

Getting the Appropriate Advice

While this national program should improve the overall treatment of women in the housing market, it's important for you to move ahead on your own to acquire housing suitable and affordable for your altered life-style. But to accomplish this, you need a strategy.

Step one of that strategy is to make yourself fully aware of your legal and economic status, and step two is to learn your rights. Find out if you have credit in your name by checking with your local credit bureau. If you and your husband held joint accounts with major creditors, such as Master Charge, VISA, or department stores, the Equal Credit Opportunity Act (ECOA) required that as of June 1, 1977, credit information be kept in separate files—one for each spouse. (For more information on credit and shared accounts, see the section on ECOA in Chapter 10, which outlines the legal rights of separated, divorced, and widowed persons and describes the practices prohibited by lenders and real-estate agents.)

If you do not have credit in your own name, the first thing you must do is establish credit. Often a personal banker can advise you how to do this. Or you can go to a Consumer Credit Counseling Center, a non-profit, community-sponsored agency that provides budgeting and financial counseling. There are two hundred of these centers around the nation. Check your telephone directory to see if there is one in your community. You can also write to the National Foundation for Consumer Credit, 1819 H Street, N.W., Washington, D.C. 20008, for a list of non-profit services across the country. Women who have difficulties with their credit histories can get help by contacting "Credit Histories," Federal Trade Commission, Washington, D.C. 20580.

Step three is to get some sound financial counseling. Marilyn Nichols, a financial counselor and founder of the firm Money Matters, Inc., warns, "Women often shy away from financial planning. Most have a bad case of the Scarlett O'Hara 'I'll-think-about-it-tomorrow' syndrome. Many women have very negative attitudes about money, and they often try to avoid financial matters by relying on friends or relatives to help or by just ignoring them altogether."

Such an ostrich approach can be downright dangerous. At this point, it's critical that you get professional advice. You must establish a realistic budget for yourself, arrange to pay off any outstanding debts, make sure you have adequate health, auto, disability, and life insurance, as well as plan for retirement and investments, such as children's educations and property management.

You can get help in some of these areas from the above-mentioned non-profit organizations. However, it's also prudent to establish yourself with a few private professionals. You should have a knowledgeable attorney whom you can depend upon for solid advice and support to get you through the rough spots. A personal banker or accountant can also provide valuable assistance and help you to take care of your transitional financial affairs.

If you have a credit record and a good job, you've got some security and have already achieved a measure of independence that should make it easier for you to step into the role of head of the household.

Displaced Homemakers

If your primary occupation has been that of homemaker and you have no outside income of your own, no credit, and are having difficulty coping with your situation, a logical place to turn for help is an agency in your community that assists displaced homemakers. It's estimated that there are now between three to six million women—mostly in their middle years—who have been displaced from their familiar roles in the home and left without any financial security.

Esther, who has not worked outside the home for thirty years, relates, "I was widowed at age 54—too young for Social Security and too old and inexperienced for a paying job and ineligible for any assistance. I have at least some insurance to live on and meet the mortgage payment for now. However, with no income, my bank account is dwindling fast. My efforts to find some source of assistance to get a job have ended up a dead-end street.

"I feel very angry at this whole impossible situation. I want to maintain my own financial independence, but how are we supposed to do that when prospective employers refuse to give us an opportunity to prove our intelligence and worth? About all I have accomplished is to beat my head against a stone wall of opposition."

The federal government and many state governments have recently allocated funds for the establishment of displaced homemaker centers to help women like Esther, and the Alliance for Displaced Homemakers is working to set up centers in cities throughout the country. See the list on page 229 of places to check for centers and assistance in your community.

Displaced homemaker centers provide several kinds of help, sometimes free of charge or for only a nominal fee.

Personal and Financial Counseling

Maxine Wilson, a Midwest-based counselor of displaced homemakers, says when she first sees a woman, the woman is often working through an intense emotional experience and not thinking clearly.

"Many displaced homemakers have low opinions of their abilities. They have accepted the stereotyped idea that women are naturally dependent and incapable of making decisions on their personal and work lives. In these cases, restoring the woman's self-esteem and self-confidence is the first step in helping her to learn to function in a productive and economically sound manner," Wilson notes.

Wilson first determines the woman's legal status. If she is separated and needs an attorney, Wilson advises the woman how to get an understanding attorney who will see that her status in the marriage is recognized. Some states have passed laws directing the courts to consider the contribution of a homemaker in determining monetary and property awards. You should find out whether your state has such a statute.

Wilson also inquires about the woman's knowledge of finances. If needed, the woman receives counseling on how to establish a budget, open a checking account, obtain credit in her own name, buy insurance, complete tax returns, get health insurance, plan for retirement income, and prepare a will. Unfortunately, many divorced women lose their right to their husbands' pensions and health-care plans.

Housing Assistance

The full-time homemaker often encounters a Catch-22 situation. Widows may have to sell their homes to pay estate taxes. In the case of divorces, either the home is sold because the husband won't support the woman there, or the court awards her the house but she gets no alimony, and with no job and no job skills she has no way of making the payments.

"When she's awarded the house, the woman thinks she's getting a good deal until she tries to live there alone and discovers that it's way beyond her means," Wilson says. "Then she's just a sitting duck for the brokers who are waiting in the wings to take advantage of her."

Wilson cautions women not to move too fast or take on things they don't understand in the sale or purchase of a home. She believes that women should not sell their family homesteads and go into rental property "where they are just throwing all of their money out the window."

Some centers may refer women to brokers who will help them find housing suitable to their means and needs. Several centers have established refuges for women who need an immediate place to stay until they can get permanently relocated. Advice is given on how to find out about special loan packages and ownership opportunities for which the woman may be eligible. Women with extremely limited financial resources are directed to inquire at the local HUD office about subsidized housing for low-income persons—an option that is meeting the needs of many displaced homemakers.

Vocational Guidance

Laurie Shields, national coordinator for the Alliance for Displaced Homemakers, notes, "Today's former full-time homemaker, lacking any record of recent paid work experience, is as vulnerable as the young person who hasn't lived long enough to acquire a work record."

Therefore, counselors trained in vocational guidance help women discover what kind of work they can do and how to use their experiences as homemakers to choose job goals.

Job Training and Placement

Counselors refer women to appropriate educational institutions or employers for training, often under special programs funded by local, state, or federal government. Many centers have established their own training and referral programs with local employers. If the center doesn't have placement capacity itself, it may have arrangements with local personnel placement offices.

If you are a displaced homemaker, here are the agencies you can contact for assistance:

- Look in your phone book for a Displaced Homemaker Center in your area. If there is none, write to the Alliance for Displaced Homemakers, 3800 Harrison Street, Oakland, California 94611, and enclose a fifteen-cent stamp. The

alliance can advise you of agencies providing services for displaced homemakers where you live and can give you information about state and federal
legislation regarding homemakers.

- Community organizations concerned with child and family welfare, such as
  the YWCA, Parents Without Partners, and local churches. You can also call
  the United Way for referral to appropriate government and UW-supported
  agencies.
- The state or city commission on the status of women. Most states, if they don't
  provide services for displaced homemakers, have commissions, which can
  provide referrals.
- The local chapter of the National Organization for Women. If it's not listed in
  your phone book, you can write to the National NOW Action Center, 425
  Thirteenth Street, N.W., Washington, D.C. 20004.
- The counseling office of your community or junior college. If a local college or
  university has a Women's Center, it often provides services for displaced
  homemakers. If you are a college graduate, contact the counseling or placement office of the college you attended if it is nearby.

Special Concerns of Widows

There are by far more widows in America than there are widowers,
because statistically women outlive their husbands by about five years and
widowed men tend to remarry younger women. According to census figures,
there are more than five million women over the age of sixty-five who live
alone, and these numbers will grow in the coming years. Sadly, it is these
older widows who are struck the cruelest blows for fulfilling traditional roles
of wife and homemaker.

Penalized by estate and inheritance tax laws, women may be forced to
sell their property to pay taxes. Instead of profiting from the appreciation of
their real estate, they must pay for it. Even if they manage to hold on to the
house initially, their incomes are cut so drastically that later they can't afford
to maintain payments for property taxes, upkeep, and utilities.

Marguerite Rawalt, a past president of the National Association of
Women Lawyers, notes, "The laws of forty-two states say that the one who
earns a salary is the one who owns the property acquired in a marriage. The
homemaker, having no earnings of her own, therefore, has no ownership in
that property. If her husband dies without a will, she may be penniless."

In any of those forty-two states, where a husband and wife own land,
such as a farm, jointly, the law makes the husband sole owner. Estate taxes at
his death will be measured by the whole value of the property. The widow
will receive only what is left after the payment of taxes, and she may have to
sell all or part of the property to pay the tax. On the other hand, if the wife
dies first, since no value is placed on her services, the husband does not have
to pay any tax.

Ironically, when they should be able to enjoy retirement in their
"golden years," many widows are struggling the hardest to make ends meet.
A HUD survey revealed that the single elderly comprise the largest segment

of our population in the lowest income categories, many of them receiving less than $3,000 per year to live on. The number one expense of Americans over age sixty-five is housing.

One life insurance study found that when the husband dies, income drops as much as 42 percent for widows fifty-five and older. Other studies indicate that money from the average policy is spent within two years. An illness at the end of a husband's life can wipe out assets the wife would have received at his death. Consequently, many women go from a comfortable standard of living to near poverty practically overnight. Then they face the same problems as this nation's chronically poor—the widowed homemaker is unable to get an adequate job or to obtain credit or a loan.

These situations can be avoided with proper financial planning. Optimally, the husband and wife should prepare for the death of either by consulting professionals, planning their estate, and drafting wills, but all too frequently they don't, and the widow suffers the catastrophic results.

For example, Harriet's husband, a minister, died six months before his planned retirement. Now fifty-seven-year-old Harriet lives on $450 a month: $300 she receives from Social Security and $150 she receives from the church. More than one-third of her income goes for a small apartment.

Overcome by grief, many widows do not take the necessary steps to get their lives and financial affairs in order. They just hang on for a couple of years and then when the money runs out, if the mortgage hasn't been paid off, they lose the house.

During the first shock of loss and loneliness, therapists and financial advisers warn there are some definite things to do and some things *not* to do.

Following the death, you should get a knowledgeable individual (a close friend or other family member) to help with the immediate paperwork and details: the funeral arrangements, death certificate, search for important papers (investments, insurance), filing for insurance benefits, applying for Social Security.

You should seek professional advice. Consult your lawyer, who can handle all estate matters. You should also contact your insurance agent and accountant or banker who can advise you how to handle transition financial affairs. If you don't have a personal financial adviser, seek assistance from your local bank, savings institution, or an accountant specializing in family finances. These individuals can also make recommendations on appropriate housing arrangements.

Anita Mandelbaum, a certified public accountant with Coopers & Lybrand, advises her widowed clients over age fifty-five to sell large, expensive family homes and purchase maintenance-free condominium apartments. Present tax laws allow home owners fifty-five and older a one-time $100,000 tax exemption from the proceeds on the sale of their primary residences.

There are a variety of ways to receive insurance benefits, and you should figure out with your agent which will be the best for you. Often it's best to ask for enough funds to tide you over the initial expenses (medical and funeral expenses and other outstanding bills). Then after you've had a chance to determine your financial status, you can make long-range plans on what to do with insurance money.

You should not do anything rash; postpone major decisions for at least one year. Resist the recommendations of family and friends to sell the house immediately. Decline real-estate brokers' offers to list the house (you may be contacted by a number of brokers who regularly read the obituaries).

You must take time to work through your grief. Many widows seek help from local organizations that provide counseling on a "widow-to-widow" basis. By talking with either a professional counselor or trained volunteer who herself is widowed, you can get solid advice and much-needed support to help you through the rough spots. If you don't know where to seek help in your community, your state commission on aging may suggest some places. You can also check the sources listed on page 229.

When you feel confident of your ability to make major decisions, you should begin to consider housing alternatives.

Above all, you should choose a home that you can afford to buy and maintain and one that will be comfortable and secure for you. Many older persons, particularly if they suffer health problems such as arthritis, want one-story homes so they won't have to worry about getting up and down stairs in later years.

Condominium and cooperative apartments are ideal, but you must be careful to select the right complex. Ask yourself whether you want to live with all older people or whether you prefer a place where there will be a mix of all ages.

Many of the government-backed cooperatives allocate a certain number of units for older and retired persons, and some adjust monthly payments to the older person's fixed income. Betty, who has a one-bedroom apartment in a large suburban co-op, says she enjoys the fellowship and family atmosphere of the community. She occasionally babysits for some of the children and regularly attends community meetings and gatherings where she can socialize and meet new people.

"I belong to a bridge group which plays late some nights. The security within the co-op is really great for the women alone; we never worry about being mugged. We older residents look after each other, and we're always reminding people to call on their older neighbors, especially if they haven't seen them for a few days."

Religious groups, particularly the Presbyterian and Baptist churches, have pioneered in constructing housing for senior citizens. If you are selling your home and seeking economical alternatives in your community, check with your church or synagogue office. Unfortunately, many northrn communities lack housing options for older citizens. In fact, there are only about three million housing units nationwide designed specifically for people over sixty-five.

The Sunbelt states offer the widest range of housing alternatives for senior citizens. They have everything from high-rise condominiums to expansive retirement communities with a full-range of sports and civic activities, as well as medical and shopping facilities.

However, before selling your home and relocating to one of these planned retirement villages, give careful deliberation to the implications of such a move. Many widows who go to a completely new place several hundred or thousand miles away from family, friends, and their old neighborhoods later regret their actions. Some senior citizens have low regard for these planned communities, which they term "retirement ghettoes," and claim they are not tuned into the personal needs of the older, single person. One psychologist, noting the absence of younger people and other age groups in the "Sun City approach," says many older widows tend to "atrophy and shrivel psychologically" in these settings without exposure to familiar elements.

If you do decide to move to a planned community, you should collect all the particulars on the facility and go over the details with your attorney. Make sure the community is a financially solvent one. You should visit it and talk with some of the residents before making any commitments.

Finally, there are a few facts the older widow should have about home financing.

If you decide to purchase a home, you may have trouble getting a mortgage. Some lenders are reluctant to make large, long-term loans to single persons over age sixty-five. You should shop around until you find a lending institution that will write you a mortgage.

Many older citizens who own their homes outright or who have paid cash for homes warn that younger prospective buyers often are unable to get mortgages. They say you are better off to have a mortgage that a younger buyer can assume when you decide to sell.

Because of the growing number of older persons in this country, plans are now being evolved to enable them to stay in their family homes. Reverse annuity mortgages (RAMs) allow retired persons on fixed incomes to tap into the equity of their homes while still living in them. With the RAM, the lender pays the home owner a fixed annuity, based on a percentage of the present value of the property. The lender collects the debt when the owner dies and the estate is settled, or when the property is sold.

There are also a number of new state and local programs which will provide reverse mortgages for low-income home owners. You should make certain you understand all the details of any reverse mortgage before you agree to it.

Suggestions for the Divorced Man

The man who has been married for a number of years and suddenly must leave the family home faces major psychological and economic adjustments. Although the man typically has more economic resources, the impact of being ejected from familiar surroundings and severing a longstanding relationship can have a shattering psychological effect.

First, he must adapt to being alone and living alone. This is often extremely difficult for the male who has traditionally depended upon his wife to do the cooking and housekeeping, particularly if he has not shared in these chores. And losing daily contact with children can also exact a devastating toll, adding to existing recriminations and doubts. Unfortunately, there are very few men's organizations or support groups that deal with the emotional needs of divorced men. Therefore, the man usually has to seek private professional counseling.

Though the man may have a substantial income, if one-half or more goes for child support and/or alimony payments, his housing and discretionary funds are reduced considerably. He often doesn't have the cash for a down payment. And because many husbands have left major housing and decorating decisions up to their wives, they don't have a strong sense of the kind of housing they really want or like. For this reason, many separated and divorced males rent furnished apartments until they develop a feel for what it's like to live alone and discover what their preferences are.

Renting for the first year or so that you're on your own usually will give you time to get yourself and your affairs in order following the divorce.

James, a lawyer who had designed and built a house with his wife a few years before their separation, rented for the first two years he was on his own.

"During that period I went through the terrible soul-searching that I think most divorced people must experience—contending with the sense of being left alone, the sense of abandonment, the sense of lack of support. You have to go through that before you can come to terms with yourself," said James.

Quite obviously, a person undergoing such internal turmoil is not ready to undertake the major decisions involved in buying a home. In fact, the best move you can make is to get some solid advice on available rental property. If you have a good friend in the real-estate business or know an agent you trust, contact that person. He or she should be able to suggest some suitable apartments or town houses. Apartment shopping can be a demoralizing experience, so enlist all the aid you can. Friends, relatives, or other divorced men may have helpful suggestions.

After you've gotten used to living alone and begun to establish a life-style of your own, then it's time to think about investing in a home. A condominium, cooperative, or small town house are the choices of many divorced men. The maintenance is included with these units, and you won't have as much space to furnish and decorate as you would with a single family dwelling. If you have children visiting on weekends or on a part-time basis, any of these three options would be a logical choice. They usually have a second bedroom or den, which can be made into a permanent room for the children.

Most single fathers say they prefer owning a place where their children can come and go freely. When you're renting, you're always subject to neighbors' complaints and criticisms if the children get rowdy.

James, who ultimately purchased a spacious older home that he duplexed, said, "I wanted to provide an environment where the kids could be
with me and feel like it was another home. Here they have a big bedroom of
their own. And for them, being able to come here any time has reduced a lot
of the alienation that they felt from me following the breakup."

If you are going to have custody of your children, see Chapter 13,
"Suggestions for the Single Parent," which points out special aspects you
will want to consider in choosing a home.

Be forewarned that many divorced men purchasing their first homes by
themselves experience intense cases of "buyer's remorse." They commit
themselves to purchase the home, thinking that it's the logical thing to do,
and then they get a sinking feeling that they have made a completely wrong
decision and will never feel at home in the place. Be patient. Real estate is
always a good investment. And once you've moved in, bought a few pieces of
furniture, and started to decorate and personalize the place, it will be a lot
more appealing and eventually will become home.

Townsend, a thirty-nine-year-old doctor with a hefty income when he
and his wife separated, exemplifies the phases and adjustments many men go
through. The first shock wave hit when a major portion of his resources were
gobbled up by lawyer's fees, house payments, child support, and alimony.
Since his practice was in a university town, he moved into a dormitory
subdivided into furnished apartments. During his fourteen-year marriage,
most of his time and effort had been devoted to getting through medical
school, a specialty, and then establishing and building his practice.

When the separation occurred, he had no idea of where or how he
wanted to live. His wife had chosen their previous houses, a detail to which
he had given no attention, and consequently, he had little confidence in his
ability to select a place for himself.

Finally, a good friend convinced him to move into a furnished duplex,
where he lived for one-and-a-half years. During that period, Townsend said,
he overcame much of the self-doubt and remorse precipitated by the
divorce. Slowly, he began to evolve a life-style of his own and gradually
acquired definite ideas about where he wanted to live.

Tired of "hot and cold running bugs and a cranky landlord," Townsend
decided to buy a new place of his own. He consulted a real-estate agent, who
showed him the floor plans for a new complex of condominiums being built
on the edge of town.

Because he still had little capital at his disposal, Townsend made a
minimum 10 percent down payment on a $40,000 condo. "But then I had an
unbelievable ambivalence about the place before I moved in. I had the
feeling, 'Oh God, I suppose I've done the right thing,' but my heart wasn't
really in it," he said. "I lived in the place for a year with only a bed and a
piano, spending as little time there as possible."

Ultimately, some friends helped him pick out a few pieces of furniture
and suggested that he seek a designer's advice on color coordination.

"Then I began to find out what I liked and developed confidence in my choices. I bought a few other pieces—a couch, table and chairs, lamps. It's been reassuring to discover that I like what I've done because I'd never paid any attention whatsoever to this type of thing," Townsend said.

Acknowledging that it's taken him a long while to feel comfortable in his condo, after one year Townsend admits that it suits his life-style perfectly. He's gone much of the time and doesn't have to worry about maintenance or security. The two-bedroom unit is easy to clean and yet is large enough for his two children to visit or for entertaining a few friends.

It is noteworthy to mention that many men who relinquish family homes as the result of a divorce often retain the first option to buy the home if their former spouses decide to sell.

Housing Alternatives for the Single-Again

If you have to move from a large family homestead to a smaller, more economical home, there are a number of logical options for you to explore. Because of the growing number of female-headed households, builders are catering to this special market with town houses and condominiums in new developments. Major builders report many divorced persons buy modestly priced cluster homes, patio homes, or tract homes. If you're a single parent in a major housing market where the big builders, such as Fox and Jacobs, Inc., of Dallas, gear their suburban homes to moderate housing budgets, this would be a reasonable option for you.

Unfortunately, in many communities there's a big void in the type of new housing available for the single-again person whose housing budget has been halved. One broker in a Midwest city says he often shows divorced buyers older, inner-city houses and low-maintenance patio homes priced under $50,000. Because it's an affluent town, he notes, the builders cater to the high-end buyer with their new homes.

As you're shopping for another home, above all work with an understanding and receptive broker, and keep these facts in mind:

- Cooperatives, particularly those with government-subsidized mortgages, may offer very reasonable buy-in rates.
- Small, new condominiums in the suburbs can often be purchased for between $20,000 and $50,000.
- Small, new suburban town houses are another low-priced option.
- Co-op and condo conversions in the suburbs may be available at very reasonable rates, depending on the market. Some cities have restricted conversions, thus driving up the demand and hence the price.
- Converted co-ops and condos in town are worth checking into, but can be quite expensive.
- Post-World War II, single-family houses often provide inexpensive, sound housing.
- Split-levels built in the fifties, while slightly more expensive, usually are a sound housing investment.

As a rule, used single-family homes are less expensive than new single-family suburban dwellings, but this will depend on the neighborhood and availability of housing. The homes in greatest demand today, and hence the most expensive, are new single-family units close to metropolitan centers.

Duplexes or houses that can be duplexed represent a solid investment for the divorced or young widowed person. You get your half to live in and have the other half to rent out for income. Plus, you can get a good tax write-off on the depreciation and expenses of the rental portion.

The key is to buy something that you can afford to maintain after you've moved in. Avoid houses with major flaws or that need extensive remodeling.

If these alternatives are all out of your price range, don't despair. You may qualify for a subsidy program and be eligible for assistance from the local, state, or federal government. For low- and medium-income persons, HUD provides the Section 235 Home-Ownership Subsidy, which pays the difference between the amount required on the mortgage at the market interest rate and the sum which the buyer can pay with one-fifth of his or her income. The 235 interest subsidy program, which serves persons with incomes ranging up to about $12,000, has been of special importance to displaced homemakers. For more information on this program, contact your local Federal Housing Administration office. In addition, check with local and state housing agencies about assistance programs they offer.

You should also find out if there are cooperatives in your community with subsidy programs. Because the majority of cooperatives have HUD-subsidized mortgages, they offer special opportunities for low- and moderate-income persons. Many displaced homemakers, unable to find affordable shelter for themselves and their families elsewhere, have turned to co-ops as the answer.

For example, twenty-eight-year-old Marty, divorced and with three pre-school-age children, couldn't find any affordable rental housing large enough in which to raise her family. Most apartments, she found, discouraged children. Since she had married and become a full-time homemaker following college graduation, Marty had to get back into the job market immediately. Meanwhile, her only income was $300 per month child support, and she had no credit record of her own. She and her ex-husband, a school teacher, had never owned a home, so there was no cash settlement.

Returning to her hometown, Marty found a subsidized cooperative and put her name on the waiting list. After one year of enduring a too-small apartment, she moved into a three-bedroom, twelve-hundred-square-foot town-house unit in the co-op. She paid $435 for her stock share and $157 per month for carrying charges, a figure based on her secretarial income then of $8,400.

"It has worked out beautifully for us here," Marty said. "My unit faces a big open field in back, so the kids have plenty of space to play. Because there are a lot of single parents here, we have shared babysitting arrangements. Plus, I'm close to bus lines, shopping, schools, and work. This place has everything going for it in terms of not having to travel a lot or be away from home a lot.

"All I have to pay for is the electricity; the heat is provided. And since the maintenance is taken care of, I don't have to bother with that and have more time for my family and career. The single parents here got together and established a medical clinic within the co-op, so I can just take my kids down there when they are sick or need a checkup."

Marty's 306-unit co-op is occupied largely by single parents, who find it both economical and convenient for them. She said single-parent families can buy a town-house unit with more space than that of single-family houses selling down the street for $45,000. Because it's a closely knit community, she added, the residents are attentive to each other's needs and are continually improvising ways to help one another—such as organizing grocery co-ops, day-care centers, and other reciprocal service agreements.

Since her income has increased from the time she moved in, Marty now pays full market value for her monthly carrying charge. And interestingly, her involvement in the co-op has led to a whole new career. After living in her unit for two years, she was asked by the co-op board to become the managing agent for the complex, which resulted in a $15,000 annual salary. She's presently in law school under a tuition grant from a firm that needs an attorney who will specialize in cooperative housing laws.

Moving Down

Finally, to save yourself a lot of grief, do not try to recreate in a smaller, more modest home the atmosphere of your former home. Accept the fact that you have to make some sacrifices, and try to make your new home as comfortable as possible and a realistic reflection of your new life-style.

Some cosmetic redecorating can make the transition surprisingly more palatable and give you confidence in your creative adaptability as an independent human being.

Marion, not exactly elated by the prospect of leaving her two-thousand-square-foot house for one half that size, nevertheless decided to capitalize on the possibilities of her new home. She budgeted $3,000 for redecorating and then set about ripping paneling off the walls and repainting and recarpeting the entire house to suit her tastes. Since the house has good window exposures, Marion has been able to create a bright and welcoming effect, which lends a special charm to the smaller home.

After tackling those projects, she painted the outside of the house, saving more than $1,000 by doing it herself, and she has learned how to handle most of the maintenance.

"When the garbage disposal broke down, I went to the library and got a book that showed how to dismantle and repair disposals. I've retiled the kitchen floor by myself, and I can handle minor plumbing repairs. I take a great deal of pride in these accomplishments because they're a sign of self-sufficiency," says Marion.

13

Suggestions for the Single Parent

Single parents need to exercise special care in selecting a safe neighborhood with good schools. If you have young children, you may want a home near recreational facilities such as playgrounds, swimming pools, and community centers. If your child has special interests, such as playing a musical instrument, you will want to locate in an area where the schools have top-notch music instructors and active bands or orchestras.

Because house prices are usually higher in the better school districts, if you have a limited buying budget, you will have to look more extensively to find a suitable house in the right area.

Rosemary, for example, looked at twenty-five houses before she found one that she could afford within the district where her two young daughters were attending school. When she and her husband separated, they had to sell their large, expensive home on four acres. Rosemary rented a duplex for one year to give herself time to adjust to being a single mother on her own. After she felt confident enough in her new status and her job, she decided to buy because she wanted her daughters to have "a permanent home environment where they would have their own private spaces."

Homes were appreciating at the rapid rate of 1½ percent a month where Rosemary was looking. She was shocked by the prices and often felt discouraged by her financial limitations because she had expected she could afford more house with the money she had. With persistence and the aid of a good real-estate agent, after about three months Rosemary bought a fifteen-year-old, three-bedroom ranch house for $47,000. It met her major priorities and enabled her girls to continue in the same school.

One of the major considerations of many single parents is providing as much continuity as possible for their children in the move to another house.

When she and her husband divorced, Muriel knew that eventually she would have to sell their home, which she couldn't afford alone. Yet she postponed the sale because she wanted to give her children, aged two and four, time to adjust to having no father at home.

"I waited one year because the kids sensed the change, and I did not want to uproot them immediately," she said.

There were only three neighborhoods where Muriel could afford to buy a home that would be within the school district she wanted. Her main concern was choosing a school where there would be other single parents. In her previous neighborhood, Muriel was the only divorced parent, and she feared that her children would suffer at school because the teachers would view them differently and treat them differently.

"So I checked out the populations of various schools and found that because of the large number of apartments in the particular area where I bought, there was a high percentage of single-parent families," Muriel said.

Muriel had a good friend on the school board who got her the statistics on the parent population of the school. Muriel also inquired about the school's philosophy of education and its teaching methodology. Then she visited with some other parents who had children in the school. She said the other parents liked the feeling in the classrooms, where the teachers showed genuine concern for their students.

Satisfied with the answers she got, Muriel bid on and bought a small, three-bedroom tract house within walking distance of the elementary school her kids would attend.

Choosing a stable, secure neighborhood (see "Neighborhood Checklist," page 82, for more on this subject) in a good school district can also greatly enhance the resale value of your home. Muriel's home, for example, has doubled in value.

Unfortunately, there is no standardized national system for rating the quality of schools. Real-estate agents are not supposed to give their opinions on whether local schools are good or bad, and often they don't have enough reliable information. School officials may not level with you—they're not going to admit they have a high incidence of drug problems or vandalism. So to get an accurate handle on the quality of the schools, you'll have to check them out with several sources. You can get a good start by visiting the schools and chatting with school officials and teachers.

Here are some guidelines to use in evaluating prospective schools:

- How much does the school district spend per year on each child? The higher the figure, the better; but you'll likely have to make a comparison with national figures or those of surrounding districts.
- Is the average class size about twenty-five students?
- How do students compare with others on a state and nationwide basis on standard student achievement tests?
- Are there modern teaching aids, such as language labs, and special services, such as guidance and career counseling?
- Is there an adequate system for transporting students to school? Are pupils bused to other schools?
- Are the junior and senior high schools considered as good as the elementary schools?
- How many high school seniors go on to college? What types of colleges do they attend? What is the average score of the senior class on standardized tests? The quality of the high school affects college admission. College admissions officials discount top grades of a student who comes from a high school known for mediocre teachers and low standards.
- How many extracurricular activities are available?
- Is the school well staffed? The better schools have a variety of specialists. Find out what the median teaching salary is and how this compares with other districts. You should determine whether the district pays high enough salaries to attract and retain good teachers.

- Is the school superintendent considered an educational leader? Are the school board members respected citizens in the community?
- Are the buildings and facilities in good condition? If not, you can expect some large capital expenditures, which may come out of your pocket.
- What percentage of school expenditures is paid by the property tax on houses? If it's high compared to the amount in neighboring districts, this could affect the resale value of the house.
- Are plans underway for new community schools? If so, your property taxes will rise sharply, which may reduce property values. On the other hand, new schools attract home owners seeking quality educations for their kids.
- What will the future school taxes be? You should be able to get a copy of the annual report on the school budget. Then you can figure the average rate of increase over the previous five years and calculate how much you can expect to pay.
- What is the record on recent budget and bond-issue elections? Consistent rejections of such proposals are a sign that the quality of education is not a major concern to citizens of the district.
- Ask the principal if you can sit in on a few classes. You should find out how well your child's previous education will translate to the new school and also observe the interaction between teachers and students. If you are refused permission to visit any classes, look for another place to live.

Some of these questions may best be answered by an official of the school board. If you have a friend or acquaintance on the board or one who works for the board, that person would be a good source of information. You can also gather considerable background at the library. Past issues of local newspapers can tell you what has been happening with the schools, and the librarian may also be a knowledgeable source.

Finally, you will want to visit with parents whose children attend the schools. Ask whether they are satisfied with the educations their children are getting.

Tax and Legal Tips

In figuring your budget, be sure to take into account whether you or your ex-spouse qualify to claim the exemption for your children. According to the IRS, if the divorce decree does not give the exemption to either parent, the one with custody is assumed to be providing more than half the child's support. There is one exception, however. If the non-custodial parent contributes a specified minimum for support, then that parent is assumed to have put up more than half unless the custodial parent clearly proves otherwise.

Regarding day care, the IRS holds that you can claim a tax credit of 20 percent of the cost of household and personal-care services for dependents who are either under age fifteen or incapable of caring for themselves if you need the help to hold a job.

As a single parent, it's important for you to make out your own will, because otherwise property may be disposed of under state law in ways that you would not want. In your will, you also must name a guardian for your children. If you do not name a guardian, the state will, if you die.

14

Investment Opportunities for the Single Person

Real estate, because it has consistently outpaced inflation over the past decade, offers the small investor some excellent opportunities. In addition to its income-producing potential, real estate enables one to obtain highly favorable tax rates—a necessity for the upwardly mobile single person. As salaries have risen an average of 6 to 7 percent annually, the IRS's tax brackets have remained about the same over the past fifteen years. Consequently, every 10 percent increase in personal income now results in about a 16 percent increase in federal taxes.

With a modest sum of money properly placed, you can reap better returns with real estate than with almost any other investment. If you have enough equity in an existing home, you can borrow against that equity to obtain the necessary capital. Real estate affords you the advantage of leveraging or maximizing your gain through the use of borrowed money. The higher your income bracket, the more sense real estate makes as an investment, because you can use borrowed money to achieve a tax-sheltered gain.

Before entering the market, you should determine what it is you want to accomplish with your money and carefully examine the alternatives. If, like many single people, your purpose is to attain a supplemental income, capital gains from appreciation, and a tax shelter through leveraging, then you would do well to invest in rental property, of which there is a variety. A duplex is the starting point for many small investors who live in one unit and rent out the other.

Dallas builder Paul York, who constructs duplexes for small investors, reports that leverage is the great lure for many of his buyers who move into one side and rent the other. With rental revenue figured in, an investor may pay as little as $300 a month for a $100,000 duplex, York said.

When twenty-seven-year-old Annette started shopping for a home, her broker suggested that she consider a duplex. After looking at a number of duplexes around town, Annette found an older, two-story brick duplex in an established neighborhood where properties were appreciating steadily. The owners, a retired couple, were asking $75,000 on a contract sale, which they needed for tax purposes. That was ideal for Annette, whose $17,500 income did not qualify her for a mortgage in the amount needed.

After several offers and counter-offers, Annette and the owners settled on a sales price of $70,000. The owners agreed to take back a $44.000 mortgage at 9 percent with $26,000 down and a balloon payment after seven-and-a-half years.

Annette had $7,000 in savings and was able to borrow $6,000 against her certificates of deposit, an amount repayable at 9½ percent with no fixed deadline and no minimum monthly payments. Her credit union loaned her the $13,000 balance, part secured by signature and part secured by using her car and stereo system as collateral. (Most company credit unions allow longstanding members to borrow substantial amounts on signature.)

Because the mortgage was made by a private party, the closing costs were low—less than $100. Annette's income from her tenants covers the $350 monthly mortgage payment to the sellers. Half of all maintenance is tax-deductible from her entire income, and she can deduct one-fifteenth or about 7 percent of the purchase price each year in depreciation for fifteen years. (The IRS bases depreciation on what it considers the "useful life" of the building.* Most older buildings, such as Annette's, are considered to have a useful life of fifteen years; hence, the one-fifteenth per year depreciation schedule.)

Thus, Annette has gained a comfortable home for herself, a second income, a sound investment that is steadily growing in value, and a favorable tax status. She has fewer out-of-pocket monthly expenses for the duplex than she would have had for a single-family house.

The decisive factors in choosing the duplex she did were structural soundness, established tenants, and a good location. The fifty-year-old building had been well maintained because it had always been owner occupied. Annette said that many of the newer duplexes she saw that were strictly rental properties were in much poorer shape. Her tenants, two retired teachers, have lived in the duplex for fifteen years and look after the place as if it belonged to them.

Many single investors also buy older dwellings in reviving city neighborhoods and do innovative things with them. Financing programs and tax incentives authorized by the federal government to encourage inner-city revitalization make these older units lucrative options. (Under the Tax Reform Act of 1976, owners of income-producing property listed in the "National Register of Historic Places" or located within a historic district listed therein are eligible to take certain tax deductions for rehab costs. For more information on this law and the federal government financing program for rehab properties see "Rehabilitation Housing," page 57.)

Frequently, two or more single persons form a partnership to buy older properties and renovate them.

Barry, a professor at a small private college, bought a huge three-story house near his inner-city campus with another professor. Before the closing, Barry had the three upstairs apartments rented. Because they both were interested in art, the two decided to divide the downstairs into art studios and an art gallery.

*The IRS considers most new buildings to have a useful life of thirty years.

The two professors formed a partnership to buy the $85,000 property and contributed equal amounts to the $17,000 down payment and the closing costs. Because neither of them wanted ongoing, out-of-pocket expenses, they chose a property that would pay for itself. The apartment rents, which easily cover the monthly mortgage payments, utilities, and taxes, eventually will also be used for remodeling and other improvements.

Because mortgage money was tight when Barry and his partner bought the house in 1979, the fact that they both owned their own homes carried substantial weight with the lender. Another factor that helped considerably was Barry's experience in renovating older property. In 1974, he purchased for $20,000 a deteriorating 1895 house, which he remodeled himself. The house is now valued at more than $75,000.

Analyze the Market

Whether you're investing in an older, inner-city dwelling to rehab or a duplex or new tract house to rent, it's imperative to analyze your market carefully before making any commitments. There are a number of factors that will affect the soundness of your investment and your ability to turn a profit on the property. Buying rental property requires consideration of some aspects not involved in the purchase of a private residence and can be a risky business. On the other hand, the right dwelling with the right financing can result in a 20 to 40 percent or more yield per year through capital appreciation, rental income, and tax shelters.

To avoid taking a serious loss on an investment, you must know your market forward and backward. This requires putting in the time to learn the ropes and acquainting yourself with local areas, property values, zoning and tax laws, and financing sources for income property. Many small investors gain much of their expertise from conversations with real-estate agents, bankers, attorneys, and other investors. Asking questions of the right people with the right information is the best way to learn quickly. The more questioning you do, the better you will be able to judge the quality of answers you are receiving.

It's advisable to contact several real-estate professionals who specialize in the areas in which you're interested and to deal only with those professionals who work regularly with investors. As you contact various realty firms, ask for the residential investment property specialist. Discuss with that individual your interests and the amount you have to invest, and visit the properties he recommends.

You need to find out about local economic trends and to follow transactions in the specific neighborhoods that have the type of housing in which you're interested. Pinpoint the specific areas within neighborhoods that you believe have the prices and income potential you're looking for.

Look for properties that are priced under the current market levels. Properties in the lower-to-middle range of the price structure return more in rent proportionate to the outlay they require. Watch also for properties in areas where there is upward movement in the rents, and avoid those where the rents are at the top of the market. The real money is made in the increasing rents.

Study the classified ads and watch for notices of tax and foreclosure sales. Visit the properties that sound promising and keep in touch with several realty firms during your search.

Don't hesitate to challenge an agent's estimates of projected rents, appreciation rates, and carrying costs for properties. Ask all brokers to explain the basis for the figures they quote you.

Evaluate the Property

When you have several specific properties in mind, you should evaluate them all according to the same factors, so that you will have comparative data on which to base your purchase.

First, analyze the location of the property. Is it in an area with a robust economic future? Are the property values rising? Is the demand for rental housing strong? Is there a mix of owner-occupied and rental housing in the area? You want to choose an area that will remain predominantly residential for as long as you will own the property.

Also consider the appeal of the location to prospective tenants. Is public transportation convenient? Is it close to employment, shopping, and recreational facilities, as well as schools? You may wish to refer to some of the factors suggested in "Neighborhood Checklist" (page 82) as you attempt to analyze the location in terms of its appeal to tenants.

Second, you need to take a close look at the structural condition of the dwelling. Refer to the "Inspection Checklist," p. 85. If you are not knowledgeable about construction nor confident of your ability to evaluate structural problems, you should hire a home inspection service to evaluate the dwelling.

After considering location and structural condition, it's time to get out your pen and start figuring the probable cost of the dwelling, the cash flow it will create for you, and projected capital gain.

First, you need to know the maximum price you will have to pay for the house. Second, you must calculate the recurring costs of ownership on a monthly and a yearly basis. To get a full picture of these costs, jot down:

- The amount of the monthly mortgage payment.
- The amount of the monthly payment that goes for property taxes and what that amount will be following the next assessment.
- The amount you will pay for utilities when all units are rented.
- The insurance premium, including liability protection.
- The monthly maintenance costs, as well as owners' association fees or any other special assessments.
- Any monthly management fees.

Now add up all of these expenses to get an estimate of how much the property will cost you on a monthly basis. Multiply that sum by twelve to get a projection of the recurring annual cost.

Next, figure your monthly rental income by totaling the rents you will charge for all the units. To calculate annual rental income, you should figure in a vacancy rate of about 5 percent. Simply subtract 5 percent of the annual rental income from the total. Bear in mind that you will have to charge rents competitive with the market to get your units quickly rented, and you will not always be able to demand top dollar.

Now calculate the net cash flow you can anticipate by subtracting the total of the projected recurring costs from the projected annual rental income.

You will also need to project your anticipated out-of-pocket costs up to the time of rental. List the amount you will pay for the down payment, any broker's fees, inspection fees, and closing costs. Add in costs for improvements you will need to make prior to renting, as well as other miscellaneous expenses.

At this point, it's necessary to take a look at all of the tax aspects of the property to find out how much its purchase can save you on taxes. First, figure the depreciation you can claim on the property based on its economic life and the depreciation method you will use. (There are several ways of depreciating income property, and it's advisable to consult your tax accountant to determine which is best for you.)

Next, add up all of your deductible costs—interest, taxes, insurance, maintenance, management fees, and capital improvements. Once you've got a total annual figure for depreciation and deductions, you can estimate how much of a tax savings you will realize based on your tax bracket. You should use this figure in comparing properties to determine which will give you the best hedge against inflation.

Finally, you need to estimate the capital appreciation of your prospective property. To do this, you need to know approximately how rapidly the property will increase in market value. Base your estimate on the performance of similar properties that have sold within the previous six months within a six-block radius, as well as inflation trends and any other relevant factors. Consider how the property does at an exceptionally low rate of appreciation, a moderate rate, and the highest reasonable rate, and project the amount of appreciation over a five-year period.

For each property you seriously consider, ask yourself how it compares with others in terms of price, overall monthly costs versus projected income, tax benefits, and anticipated appreciation.

Financing Your Investment Property

Proper financing of your property should be a key factor in your overall investment strategy. Your financing arrangements will determine how much up-front cash you'll have to put into the deal and how much you'll have to pay out on a monthly basis, which in turn affects your cash flow.

The time to work out your financial arrangements is *before* you enter into serious negotiations with the seller or commit yourself to an offer to buy. You should explore all of your financing options and weigh the advantages and disadvantages of one method against another. Ultimately, your overall investment objectives should determine the method of financing you choose. This is where a tax accountant versed in income property investments can come in very handy. Such a person should be able to discuss the alternatives with you and advise you which financing method will help you best achieve your objectives. You should concentrate on financing methods that will minimize your down payment without overburdening you with large monthly payments.

Here are some of the financial devices that can enable you to break into the market with the minimum amount down:

- Assume the seller's existing loan. This method is most advantageous for the small investor who can negotiate favorable terms.
- Contract sale. The terms are negotiated by you and the seller; you make direct payments to the seller. There are no closing costs involved, and you may be able to negotiate for no down payment or a very small one. (For details on this method of financing see "Other Methods of Financing," page 156.)
- FHA- and VA-backed mortgages.
- FNMA Two-to-Four Unit Program. The Federal National Mortgage Association's (FNMA) program, designed to provide incentives for inner-city revitalization, offers mortgages of more than $100,000 with 5 percent down payments for persons who buy two- to four-unit dwellings in urban areas and live in one of the units. The program also offers mortgages with a slightly higher down payment for non-occupant investors of small apartment buildings. These mortgage packages are available through savings-and-loan associations and mortgage bankers participating in this FNMA program.
- Secondary financing. Many small investors find it necessary to have some form of secondary financing to purchase their properties. (You will find a discussion of second mortgages in "Other Methods of Financing," page 156.) It is advisable to visit with local mortgage officers, mortgage brokers, and residential real-estate investment specialists about the type of secondary financing available in your area.

When you make an offer to buy on a prospective property, it's a good idea to have an attorney knowledgeable in investment purchases look over the document to ensure that your interests are adequately protected.

Landlord-Tenant Relations

Once you're in the rental business, part of your life becomes coping with the problems of tenants and the maintenance of your property. That often means calls in the middle of the night with complaints of malfunctioning furnaces, air conditioners, toilets, and the like. You'll have to handle these problems yourself until your cash flow grows to the point where you can afford a management/maintenance service. Plus, you'll have to contend with non-paying tenants and evictions. There are a few ways you can protect yourself going into the rental business, but much of your expertise, such as judging and choosing tenants, will have to be gained on a trial-and-error basis.

To protect yourself from lawsuits and charges of discrimination you must know the law. As a result of the consumer movement and the formation of tenants' unions, many states and cities have passed stringent laws governing landlord-tenant relations. These laws usually spell out the provisions a lease must contain, the amount you can charge for a security deposit, the manner in which you must serve an eviction notice, and other rules. Many cities have recently established special housing courts to deal with tenant problems, and they, in fact, encourage tenants to take their grievances into court. You should study all the local and state provisions governing rental property and familiarize yourself with rental practices.

Most cities require landlords to get a certificate of compliance from the local housing code inspection department stating that the property meets code standards. If it fails to meet the standards, tenants legally can withhold rents until the property is in compliance with the code. If you are in violation of this code and the tenants damage your property extensively, you may not be able to get the city inspection division to come out and assess the damages. Hence, you will have no evidence that will stand up in court, and you might have a hard time collecting on your insurance.

You will need to know what special equipment, such as smoke detectors, the law requires, and make certain that it is properly installed.

You will need application/lease forms that enable you to collect enough information on prospective tenants to check their credit, income, and personal references. For help in designing your application/lease form you should contact your local apartment-owners' association or Board of Realtors to see whether they have recommended forms you can obtain. You may also be able to get a copy of a standard legal form from a local realty firm that handles rentals.

The lease should describe the period and type of occupancy—whether the lease is on a month-to-month basis or for a minimum period of one year. In addition, the lease must spell out all of the operating rules, such as provisions for pets, subletting, maximum number of tenants allowed, and so on.

You will also need some check-in/check-out lists that describe all the components of the rental unit and allow you to note their condition. You will have to go through the unit and fill out this checklist with each new tenant, who should receive a copy of the completed form. When the tenant departs, you should do a similar inspection. The check-out list will determine how much of the security deposit you return so you will have to assign repair values to all damages. Your lease should include a provision stating that the new tenant acknowledges the unit has been rented in good repair and working order unless otherwise specified on the checklist. Following this check-in/check-out procedure methodically can save you money and eliminate disputes with tenants.

Record-Keeping

You should keep copies of all application/lease forms and inspection checklists, and maintain records of all the credit checks and personal references made on tenants and prospective tenants.

You will need to document and keep precise records on all money spent in your rental business. Keep track of all you spend for a home office, rental ads, travel associated with your business, operating and maintenance expenses, and all other related funds. You'll have to establish ledgers showing receipts from rental income and expenditures. Your tax accountant should be able to help you set up these ledgers. At the end of the tax year, you can turn all the ledgers and files over to your accountant, who will calculate how it all stacks up for your tax filing. Your accountant can also advise you which expenses count as routine maintenance, and can be deducted 100 percent in the year they occur, and which count as capital improvements and must be depreciated over their life.

Other Investment Alternatives

As you can see, investing in property is a substantial undertaking, requiring strategy and great attention to detail. It can be both a lucrative and rewarding experience if you know what you are doing and proceed judiciously, but it is not a course on which you should embark precipitously or without study.

If you are unsure of the best investment course to pursue or if you doubt that you would have the time to manage and maintain rental property, there are alternatives you can explore. However, you should consult a professional real-estate counselor, who can advise you which real-estate investments would best meet your means and objectives.

Members of the American Society of Real Estate Counselors, who have earned the professional designation of Counselor Real Estate (CRE), will consult with you on a fee basis. CREs, who must have a minimum of ten years' experience in the real-estate field, are qualified to advise you about real-estate securities, such as syndications, real-estate investment trusts, and limited partnerships. These are often the logical choices of high-income professionals who want the yield and tax advantages of real estate without the day-to-day hassles of property management. All real-estate securities are group, as opposed to individual, investments in real estate.

These certified counselors can also discuss with you the potential for investments in cooperatives and condominiums and the special tax advantages of investing in rehabilitation or subsidized housing. Check your phone book for a list of these counselors or contact the American Society of Real Estate Counselors, 430 N. Michigan Avenue, Suite 607, Chicago, Illinois 60611.

Before commissioning a real-estate counselor, check his or her references and background. Whether you are buying rental property or securities, a good counselor can save you a bundle of money. Many unsophisticated investors, who proceed without sufficient advice, pay premium prices for their acquisitions because they get misleading or inaccurate information. A qualified counselor can help you avoid these traps.

15

Vacation Homes

Jake, a Boston city official who lives in a small apartment, bought a house on property in Vermont ski country with two couples. The five partners worked out their own contract stipulating each one's rights, responsibilities, and share of ownership proportionate to his or her capital and sweat-equity investment in the property.

Now Jake, who could not afford the property by himself, has an occasional weekend retreat without the full responsibility of maintenance. In addition, he gets the advantage of tax deductions on interest and property taxes, as well as the benefit of appreciation on the well-located property. He can sell out his share of ownership at its appreciated value to his partners anytime he wants.

Joining with friends to buy a vacation home is one approach. But there are a variety of other ways that a single person with a limited amount of capital can manage to get a vacation retreat in the location of his or her choice. Investing in a second property for recreational purposes often is financially impossible and impractical for the single person with a demanding career. Therefore, you should consider one of the innovative vacation investments on the market today. Since inflation presently is driving up the rate of resort accommodations at the rate of 10 percent annually, you want a guarantee that you will be able to afford the vacation of your choice in the years ahead. This chapter will discuss the most economical and feasible alternatives—resort condominiums, time shares, and house-swapping programs.

Resort Condominiums

If you invest in a condominium in a resort area, either by yourself or with others, you can expect to pay anywhere from $35,000 to $100,000 or more, depending on the location. Prices for these type units are rising at the rate of about 15 percent annually. Condos in Vail, Colorado, that cost $50,000 in 1975, were selling for around $100,000 in 1979. The best time to buy a vacation condo is in the early stages of the development, while prices are still low. However, there are some hazards involved in buying into a new resort development (see "Condominiums," page 37, for guidelines on how to evaluate condo developments).

Before buying a vacation condo, you should analyze its rentability and how it will affect you financially. Calculate what you're going to have to spend on the place for the first two years; then calculate possible offsetting income and tax breaks and assess the bottom line. If you rent out the property, you will come under the provisions of the Tax Reform Act of 1976.

This law stipulates that if you make personal use of your vacation home no more than 10 percent of the total days it is rented in one year (or fourteen days, whichever is greater), you can deduct as expenses such items as mortgage interest, property taxes, fees paid to brokers, maintenance, utilities, insurance premiums, casualty losses, depreciation, and any other costs involved in your effort to generate rental income. Under these circumstances, the property is not considered a residence but a business enterprise, similar to any rental property, and as such, it can be used to shelter all of your income. You will, however, have to demonstrate to the IRS that it is rental property. You will have to show that the property has turned a profit in at least two years during a consecutive five-year period or provide other proof acceptable to the IRS.

If your personal use of the condo goes beyond 10 percent of the total days it was rented or the fourteen-day ceiling, your unit will be considered to have been used as a residence for some portion of the tax year. Consequently, your deductions for expenses can be no greater than your gross rental income, reduced by the portion of mortgage interest and property taxes that can be attributed to the rental use. Once you exceed the 10 percent or fourteen-day limit, you can't take losses on the property because you're using it for personal pleasure. (The IRS also considers as personal use any occupancy by brothers, sisters, parents, or rental to friends or anyone else at reduced rates in exchange for something of value.)

Rental Pool Condominiums

To avoid the time-consuming duty of renting, managing, and maintaining your condo—particularly if it's some distance from your primary residence—you might consider buying a rental pool condominium.

Here's how this operation works. You buy a condominium unit, which is then put into a rental pool along with other units in the same condo development. The developer or some management firm contracts to rent your unit when you're not using it. The rental income and operating costs of all the units in the project are combined and you receive your share, regardless of whether your unit was rented.

So, assume that you buy a two-bedroom condo for $80,000 and put 20 percent down. If you finance the rest over thirty years, your annual mortgage cost at 11 percent interest will come to $7,314. You'll also have to pay about $25 a day for services while you occupy your unit. Those who rent units from the pool pay around $75 per day. Assuming that all units were rented for forty-eight weeks each year (allowing two weeks for maintenance), the pool would pay you $25,200 annually, minus management expenses. And as long as you use the unit for two weeks or less, you can claim it as income property and use deductions to shelter your total earnings.

If you decide to go this route, first evaluate the management team carefully—competent management is essential to successful vacation developments. The staff should have extensive condominium or resort hotel experience. Unfortunately, you can't always be assured that the rental agent will select the best tenants and so you may incur damages to your property. Be wary of promoters who claim that if you turn over your unit to their rental pool for ten months or so, it will pay for itself. There's no guarantee of full occupancy and the possible pilferage and wear and tear involved in short-term renting can cut deeply into your return.

Take time to read the management contract; it can tell you a lot. If it provides a day between occupants to give the unit a thorough cleanup, as well as a period during the year for extensive maintenance, you can tell you're dealing with professionals. The management should also establish reserves for furniture and appliance replacement.

Look for developments that are designed for year-round use so that costs can be spread over many owners and renters. The condo development as well as the surrounding area should offer the kind of vacation amenities and recreational facilities that will attract other owners and renters.

Developers of rental pool condos, or any condo units sold with a rental arrangement handled by an agent designated by the seller, come under supervision of the Securities and Exchange Commission (SEC). Developers selling such units must register with the SEC and give buyers a prospectus disclosing in detail the costs of buying and owning the property, and such other information as the background of the project sponsors, sales and management fees, and tax considerations.

If a developer covered by the securities laws fails to register with the SEC and deliver a prospectus, the buyer has the right to rescind the contract and claim a refund with interest within one year—and in some cases up to three years—from the time of the purchase. You can check whether a condominium is registered or should be registered by writing to the Office of Registration and Reports, Securities and Exchange Commission, 500 N. Capitol Street, Washington, D.C. 20549. Enclose sales literature or other material showing the terms on which the units are being offered or were offered when you signed your contract.

Time Sharing

If you have only a few thousand dollars to invest in a vacation home and can't afford to take on a large second mortgage, then you should consider a condominium time-sharing plan. This is one of the cheapest, yet most convenient and flexible, vacation arrangements you'll find. Time shares can be purchased in resort condominiums and hotels in the U.S., Mexico, the

Caribbean, or Europe. More than half a million Americans now own time shares.

"Everyone has a dream of owning a second home. But unless you have an income in excess of $50,000 and additional savings, owning a whole condominium or second home is out of the picture. Time sharing is an affordable way to have a vacation home in the mountains or on the beach," says Carl Burlingame, author of *The Buyer's Guide To Resort Time Sharing*.

Time sharing works like this. You and a number of people buy shares in the same condominium unit. What you're actually buying is the right to use the condominium for a specified time of the year—say, the first two weeks in January. Unlike a whole unit buyer of a condo, you get a break on prices because you pay for no more than you use.

For example, a 1/22 share of a two-bedroom condominium might cost you $7,000 plus $350 to cover your share of the furnishings. Spread over the length of your time share, which could be thirty years, the cost of owning an annual two-week stay at the condominium would run around $245, and expenses for two weeks during a peak month might come to another $200. That covers your share of utilities, maid and linen service, insurance, use of recreational facilities, administrative costs, and the home-owners' association fee. All told, a two-week vacation would cost you less than $31 per day.

But you're not tied indefinitely into that two-week time slot in January. You can swap with other owners and spend one week at the condo in August if you wish. Or if you don't feel like going to the same place each year, you can take advantage of a time-sharing exchange program. Instead of going to your condo at the beach, you can swap for a condo in the mountains for a week. Most time-sharing resort developments have exchange programs that allow their members to vacation almost anywhere in the world.

A well-designed time-share program offers a hedge against inflation in resort accommodations because you buy future vacations at today's prices. And you can deduct the interest on your loan and your share of the real-estate taxes.

Types of Time Shares

There are two types of time-sharing arrangements. Either you *own* an interest in real estate or you buy a *right-to-use* option on the facilities for a specified period of time without owning an interest in real estate. And there are several variations on both types of arrangements.

Ownership Types

There are two types of time-sharing ownership:

TENANCY-IN-COMMON OWNERSHIP. Under this arrangement, also called time-span ownership (TSO), you buy an undivided interest in the whole living unit based on the length of time you select. This does not give you any direct interest in a specific time period, because the particular time period you will use is established by a separate agreement. This type of ownership can be restrictive, because you have to act in conjunction with other owners.

For example, assume that you buy a one-week period in a beachfront condominium for the first week in February. You will own a $1/52$ undivided interest in the building, and under a separate agreement, which all buyers are bound by, you are guaranteed the exclusive use of the living unit every first week in February for as long as the other buyers keep their $1/52$ interests.

INTERVAL OWNERSHIP. This type of ownership, the most popular, also consists of two parts. The first part is an *estate for years,* during which you own the condo unit for the period of time you have selected each year. You own it every year for a specified number of years—usually corresponding to the estimated useful life of the building—twenty to forty years. At the end of this period, you and all other owners become tenants-in-common in ownership of the unit. Your undivided interest in the unit is then based on predetermined percentages, usually in proportion to the length of the time period you originally selected.

Assume that you buy a one-week period for the first week in January at a condominium in Steamboat Springs, Colorado. You will own and have exclusive use of the condo every first week of January for thirty years. At the end of that time, you and all others who bought time shares in the same condo unit will own it outright.

Non-Ownership Types

There are three types of non-ownership time sharing:

VACATION LICENSE. The most widely used form of non-ownership time share, vacation license is typically found where time shares involving an operating hotel are being sold. The license gives you the right to use a selected living unit for a specified week or weeks for a term of years. Although you can sell your license, you probably will not be allowed under the contract to sell at a profit or to rent your living unit. Some licenses allow you to select each year the time period you choose to spend at your unit.

VACATION LEASE. This type is similar to a vacation license. You buy a lease on a particular living unit, which entitles you to a fixed annual occupancy. The lease may be transferable, and subletting may be allowed.

CLUB MEMBERSHIP TIME SHARES. In this case, you buy a club membership which gives you the right to occupy a living space for a specified period of time each year. The club, a non-profit association, buys or leases a building or group of buildings at a resort for the club members. The time period may be fixed or may be a given number of days to be selected annually.

Pros and Cons of Ownership Time Shares

With an ownership time share, you have the security of a warranty deed, and acquire equity and benefit from the real-estate appreciation. You have a right to mortage your property, rent it, sell it, and pass it on to your heirs. You can deduct for real-estate taxes and interest payments and sell at a profit.

A major problem with ownership time shares, however, is their presently questionable legal status under the laws of many states. Among the issues still being debated are whether time shares are legally classifiable as securities and require complete financial disclosures by developers and promoters. Some states with tough condo disclosure rules now enforce such requirements on time-share developers.

With interval ownership, the question arises whether it is really a lease instead of ownership until the initial thirty or forty year period is up. Before buying, you should find out whether you can obtain title insurance to guarantee your legal claim to your $1/52$ interest in Unit 8C at Steamboat Springs. If you can't, then you may have difficulty selling your time share.

There is also a disadvantage to the tenancy-in-common time share, or TSO. In most states, a co-owner can sue for partition of real estate. So in the case of a TSO, any one owner could theoretically sue to have the building sold and the proceeds distributed pro rata among the co-owners. Moreover, federal tax laws allow the government to force the sale of the entire living unit to satisfy a lien against any tenancy-in-common owner.

Pros and Cons of Non-Ownership Time Shares

Right-to-use time-sharing plans are usually less expensive than the ownership plans. You don't get involved with management or a homeowners' association, and many of these plans allow you to choose a "floating week" versus fixed time periods.

You, of course, receive no real-estate title, tax benefits, or say in the way the place is run. Moreover, there may be limitations on the rental, sale, or transfer by gift of non-ownership time shares. At the end of the time-share period, full ownership reverts to the seller.

If you buy into a non-ownership time share encumbered by a construction loan, you must make sure your purchase is protected from claims by the lender. You can do this either by getting a recorded non-disturbance clause from the lender or through establishment of an escrow fund to ensure that proceeds from time-share sales are used to pay off the construction loan. You also should make certain that there is a restriction preventing the owner of the property from placing new encumbrances on the building without providing protection for time-share buyers.

The Financial Picture

The average price for a one-week ownership of a one-bedroom resort condominium unit in 1979 ranged from about $5,100 at peak season to about

$2,255 at low season, according to Carl Burlingame. Prices for right-to-use time shares were slightly less. Prices have jumped by several hundred dollars annually since the time-share concept gained U.S. acceptance in 1974, and they should continue to escalate as time shares grow in popularity.

Time shares are priced according to the size and location of the unit, the quality of the resort, the available facilities, and the season that you buy. In some cases, you can buy an off-season week for about half the price of a peak-season one. If you're buying an off-season week, however, the developer might insist that it be part of a package deal and require you to also buy a peak-season week. Many developers offer a discount if you buy more than a two-week time share.

In addition to the initial cost of the time share, you will be charged a management and maintenance fee. Average annual maintenance fees in 1979 ranged from $100 to $150 per week of ownership, although some weekly maintenance fees ran as high as $250. On top of the maintenance fee, you may have to pay a "use" fee of about $10 daily while you're staying at your unit. Collectively, these fees should cover property management, taxes, utilities, furnishings and furniture replacement, upkeep of the complex, and maid service. Ask for a complete breakdown of these prices before you buy.

To determine whether the price of the time share is reasonable, estimate what your whole unit would sell for and divide that amount by fifty (assuming two unsold weeks for maintenance). If your weekly cost is more than three times that amount, the unit is overpriced. Most experts agree that a time share is a good value if you can project that your savings on rent, meals, and recreational expenses will equal in ten years the total amount you pay for the time share.

Most time-share units are financed over a five to seven year period with 20 to 25 percent down. Financing is available through the usual mortgage loan sources. You will probably be charged a consumer-loan interest rate at about the same level you would pay for a car loan. You may find that lenders in the resort area are more willing to write the loan than local lenders where you live.

It's hard to predict the resale value of time-share units, since there is not sufficient history from which to project. Burlingame said in the resale cases he has studied, the owners have gotten out what they put in and in some cases a little more.

"I think the ownership will go up in value if the unit is in a good location," he said. "But 75 percent of the people involved in time sharing have only owned their units for two years, and there hasn't been much resale activity."

Time-Share Exchange Programs

If the idea of vacationing at the same place the same time each year seems dreary to you, then you should shop for a time-share development with an exchange service. Through exchange programs, you can vacation at a different place in the world each year for the week or weeks you choose.

Exchange services offer your unit for swapping, and in return, you can reserve a unit in another development.

There are three types of exchange services:

- Trading networks, between owners of resort homes or time shares. These networks are arrangements between individual owners who agree to swap accommodations; they do not involve the builder or seller of the time-share units.
- Internal exchange services operate among affiliated facilities offered by the some builder/seller. In other words, you can swap your time share in XYZ Developer's Florida resort for a week in XYZ Developer's Colorado ski resort. Holiday Inn, which sells right-to-use time shares, offers twenty-three locations through its internal exchange service.
- External exchange services are run by independent companies that specialize in arranging exchanges for time-share owners in unaffiliated resorts. The time-share development must belong to one of these services in order for you to participate in its exchange program. Two of the largest external exchange services are Resort Condominiums International (about 250-member resorts located throughout the U.S., Canada, the Caribbean, Europe, South America, and Australia) and Interval International (more than 150-member resorts).

    RCI charges an initiation fee of $100, which is paid by the developer. After the first year, the time sharer pays $36 for an annual membership and a nominal fee for processing. Interval International charges the time sharer an $18 annual membership fee and a $14 exchange fee. Both services send members their directories of participating resorts. For more information, write: Resort Condominiums International, Box 80229, Indianapolis, Indiana 46240; Interval International, 6075 Sunset Drive, South Miami, Florida 33143.

A few warnings are in order regarding exchange services:

- Don't expect to buy low and trade high. Don't buy a $1,200 discount week at a Florida resort with the expectation of trading up for a $10,000 week in Aspen over Christmas. You will be most successful in your trades if you swap for similar accommodations and similar times.
- Exchange programs cannot guarantee that specific exchanges can be made year after year. Exchanges generally go on a first-come, first-served basis, but priority is given to comparable units in the same season and availability changes constantly. Beware of any salesperson who guarantees you specific trades.
- Make certain that the exchange service is fully operating before buying in. Get references and check them out; talk to purchasers who have made exchanges.
- Make sure that the builder/seller has a valid contract with the exchange service.

Time-Share Recreational Vehicle Parks and Campgrounds

If you own an RV or are a camper, you may be interested in buying a time share in an RV park or a campground site. These time shares work similarly to condo resort time shares. You buy an ownership or right-to-use time share in an improved RV lot or campsite for a certain time period. Your time share is usually exchangeable with other sites across the country on a space-available basis. Before buying, make sure the time share is tied in with other parks on a reciprocal trading or exchange basis. Many of these time-share sites offer such recreational activities as golf, tennis, swimming, fishing, and horseback riding.

Shopping for Your Time Share

Before putting down any money on a time share, look over the resort and its location. If you can, vacation there first. Ask yourself if the resort will retain those features which attracted you to it. Make sure the building is well constructed and clean. The furnishings should be durable and easily cleaned. The units should be equipped with quality appliances that are backed by warranties. Is the place well landscaped and are the recreational facilities well maintained? Talk to some present owners and find out what steps have been taken to hold down building and grounds maintenance costs and how satisfied they are with the management and home-owners' association.

Take time to check out the reputation of the builder/developer and the management company. Do they have experience in the resort or hotel business? Check for complaints with the Chamber of Commerce and Better Business Bureau where the resort is located. Get a financial statement from the condominium association; your lawyer or a bank's commercial loan officer can help you analyze it. Also ask your banker to run a credit check and get a Dun & Bradstreet report (it will cost you about $50). You may not be able to get all of the particulars, but the banker should be able to tell you whether it's a reasonable investment.

If the property is mortgaged, find out when the mortgage is to be paid off and by what means. Do some calculating to see whether the time-share prices multiplied by the number of time shares being offered will produce enough cash to pay the mortgage. Ask when sales were started and how many sales have been made. If the development is still under construction, your money should be put in an escrow account until your unit is free and clear. In some states, this is required by law. If not, get this stipulation written into your contract. Avoid buying from small developers who may not be in business in the future.

Competent management at affordable prices is the key to the success of any time-sharing project. Hotel-type management is essential in a large development. Ask to see the management and/or maintenance agreement. You should avoid buying where management contracts run for many years and allow substantial fee increases. Management contracts should be renewable every three to five years. (Time-shared hotels managed by large hotel management companies are the exception; they usually operate with long-term contracts to assure they can attract skilled management.)

The management contract should spell out the responsibilities of the management firm, and the home-owners' association should have the right to replace the firm for failure to adequately perform its duties. Be wary of exceptionally low management or maintenance fees. If the fee is under $100, that could be an unrealistic projection. And watch out for agreements that call for automatic maintenance increases or increases tied to the consumer price index. You should also make certain that the budget includes a contingencies fund which will prevent you from being hit with emergency assessments at a later date.

If you're buying an ownership time share, you should get a waiver of partition in your agreement to buy. Without it, any of the co-owners may sue to have a unit sold and the proceeds distributed pro rata among you. Make certain that the waiver is enforceable against present and future owners in the state where the development is located.

See if the management company or home-owners' association has the right to take action against owners who damage a unit, stay beyond their allotted time, or fail to pay their annual fees. The management should have lien and foreclosure powers and the ability to deny future use to delinquent and offending co-owners.

Determine that adequate security is provided by the builder/seller and the management. Although the home-owners' association should provide fire, damage, and liability insurance, you may need extra insurance for personal property. Check with your agent.

You should have your attorney go over your contract before signing it. Because time sharing is a new concept, there aren't legal precedents to protect you and a careful reading of all documents by your attorney is essential.

If the building is being converted to a time-sharing development, find out why. Is it because the area lends itself well to the time-sharing concept or because the project has not gotten off the ground? If the project has been grounded because of a stagnant economy that is now reviving, you may be making a good investment. On the other hand, if the project has done poorly because of a bad location, poor design, or shoddy construction, avoid it.

For more information on time sharing, you can write to the Resort Time Sharing Council, a division of the American Land Development Association, 1000-16th Street, N.W., Suite 604, Washington, D.C. 20036. For the booklet, *A Consumer's Guide To Time Sharing*, send fifty cents and a self-addressed, stamped envelope. You can also request free of charge a list of all time-sharing developers who belong to the council, as well as information on the currently operating trading networks and exchange programs.

House Swapping

The cheapest, and perhaps most personal and creative, way to arrange for a vacation home is to engage in a house swap with another single person or a family. This method provides you maximum flexibility—you conceivably could vacation in a different part of the country or of the world each year. And the only tab is the use of your own home and your transportation.

You work out with the other swapper the time and period of the exchange. You can find people to swap with simply by placing an ad in the classified columns of a magazine like *Saturday Review* or *Quest* or in newspapers in areas you want to visit. Or you can subscribe to one of the home-exchange agencies that circulate lists of homes up for swaps and rentals in the U.S. and other countries. (Some of these agencies and their subscription rates are listed on pages 261–262).

Exchange agencies serve as clearinghouses for information about homes available for swapping. They provide names and addresses of the owners, descriptions of the homes, other facilities included (such as car, pool, boat), date and location preferences of the owners, and special stipulations regarding pets, children, and other matters. Some exchange services will find you a matching home and make all the necessary arrangements for a fee.

In order to join an exchange service or get its directory of available homes, you need not list your home for exchange. However, some agencies' subscription fees include the cost of listing your home. If you're seriously interested in swapping, listing your home will help generate inquiries and improve your chances of finding a good match. Listing your home does not obligate you to go through with a swap.

Finding a Swapper

The logical starting point is to circulate a form letter to owners of homes listed in areas you want to visit. State particulars about the accommodations you are offering, tell something about yourself, and indicate when you want to swap. If you're listed in an exchange service directory, you'll receive similar letters.

You should allow plenty of time for arrangements. A satisfactory house swap requires advance planning and correspondence to locate the right swapper and work out details of the exchange. One veteran house swapper advises that if you want to vacation in August, you should begin shopping for a swap in April.

Of course, there are some risks involved in allowing someone you've met only by phone or letter to use your house and perhaps your car. Exchange operators report, however, that they have heard very few complaints from swappers. Most parties treat the other's home as though it were their own and leave it in the shape in which they found it.

Taking Precautions

There are some precautions you can take in advance to ensure that your swap will be a satisfactory experience. Handle these details through letters or phone calls:

- Exchange pictures of your homes and yourselves. Tell the swapper a bit about yourself and get similar information from that person or persons.
- Give and ask for references, especially the names of people swapped with before, neighbors, or work associates. Write or call the references.

- Make a written agreement about housekeeping rules each party will follow, including such things as seeing that the lawn is cut, paying for excessive use of utilities and long-distance phone calls, not using certain equipment and facilities.
- Type up instructions about your respective homes—when the trash is collected, special problems with household equipment, who to contact in emergencies.
- Make certain you and your swapper have adequate insurance on your homes, cars, and other belongings.
- Agree to clear out some dressers and closets for the use of your visitors, and lock up all valuables.

If you don't feel comfortable handling these details yourself, there is one exchange service—Inquiline—which will check out persons and their homes through a national investigation agency. Of course, both parties must agree to such an investigation.

Home Exchange Agencies

These are some of the U.S.-based home exchange agencies and the services they provide:

- *Adventures in Living*, Box 278, Winnetka, Illinois 60093; mail inquiries only. Prices: $25 for subscription and listing in annual directory plus two supplements. Listing deadlines: January 1; May 1 for supplements. You'll also receive a handbook on house-swapping tips. Exchanges only; no rentals included.
- *Holiday Exchanges*, Box 878, Belen, New Mexico 87002; 505/864-8680. Prices: $15 for listing and subscription to either past twelve or next twelve monthly issues of directory; $25 for listing and all twenty-four issues; $5 for listing only, with no subscription to directories. No listing deadlines.
- *Inquiline, Inc.*, 35 Adams St., Bedford Hills, New York 10507; 914/241-0102. Prices: $30 for subscription to annual directory or for a listing with photo in directory. $50 for both; $10 registration fee for match-up service; $100 for completed swap arrangements. With a subscription you'll also receive quarterly newsletters and a brochure of homes for vacation rental in Europe. Listing deadline: November 15. This agency specializes in the homes of professionals and executives and in lining up swaps—including long-term exchanges—for subscribers.
- *Interchange Home Exchange*, 888 Seventh Avenue, Suite 400, New York, New York 10019; 212/265-4300. Inquire also at 2233 Beverley Glen Place, Los Angeles, California 90024; 213/475-3858. Prices: $12 for subscription to annual directory; including listing with photo and supplement to directory; $110 for completed matching and swap arrangments, which include a guidelines booklet and model exchange agreement. No names or addresses listed; all swaps arranged by this service. No listing deadline.
- *InterService Home Exchange*, Box 87, Glen Echo, Maryland 20768; 301/320-3558. Prices: $15 for annual directory and periodic bulletins, with or without listing of your home; $5 extra for listing without address (inquiries are forwarded to you); $3 for photo with listing. Worldwide exchanges and rental

listings, with sample agreements and checklists provided. No listing deadlines.

- *The International Spareroom,* Box 518, Solana Beach, California 92075; 714/755-3194. This agency deals primarily with swaps and rentals of hosted accommodations—persons visit each other at home on an exchange basis or as paying guests. Prices: $1 for a year's lists; $20 for arranging a one-week swap, $10 for each additional week; charge for arranging rental is included in the stated rental amount. No charge for listing, no listing deadlines.
- *Vacation Exchange Club,* 350 Broadway, New York, New York 10013; 212/966-2576. Prices: $12 for a subscription to the annual directory and supplement, $15 with a listing (add $5 for inclusion of photo) plus $2 if you want first-class mailings. Listing deadlines: December 17; February 15 for supplement. You'll also receive a directory and supplement with overseas listings from Intervac, an affiliated service. Some rentals are included in the listings.

Glossary

ABSTRACT: A summary of the history of the title transfers, as well as any liens and encumbrances on the property from the original source of the title up to the present. The abstract reports on all the legal documents—contracts, deeds, or wills—that affect the parcel of real estate and its present status.

APPRECIATION: The increase in value of a property.

BALLOON PAYMENT: The final lump-sum payment of a note or mortgage which repays the debt in full.

CAPITAL GAIN: The taxable profit derived from the sale of a capital asset.

CLOSING: The conclusion of a real-estate transaction at which time the balance of money above the down payment is exchanged for the deed, and all other funds necessary to complete the transaction are exchanged. Also referred to as "settlement."

CLOSING COSTS: Expenses incurred in purchasing real estate above the purchase price (in the case of the buyer) and those which must be deducted from the proceeds of the sale (in the case of the seller). Buyer's expenses typically include loan fees, points, appraisal and attorney's fees, deed and mortgage recording costs, and the title search and title insurance. Also called "settlement costs."

CRAWL SPACE: In basementless houses, the open space between the underside of the floor and the ground.

DEED: A written document by which the ownership of land is transferred from one party to another.

DEED OF TRUST: A security instrument conveying title in trust to a third party for a particular piece of real estate. In some states, such as California, a deed of trust is used instead of a mortgage. Also known as a "trust deed."

DEPRECIATION: The loss of value in real property through physical deterioration, or functional or economic obsolescence.

DRY ROT: Disintegration of wood caused by fungi growing in moist sections.

EARNEST MONEY: Funds the buyer deposits in escrow when making an offer to buy as an indication of serious intent to follow through with the transaction.

EQUITY: An owner's interest in a property after payment of all liens or other charges on the property.

ESCALATION CLAUSE: A clause included in the mortgage agreement by the lender stipulating that the interest rate can be increased in the future.

ESCROW or ESCROW ACCOUNT: Money placed in a reserve account. Lenders often require home buyers to place money in escrow accounts to cover such expenses as property taxes, home insurance, and private mortgage insurance.

FARMERS HOME ADMINISTRATION (FmHA): A government agency within the Department of Agriculture that makes loans to qualified rural home buyers.

FASCIA BOARD: The horizontal board covering the joint between the top of a wall and the projecting eaves.

263

FEDERAL HOUSING ADMINISTRATION (FHA): A division of the Department of Housing and Urban Development that insures residential mortgage loans made by private lenders and sets standards for construction and underwriting.

FEDERAL TRADE COMMISSION (FTC): A federal agency that monitors business activities for unfair, deceptive, and anticompetitive trade practices and issues cease-and-desist orders to organizations found in violation of fair trade practices. In 1978, the FTC launched a major investigation into the home-building and real-estate industry.

FEE SIMPLE: Outright ownership of land in the highest degree. The only limitations on this type of ownership are governmental limitations.

FLASHING: Sheet metal or other material used around chimneys, projecting pipes, in roof valleys, or where two exterior surfaces join, to protect against water leakage to a dwelling's interior.

FORECLOSURE: A legal procedure, under the terms of a mortgage or deed of trust, in which the title of the property is passed to the holder of the note or to a third party who buys the property at a foreclosure sale, usually prompted by the owner's defaulting on the mortgage payments.

GRADUATED PAYMENT MORTGAGE (GPM): A mortgage designed to meet a borrower's financial position; payments are smaller in the early years of the mortgage and larger in subsequent years when, theoretically, the buyer's income should increase.

HOME-OWNERS' ASSOCIATION: An association of home owners sharing interest in and responsibilities for common property of a housing project, such as a condominium, or for a specific area or subdivision.

DEPARTMENT OF HOUSING AND URBAN DEVELOPMENT (HUD): A federal agency responsible for the implementation and administration of government housing and urban development programs. The agency's programs include community planning and development, housing production and mortgage credit, equal opportunity in housing, research and technology.

JOINT TENANCY: An interest in a piece of real estate held by two or more individuals equally. In the event of the death of one person, the property is divided equally among the surviving owners. Also called "joint tenancy with the right of survivorship."

JOISTS: Heavy boards placed on edge to support walls, floors, and ceilings. Usually 2 by 8's or 2 by 10's.

LEVERAGE: In real-estate investments, the use of borrowed funds to maximize returns.

LIEN: A claim made on one's property as security for a debt or obligation.

MARKET VALUE: The highest price a property will command on the market.

MORTGAGE: The legal document pledging the property as security for a debt.

MORTGAGE NOTE: The document in which the buyer promises to repay the loan. The mortgage note states the amount of the loan, the interest rate, the first and last payment dates, and other conditions of the loan.

MORTGAGEE: The lender.

MORTGAGOR: The borrower.

NATIONAL ASSOCIATION OF HOME BUILDERS (NAHB): National trade organization of builders.

NATIONAL ASSOCIATION OF REALTORS: Trade organization of real-estate agents and brokers whose members carry the designation Realtor.

NATIONAL ASSOCIATION OF REALTISTS: Trade organization of real-estate agents and brokers whose members carry the designation Realtist.

OFFER TO BUY: A legal contract in which the buyer offers to purchase a piece of property for a certain price and subject to certain conditions.

ORIGINATION FEE: The fee charged by a lender to prepare loan documents, make credit checks, and sometimes appraise the property. The fee is usually computed as a percentage of the loan amount.

PLANNED UNIT DEVELOPMENT (PUD): A subdivision with a comprehensive development plan providing for schools, recreational and service facilities, commercial and office areas. Open spaces within PUDs are often owned in common by the home owners.

POINTS: Actually a disguised form of interest, a point is a fee a lender charges to compensate for making a loan at less than the going market interest rate. Where the interest ceiling is set by state law, lenders often charge points. One point is equal to one percent of the loan amount. Also called "loan discount" or "discount points."

PREPAYMENT PENALTY: A clause in the mortgage note that requires the borrower to pay a penalty if the mortgage is prepaid prior to its maturity. Most mortgage contracts have a penalty for prepayment in the first year of the mortgage.

PRIVATE MORTGAGE INSURANCE (PMI): Insurance written by a private insurance company protecting the lender against loss in case the borrower defaults on the loan. Usually required if the borrower puts less than 20 percent down.

PRORATION: A division of the continuing costs of owning a piece of real estate between the buyer and the seller so that each pays a fair share. Items typically prorated at the closing include taxes; water, gas, and electric bills; and any home-owners' association fees.

QUITCLAIM DEED: Document by which the seller conveys whatever interest he or she has in the title to the purchaser. This is the least desirable type of deed because it contains no warranties.

REAL ESTATE SETTLEMENT PROCEDURES ACT (RESPA): The law that requires a lender to give the borrower a good-faith estimate of settlement costs and an informational booklet on these costs at the time of loan application. RESPA also requires that the borrower receive a uniform settlement statement listing actual settlement costs at the time of the closing.

RED-LINING: Practice by mortgage lenders of not making loans in certain undesirable or low-income "red-lined" areas. This practice has been declared illegal in some areas and is decreasing as a result of the growing emphasis on urban rehabilitation.

RESTRICTIVE COVENANT: Rules often imposed by a developer or home-owners' association that place certain limitations on an owner's use of property. For example, a restrictive covenant may prohibit parking recreational vehicles or boats in the driveways or yards within a development.

R-VALUE: A number that indicates thermal resistance of insulation to heat flowing out during the winter and in during the summer. The higher the R-value, the better the performance of the insulation. Also called "R-factor."

SALES CONTRACT: See "offer to buy."

SAVINGS AND LOAN ASSOCIATION (S&L): Association founded to promote savings and home ownership. Deposits are invested in residential mortgage loans.

SECOND MORTGAGE: A second mortgage that is subordinate to the first mortgage on a property. Usually the term of a second mortgage is shorter and the interest rate higher than that on a first mortgage. Also called "junior mortgage."

SECONDARY MORTGAGE MARKET: A system whereby lenders and investors buy existing mortgages as long-term investments, and in so doing, provide more funds with which banks and savings and loan associations can make mortgage loans.

SETTLEMENT: See "closing."

SITE BUILT: A dwelling that is built at the construction site, as opposed to manufactured homes which are built in factories.

SWEAT EQUITY: Equity created in a dwelling through one's own labor. Owners who finish off part of their homes to save money are considered to have built equity through their own sweat.

TENANTS IN COMMON: A form of ownership in which two or more persons own a share in common property. Upon the death of one owner, the decedent's share becomes part of his or her estate and is distributed according to the will.

TITLE: Legal term indicating that the owner of land has the just and legitimate possession of it.

TITLE INSURANCE: Insurance providing the policyholder with protection against losses that might occur due to any encumbrances on the title.

TITLE SEARCH: An examination of public record to determine whether the title is free and clear of liens and encumbrances. A title search is required before property can be conveyed from a seller to a buyer.

USURY CEILING: A maximum legal rate, established by state law, on the interest that can be charged by lenders on loans. Usury rates or ceilings vary from state to state.

VAPOR BARRIER: A waterproof shield placed on the warm side of insulation to prevent moisture from the living quarters from seeping into the insulation.

VARIABLE RATE MORTGAGE (VRM): A mortgage that allows for the adjustment of the interest rate in accordance with the economy and subject to terms stipulated in the mortgage note.

VETERANS ADMINISTRATION (VA): Federal agency which administers the VA home loan guaranty program to encourage lenders to provide long-term, no-down-payment mortgages to eligible veterans.

WALL PLATE: Horizontal piece of lumber placed on top of a masonry wall and under joists and other load-bearing members to distribute their weight evenly to the wall.

WARRANTY DEED: A deed in which the seller of the property guarantees that the title being conveyed is good and marketable. This is the most desirable type of deed for the buyer to receive.

Bibliography

AMERICAN BANKERS ASSOCIATION. *Your Guide to Settlement Costs*. Washington, D.C.: American Bankers Association, 1978.

BARRON, PAUL. *Federal Regulation of Real Estate: The Real Estate Settlement Procedures Act, 1979 Cumulative Supplement No. 1*. Boston: Warren, Gorham & Lamont, 1979.

COBB, HUBBARD H. *How To Buy and Remodel the Older House*. New York: Collier Books, 1974.

DAVIS, JOSEPH C. and CLAXTON WALKER. *Buying Your House: A Complete Guide to Inspection and Evaluation*. Buchanan: Emerson Books, Inc., 1975.

DE BENEDICTIS, DANIEL J. *The Complete Real Estate Adviser*. New York: Cornerstone Library, 1977.

ECCLI, EUGENE. *Low-Cost, Energy-Efficient Shelter for the Owner and Builder*. Emmaus: Rodale Press, 1976.

FAIRBRIDGE, KINGSLEY C. and KOWAL, HARVEY-JANE. *Loft Living: Recycling Warehouse Space for Residential Use*. New York: Saturday Review Press/E.P. Dutton Co., Inc., 1976.

FEDERAL TRADE COMMISSION. *Housing Policy Session*. Washington, D.C.: Federal Trade Commission, 1978.

HARRISON, HENRY S. *Houses: The Illustrated Guide to Construction, Design and Systems*. Chicago: Realtors National Marketing Institute, 1973.

IRWIN, ROBERT. *How To Buy a Home at a Reasonable Price*. New York: McGraw-Hill, Inc., 1979.

LEE, STEVEN JAMES. *Buyer's Handbook for the Single Family Home*. New York: Van Nostrand Reinhold Company, 1979.

MENCHER, MELVIN, ed. *The Fannie Mae Guide to Buying, Financing & Selling Your Home*. Garden City: Dolphin Books, 1973.

MUIR, DORIS L., ed. *The Log Home Guide for Builders and Buyers*. Fort Irwin, Ontario: Muir Publishing Company, Ltd., 1978.

NATIONAL ASSOCIATION OF HOME MANUFACTURERS. *1979 Guide to Manufactured Homes*. Washington, D.C.: National Association of Home Manufacturers, 1979.

NATIONAL ASSOCIATION OF HOUSING COOPERATIVES. *Cooperative Housing: People Helping Each Other*. Washington, D.C.: National Association of Housing Cooperatives, 1977.

SCHRAM, JOSEPH F. *Finding and Fixing the Older Home*. Farmington: Structures Publishing Company, 1976.

SHEEHAN, PHILIP BROWN, ed. *The McGraw-Hill Home Book*. New York: McGraw-Hill, 1979.

SHERWOOD, GERALD E. *New Life for Old Dwellings*. Washington, D.C.: U.S. Government Printing Office, 1975.

SORIANO, NICHOLAS M. *Handling Your House Closing: A Practical Guide*. White Plains: Penchant Press, Inc., 1974.

TROUTMAN, CURT, et al. *Settle for Less: The Expensive Failure of HUD's Real Estate Practices Staff*. Washington, D.C.: Housing Research Group, Center for the Study of Responsive Law, 1977.

TYMON, DOROTHY. *The Condominium: A Guide for the Alert Buyer*. New York: Avon Books, 1976.

U.S. DEPARTMENT OF HOUSING AND URBAN DEVELOPMENT. *How Well Are We Housed? Female-Headed Households*. Washington, D.C.: U.S. Government Printing Office, 1978.

U.S. DEPARTMENT OF HOUSING AND URBAN DEVELOPMENT. *Questions about Condominiums*. Washington, D.C.: U.S. Government Printing Office, 1979.

U.S. DEPARTMENT OF HOUSING AND URGAN DEVELOPMENT. *The President's National Urban Policy Report*. Washington, D.C.: U.S. Government Printing Office, 1978.

U.S. DEPARTMENT OF HOUSING AND URBAN DEVELOPMENT. *The President's National Report on Sex Discrimination in Five American Cities*. Washington, D.C.: U.S. Government Printing Office, 1975.

U.S. LEAGUE OF SAVINGS ASSOCIATIONS. *Homeownership: Affording the Single-Family Home*. Chicago: U.S. League of Savings Associations, 1978.

WATKINS, A.M. *Buying Land: How To Profit from the Last Great Land Boom*. New York: Quadrangle, 1975.

WASCHEK, CARMEN and BROWNLEE. *Your Guide to Good Shelter: How To Plan, Build or Convert for Energy Conservation*. Reston: Reston Publishing Company, Inc., 1978.

WEDIN, CAROL S. and L. GERTRUDE NYGREN, eds. *Housing Perspectives: Individuals and Families*. Minneapolis: Burgess Publishing Company, 1976.

Index